The

Companion to
FOSTER CARE

Edited by Ann Wheal

Russell House Publishing

First published in 1999 by:
Russell House Publishing Limited
4 St. George's House
The Business Park
Uplyme Road
Lyme Regis
Dorset DT7 3LS

British Library Cataloguing-in-Publication Data:
A catalogue record for this manual is available from the British Library.

ISBN: 1-898924-34-1

Text design and layout by The Hallamshire Press Limited, Sheffield

Printed by Cromwell Press, Trowbridge

THE COMPANION TO
FOSTER CARE

Contents

SECTION THREE   Issues

CONCLUSION

Acknowledgements

My grateful thanks must go to:

Russell House Publishing, the publishers, for identifying the need for this book and for persuading me to be the editor.

My critical readers, Ena Fry from the National Foster Care Association and John Hudson, consultant.

Sarah Bray and Sue Blundell for their clear heads in checking and organising the book and me.

My husband Peter, who as usual, has been patient and understanding.

Most of all my thanks must go to the authors whose wealth of knowledge and experience is so evident in their chapters.

Foreword

Ann Wheal

The diversity of backgrounds and personal experience of the authors of this book's chapters ensures that it is lively, interesting and up-to-date. It offers suggested solutions to the current challenges in foster care, combined with a sound theoretical base.

The chapters contain contributions from:

– a care leaver

– foster carers

– National Standards Project

– managers and practioners in health and social care

– voluntary and independent agencies

– BAAF

– NFCA

– academics

– consultants

– planners

– policy makers.

The aim is to provide the reader with both a deep understanding and a broad perspective of foster care. It is intended that this will enable those studying and working in the field to better understand the complexities of this exacting activity.

The book has been divided into three sections - The **Wider Context**, **Foster Care Practice**, and **Issues**. Key references are highlighted in each chapter. All the authors are specialists in their chosen fields and they have between them a wealth of experience in foster care. Each chapter stands alone and can be read alone. It is not anticipated that the book will necessarily be read from cover to cover; the reader will find that they are able to 'dip in' and find the appropriate information as required, and thus this book will act as an easy reference guide that will:

- help **social workers** and other practitioners to develop their skills and knowledge whether they are new to this work, face particular challenges for the first time, or want a convenient way of staying abreast of current thinking and practice

- provide background information and guidance to those **trainers** who are not specialists in this area but might be called on to work with foster carers, social workers and others

- give support and guidance to **foster carers** themselves when they are trying to develop their skills and improve the care they provide

- enable **policy makers** to understand better the dilemmas that face front line workers, carers and young people; and to develop new policies on a sound knowledge of current thinking

- give **students** a convenient source of reference both on foster care as a whole and on specific topics.

All the opinions expressed are those of the authors of the chapters.

All reference to the Children Act refers to Children Act 1989, Children Act Scotland 1995 and The Children (Northern Ireland) Order 1995.

Utting (1997) HMSO and Kent, The Scottish Office reports have both highlighted the need for improvements in the foster care service. It is hoped that this book will assist in this development.

The following quotations from young people currently in foster care really highlight the vital role that carers play in the life of young people. It is hoped that this book will help all those involved to further improve this most valuable service:

I can trust them

They treat you with respect

Kind and caring

You can talk to your foster carer and get an honest answer

You are safe

You feel as though someone cares

You feel as though you belong to a family

They help me through the bad times

NFCA Consultation with Children and Young People on National Standards in Foster Care 1998

About the Authors

Shelagh Beckett is a freelance trainer and consultant in child care, specialising predominantly in family placement. She regularly acts as an expert witness in respect of sibling contact, adoption and other placement options.

Moira Borland is a research fellow at the Centre for the Child and Society, University of Glasgow, having previously worked as a social worker and in social work education and training. Recent work includes a survey of foster carers in Scotland and evaluating a professional fostering project run by the NCH Action for Children.

Dr Ann Buchanan is a lecturer in the Department of Applied Social Science and Social Research, University of Oxford. She is a very experienced researcher and has published widely in the area of children and families.

Dr Bob Broad is a senior research fellow in the Department of Social and Community Studies at De Montfort University, Leicester. Previously, he was a social work lecturer at the London School of Economics and Science, a senior child care manager, and earlier a qualified probation officer.

Marion Burch is a retired foster carer who now runs workshops for local authorities on life story work.

Cathy Caine joined West Sussex County Council to be their first GALRO panel manager, and went on to chair the National Association of GALRO Panel Managers. Her current position is Policy Officer (Child Care).

Martin C. Calder is a Child Protection Co-ordinator and Reviewing Officer with City of Salford Community and Social Services Directorate. He has published on a wide range of child protection issues.

Sue Cart is the County Child Protection Advisor for West Sussex Social Services Department. She qualified as a social worker in 1984 and has always worked with children and families as well as lecturing at several universities.

Beverley Clarke is a health visitor. She is also chairperson of the CPHVA Private Fostering Special Interest Group. She is an RGN and RMM and has 12 years experience as a qualified health visitor.

Felicity Collier is director of BAAF. She has worked in child care social work, family court welfare and the probation service as practitioner, training manager and assistant chief officer. She was a guardian ad litem for several years and obtained her M. Phil in Social Work in 1994 at Brunel University and the Tavistock Clinic.

Hilary Corrick is Policy and Development Officer for children and families in Southampton exploring the implication of Best Value for children's services. She has worked in all aspects of child care since 1966. She was also involved with the development of the Looking After Children (LAC) materials, including supporting the implementation in England and elsewhere, including New Zealand and Australia.

Pat Doorbar is a psychologist with a commitment to social research. She is particularly interested in developing methodologies which enable vulnerable service users to communicate their views. She is an independent researcher whose clients include health authorities, social service departments and charitable foundations.

Ena Fry has been development worker for NFCA's Young People's Project since 1990. The project provides information, advice and training on teenage fostering as well as working with local authorities to develop better services for young people leaving foster care. Prior to joining NFCA Ena worked directly with young people in a range of local authority settings including ten years developing leaving care resources in an inner London authority.

Roger Greeff worked as a social worker with children and families in social services. He now teaches social work at Sheffield Hallam University. He has interests in children's rights, social work with children and families, and in anti discriminatory social work, especially in area of racism.

Jan Hawkins is a foster carer and trainer. She is also a support carer and has been on a variety of working parties set up to discuss foster care issues.

John Hudson is an experienced child care worker and consultant. He is also treasurer of Caring For Children, the UK arm of FICE (Federation Internationale des Communicatives Educatives).

Sheah Johansen began her career as a special needs teacher and then as deputy head of a remand unit, before going in to social work. She has worked in fostering and adoption, family placement and then joined NCH, Action For Children Family Finders Project in 1988. She is also an adoptive parent.

Kevin Lowe is Head of Services at the National Foster Care Association which he joined in 1989. Kevin wrote the training material 'Choosing to Foster - The Challenge To Care' and has led NFCA's role in helping to establish (S)NVQ qualifications for foster carers.

Dr Marion Miles is a consultant paediatrician and clinical director in child health to a community health trust in London. She is medical advisor to two local authorities and two voluntary agencies and is regularly concerned with medico-legal issues.

Simon Newstone works for Families for Children an independent fostering agency as a foster carer resource manager. He also offers consultancy, training and group work in foster care and HIV/AIDS.

Mari Piper spent five years in public care moving home a total of 25 times. In 1997 she started studying for an English degree at Leeds University and in 1998 she became a member of the Ministerial Task Force created to respond to the Utting Report - "People Like Us".

Linda Rayfield is a part time Education Welfare Officer employed by Milton Keynes council. She has been a youth worker, a community development worker and has recently qualified as a social worker. She is on the committee of the local foster carers' association.

Kate Rose is a qualified social worker employed by Salford Social Services. Her current project in Salford, Greater Manchester, concentrates on the issues for children and their carers following sexual abuse.

Maria Ruegger is a senior lecturer in social work in the Department of Social and Community Studies as De Montfort University. She is also a guardian ad litem on the Hertfordshire Panel of Guardians ad Litem and Reporting Officers.

Peter Sandiford is Senior Development Officer at the National Children's Bureau. Barbara Kahan says 'he has been in the care system for 43 years' - he was in care as a baby, an adopted child and as a worker.

Anne Savage is a qualified social worker, employed by the NSPCC. Her current project in Salford, Greater Manchester, concentrates on the issues for children and their carers following sexual abuse.

Clive Sellick is a lecturer in social work at the University of East Anglia where he is responsible for international programmes. He is a former social worker, team manager, magistrate and guardian ad litem.

Vivien Stuart is a family placement social worker for Wakefield Community and Social Services Department. She has been a social worker for over 14 years and is particularly interested in developing support and training groups for foster carers.

Pat Verity is Deputy Director of the National Foster Care Association. She has been involved in foster care, both as a carer and worker at NFCA for over 25 years.

Derek Warren trained as a newspaper journalist. He has spent the last 18 years working in media and communications for voluntary sector organisations, such as working on children's rights with UNICEF, in Central America. He is the secretary of the National Standards in Foster Care Project. He is also an adoptive parent.

Carol Woollard is a social worker. From 1990 - 1993 she was an advisor on policy and development for the African Family Advisory Service under the auspices of Save The Children.

Julia Waldman is an independent researcher, working on social work university programmes and is an associate for a human resource consultancy. She is also a family link carer.

Ann Wheal is in the Department of Social Work Studies at the University of Southampton. She previously spent 17 years teaching young people in inner-city, multi-racial schools and colleges. Her publications include the Foster Carer's Handbook.

The Nature and the Dilemmas of Fostering in the Nineties

Maria Ruegger and Linda Rayfield

Foster care is the term used to cover the wide range of activities undertaken by those who care for other people's children, usually with the state acting as intermediary between the child's natural family and those who are given responsibility for the care of its children. Foster-carers have a vital role to play in looking after children who cannot live at home both for short and lengthy periods. The nature of foster care provision has changed and developed since its inception in response to research findings, to changes in society that have led to changes in the population of those who require care, and to changes in the legal and organisational framework within which the service is provided.

In order to understand how fostering has arrived at its present state it is necessary first to understand where it has come from. Our aim in this introductory chapter is to take the reader on an albeit brief journey that traces the historical development of fostering, highlighting the major factors that influenced it along the way, with a view to defining current nature of the fostering task. We then go on to explore what we believe to be one of the most complex aspects of foster care practice today, namely drift from short to long term placement.

One of us has much direct personal experience of the difficulties and challenges involved in providing care for other people's children, and continues to struggle daily with the dilemmas that providing a repairing family environment, working alongside children's natural families and caring for one's own family present. The other is an academic and guardian ad litem who brings to the debate her knowledge and understanding of the factors that enhance children's emotional development, together with her experience of working with children in foster care who have been separated from their families. The debates we have engaged in with each other, often from opposite ends of the spectrum, have served to deepen our own understanding of the complexities of the fostering task. We share some of this here in the hope that others will be encouraged to take forward the development of knowledge in this under-researched area of foster care practice.

References to fostering go back to earliest times with mention being made in the Bible to children being cared for by adults not related to them, although the arrangements may not have been given a formal descriptive title. As with much history there are different versions of the same event. Readers are also referred to Heywood, J. (1978) an ackowledged leading authority on the history of childcare.

Records relating to the 16th century refer to young orphans being placed with nurses in the suburbs of London, although it was more common for care to be provided by institutions. By mid-Victorian times the numbers of destitute children requiring care were so great that many institutions housed upwards of 2000 children. Regimes were strict, so much so that many children preferred to live rough in order to have their freedom. These institutions had been set up with the good intention of rescuing children and thus containing the problems they presented to society, but they were not judged successful. Philanthropists in the mid 1800s such as Doctors Stephenson and Barnado, and Father Nugent began to advocate that different solutions were required if the hoards of destitute children were to become respectable citizens. They suggested that whilst institutions met the children's basic physical needs, they had an adverse effect on their emotional and social development. It was during the 19th century that developments took place which laid the foundation for fostering as it is known today.

The earliest known incidence of fostering in the modern sense was in 1853 when a Reverend Armistead in Cheshire placed children from a work house with foster parents. The local council was legally responsible for the children and paid carers an allowance equivalent to the amount required to maintain them in the workhouse. A few years later a Mrs. Hannah Archer in Swindon placed a number of orphan girls with foster carers who received the basic workhouse allowance supplemented by voluntary contributions. The following quotations are from a pamphlet which she wrote:

> In the workhouse the children's minds are contracted and their affections stifled... The workhouse school mistress cannot do a mother's part to the many little girls placed under her charge. She can be gentle with them as a shepherd with a flock of lambs, but they are to her as a mass of human life and one rule must answer for all.

Initially there was much opposition to fostering. It was feared that it would encourage feckless parents to be more irresponsible, producing and abandoning more children when they saw that their children had better care than they could afford to provide. It was also thought that foster children may be ill-treated or neglected by those who wished to profit financially from their care. However, its advantages over institutional care slowly came to be recognised and as fostering became more established, boarding out committees were formed throughout the country. These committees were responsible for recruiting foster parents, paying fostering allowances and supervising placements. The supervision of placements was initially undertaken by unpaid volunteer workers who gradually came to be replaced by paid full-time officials, the precursors of our modern day social workers. In 1908 there were 98 such officials, only six of whom were solely responsible for overseeing placements, the remainder having various other social and medical functions in the community. The duties of these boarding out committees were later taken over by children's departments and then social services departments. Fostering was at this time seen as a service for deserving children, a charitable act for which the recipients were expected to show gratitude. Until as recently as 1911 only orphaned or abandoned children between the ages of two and ten years could be fostered, and only then if they were considered to be healthy, normal and well behaved. Only very gradually did it come to be recognised that physically and mentally disabled children, and delinquents,

could benefit from specially selected foster homes. The provision of foster care continued to be seen as a charitable service, but both for the deserving and the undeserving poor and this remained the case until the outbreak of the Second World War.

As a result of the war more than a million children had to be evacuated from the cities and hence the practice of caring for other people's children became the subject of national attention. Whilst many had happy experiences of giving and receiving substitute family care, some did not. The neglect and violent death of Dennis O'Neill in 1945 at the hands of his foster father caused public disquiet at a time when there was a great idealistic upsurge to create a better society. Health, education and welfare systems were being reconstructed in accordance with new or revised concepts about sharing the national cake and sweeping aside the old indignities and equalities. The Curtis committee was set up to investigate the services provided to children cared for by the state and its conclusions resulted in a thorough overhaul of provision. The haphazard system of meeting children's needs through charitable deeds was finally brought to an end. Children's departments were set up and run by qualified social workers.

Amongst the first tasks of the newly created children's departments was the provision of care for some 5000 war orphans. Fostering came to be seen as a most valuable and economic way of providing good standards of substitute family care. Bowlby, in his seminal thesis *Child Care and the Growth of Love*, (Bowlby, 1953), had drawn attention to the importance for infants to have opportunities for close and loving relationships with a primary carer if their emotional and intellectual development was to be facilitated. Recognition of the importance of close and loving human contact for children alongside meeting their physical needs led to a rise in the popularity of foster care, although foster care was still regarded as a natural activity for women, and one that required little or no special training. There were still many lessons to be learnt about the nature of successful fostering, and how best to recruit and support foster carers in their task. For example, the pioneering work of James and Joyce Robertson, (Robertsons, 1969) led to the establishment of knowledge about how best to prepare children for placement, the nature of their needs in placement and how these might be met. The idea that children could be helped by being provided with reminders of their parents and previous home rather than being protected by denying the existence of their past was identified. The notion that young pre-verbal children needed only good physical care was successfully challenged and the traumatic impact of separating children from their primary carers was highlighted.

As knowledge about the complexities of the fostering task grew so did the demands made on foster carers. Rowe and Lamberts' study *Children who Wait*, (1973) drew attention to the great numbers of children who were removed from their parents and allowed to drift in care without any plans being made for their future. Through their work they drew attention to children's need to have a sense of belonging to a family who were committed to them, rather than the state delegating it's responsibility for their temporary care to others. In *Beyond the Best Interest of the Child*, Freud, Goldstein and Solnit (1973) it is argued, that, with hindsight it must be said, on the basis of largely anecdotal evidence, that children could not cope with more than one set of 'psychological' parents. The joint impact of these two extremely influential publications led to what has since been termed 'permanency planning' coming into vogue. Great efforts were made to find permanent substitute families for children who it was thought could not be rehabilitated to their natural families. It was considered best for these children if all contact and legal ties with the birth family were severed.

The importance of the different things that could be offered to children by people who were able to provide short term care as compared to those who were able to offer permanent homes began to be recognised. However, further research has called into question the benefits of severing ties and cutting off contact between children in long term care and their families, see Tristeliotis, J P. (1983), Fratter, J. (1989). Such findings were embodied in the Children Act 1989 which moves away from the concept of rescuing children from their families to providing a service for families. The emphasis is on ensuring that, wherever possible, children are brought up by their own families and that appropriate services are provided to support them. It is now recognised that the dangers of removing children from their families are such that the child is likely to suffer a loss of self esteem and lack confidence in themselves as being worthy of love and care. Research and experience has shown that these problems are not easily solved through the provision of good substitute family care.

The foster carers' task, once considered so natural as to require little in the way of training or special expertise, has come to be regarded as so fraught with difficulties that it should only be attempted when there is no alternative. The manner in which the scales are balanced in determining what is good enough parenting has changed, and much thought is given to supporting and supplementing poor parenting before risking the potentially damaging emotional consequences of removing children from their families. Where children have to be removed it is thought that for the most part, particularly with children who are old enough to have a strong sense of who their families are, that their development is likely to be enhanced through continued contact with their natural families. Thus foster carers are having to develop skills in working alongside natural families not only when rehabilitation is being considered but also when offering a child a permanent home.

The recognition of the need for special training and the expertise, that must be continually updated in the light of research and knowledge, is now well established. Today foster care is seen as a professional vocation that requires different skills and knowledge from that which parents typically possess, although it must be pointed out that it is not often remunerated as such. Foster carers require training in child development generally and attachment theory in particular, an understanding of how the various unfortunate experiences that most of the children they care for will have affected their development, and knowledge of how best to help them recover. They need to know what to expect from children who have been emotionally, physically and sexually abused and to be able to cope with the low expectations that these vulnerable damaged young people will have of their carers and what they have to offer. They need to have techniques available to them to assist the young people they care for in the process of building their trust and self esteem, and at the same time to be able to balance the competing demands of their own families. In many circumstances they must also be able to work alongside the child's natural family, tolerate their rejection or even hostility, and yet help the child they care for to recognise all that is positive in their blood relations. In addition to training they need to be professionally supported in order to meet the needs of the children they care for.

Fostering then has evolved and developed to become a multifaceted and complex task. It can usefully be subdivided under three different headings; short term fostering, long-term fostering and intermediate fostering, each requiring different skills, knowledge and abilities. Short term fostering involves looking after other people's children for short periods of up to six months. The majority of children who are fostered fall into this category. These placements are often initiated in response to a crisis but they may be planned, as in the case of respite care provision. The usual aim in short term placements is to return the child to their family. Research indicates that rehabilitation is more likely to be successful if the child is returned home within weeks of being separated from his family, (Parker and Farmer, 1991) The task of the foster carer, in addition to providing for the daily needs of the child, is to assist the process of rehabilitation. These placements tend to be busy and involve frequent contact between the child and his family, possible visits for medical or psychiatric assessments, supervision of contact, attendance at meetings and occasionally giving evidence in court proceedings.

Long-term foster carers provide permanent substitute families for children. Often the child will retain at least some tenuous link with their natural family, notwithstanding the fact that it is expected that they will be cared for outside their natural family for the remainder of their childhood.

Intermediate placements are defined here as those short term placements which extend beyond six months. Typically children in such placements are those for whom rehabilitation was unsuccessful and who are awaiting a permanent placement, or those for whom there has been a delay in finding a permanent family following identification of the need. The primary task for carers will be to assist the child in coming to terms with the plans that have been made for them. This may become complicated by the child forming a strong attachment to the carers and expressing the wish to remain with them. Often the carers too have formed an emotional bond with the child and do not wish to cause them further distress through yet another separation from those they have begun to trust. Well informed foster carers will be only too aware of the research that demonstrates increasing vulnerability with each placement. They will want to protect children from moves within the care system if possible. The carers face a dilemma: the needs of the child for whom they have sought to provide the highest possible standard of care may be in conflict with the needs of the foster carers and their own families. Their own personal conflict may be further compounded by pressure, either overt or covert, from the child's social worker who will have their clients needs to the forefront of her thinking.

The following account of the experience of short term foster carers who drifted into intermediate caring, and then became long term carers by default illustrates the enormous difficulties facing carers and those they seek to help. It poses difficult and uncomfortable questions that highlight the limitations on what we can do for children through the provision of alternative family care, and identifies the challenges currently facing carers and those responsible for the organisation, delivery and development of substitute family care services.

Linda's story

Whilst working as a youth worker I had often considered what else I could do to support vulnerable young people. I chose to foster as I felt that I could offer children in need some of the benefits that come from the stable and secure family environment I shared with my husband and four daughters. Initially we had three 'lodgers' from the 16 plus age group over a period of two years. Following this we were approved to provide a short term placement for one, 8-12 year old girl. We wanted to help a child in need by offering them acceptance, providing time out and the opportunity to think clearly about the past, talk about the present and plan for the future. We understood that a short-term placement would be for a period of no longer than six months, during which time the child either returned home, or long term arrangements would have been made for their permanent care. My expectations were that contact visits between the child and her family would be frequent, conversations and meetings with natural parents difficult but necessary, and visits and telephone calls from social workers likely to happen at the most inconvenient times! My family agreed to this, enjoying the challenges presented by new relationships whilst knowing that no matter how difficult and unsociable some young people were, their stay was time limited and they would eventually be moving on. We also expected that if we were not able to provide a 'repairing' environment for any individual child that our views would be valued and our decisions respected.

Over a period of two to three years we had several placements ranging from overnight to six months in duration. I thrive on the constant activity and achieve immense satisfaction from the knowledge that whilst we may not make things right, accommodating young people provides families with the time to reflect upon why and where things had gone wrong. This often assisted in helping the family establish ways of coping with adolescent behaviour which eventually led to the child's return home. Naturally there are many challenges and obstacles to be overcome in every placement. Contact with natural parents is frequent and demanding. Natural parents typically see carers as a threat and there were often disagreements between us about differences in house rules and routines. Initial negotiations require considerable patience, tact and understanding. The aim is to reinforce and support the parental relationship where possible so as to preserve it for the future, whilst at the same time introducing the child to our own domestic routines. I constantly find myself in a dilemma as to how everyone's needs can be met, including those of my own family, particularly at the beginning of any new placement, and many compromises are necessary along the way. However, after the initial settling in process, short-term placements in our experience have been rewarding and successful. Naturally there are plenty of disagreements, but I consider problem solving a useful skill for managing adult life and see it as a potential advantage that my daughters have had more opportunities to practice this skill than they otherwise might.

However, problems arose when a teenager who joined us was later assessed as being in need of long term family care. Social workers, happy with the positive changes to the young person's behaviour during her early stay with us, saw no reason why we should not continue to meet her needs in a long term placement until she was ready to leave the care system. Understandably, social workers appear anxious to maintain the positive attachments the child has made to short term carers and convey the view, consciously or

otherwise, that if something is working it is best to allow it to continue to do so. Offering children a long term placement can mean the initial six months being extended over many years as local authorities have a legal duty to offer 'looked after' children assistance until they reach the age of twenty-one.

My family agreed that we would offer this particular child a place in our family on a long term basis without any real idea of the complexities involved in so doing. Having made the decision to offer her a semi-permanent place in our home, everyone in the family sub-consciously began to expect more from the changing and enduring nature of the relationship. For example my younger children found it difficult to understand how their foster sister could still be under considerable influence from her natural parents if there were no plans for her to return home. They expected her to obey the same rules, and to be treated the same as themselves, when it came to punishments. At a deeper level they expected their growing affection for and attachment to their foster sister to be reciprocated in a manner similar to that which characterises their relationship with their birth sisters. Family life had by then taken on routines that included the foster child and it is true that we all began to have similar expectations of her as of each other. To us she was now one of the family in many respects, but there were some very obvious differences, in addition to the influence exerted by her parents, that acted as a barrier to full integration. For example one that stands out is the arguments between sisters that occasionally erupt into physical encounters. At such times our children must be reminded of the existence of child protection procedures. "You can't hit me or I'll tell my social worker", does not assist in the development of sisterly bonds! Another more serious issue that has been a constant source of family conflict concerned fostering allowances. There are nationally agreed rates which are in my opinion unrealistic when looked at in comparison to what I can allow my own children. These are two examples that serve to highlight our foster daughter's 'alien' status within our family.

On reflection it seems to me that our expectations as to how a temporary guest could join our family on a permanent basis were unrealistic in other respects as well. We were 'lulled' into a false sense of security because we felt that we had been accepted, and that we had succeeded in making available to someone else what we all share with each other. In my own naivety I had assumed that by offering this child the security of a long term placement that she would eventually recognise genuine care and concern and be able to differentiate between 'confusion' and 'order'. The 'confusion' being the uncertainty about her relationships with her birth family experienced regularly at contact visits, and the 'order' being the sense of security achieved through the predictable daily routines maintained in our family.

It seems to us now that it would be unwise for those providing long term foster care to a child who initially came as a temporary guest and who remains in contact with her natural parents to hope that the relationship is likely to be anything other than superficial. The blood tie is strong and can withstand much ill treatment and inconsistent emotional care. For the child's part, how can she deal with divided loyalties other than to rely on the one thing that she is sure of; the only tie that cannot be broken or changed as a result of other people's commitment or planning meetings at social services offices is surely the blood tie?

Our long stay foster child has been with us for over three years now. She should be moving on shortly as she is now 17 and I cannot see that we as a family have anything else to offer. I believe I have honoured my commitment to this young person, accommodation has been her 'lifeline' and she is now experiencing life and its challenges as an average 17-year-old. Problems that children have acquired as a result of abuse, neglect and rejection are difficult to overcome completely and often we must be satisfied with less that we would wish for. I have to come to terms with the limitations of fostering as compared to parenting and am proud of my own and my family's achievements. It would be both unrealistic and counter productive to think in any other way.

Fostering is a challenging occupation. If those fostering have a realistic attitude to young people and their families they will know and accept that with short-term placements they are one of life's 'sticky plasters.' They are there to protect, keep safe and help in the healing of wounds. The 'plaster' is essential to keep the wound infection free, however, once the wound is clean the 'plaster' is discarded its importance fades into insignificance. Any future contact is seen as a bonus and not an expectation.

Carers that wish to take on the role of 'sticky plasters' should be respected for that and careful thought must be given before any change is made to their role. Whilst we must all consider what is in the best interests of the child when reviewing placements, and secure attachments are indeed key elements to a successful fostering relationship, attention must be given to the complexities involved in delivering the care required. As Lindsey points out when speaking of the dangers inherent in allowing drift between short and long term placements, 'there is a serious risk that the psychological commitment needed to parent a child on a permanent basis is not there'. (Lindsay, 1995). Pressure on foster carers to agree to make a further commitment on the strength of the needs of the child, shows a lack of understanding on the part of social workers of the emotive family issues that are uppermost in the minds of the carers. There are no easy solutions as every placement presents different problems.

We need to develop a better understanding of the complexities involved in changing from short to long term carers if children and foster families are to be properly prepared and supported. Foster carers could contribute much to this body of knowledge from their experiences. This requires a move on the part of academics and policy makers towards acknowledging the important information, knowledge and skills that carers have developed through their experiences, and which are not available to social workers or others professionally involved in providing substitute care for children. In addition consideration must be given as to how children, both those who have been fostered and those who have taken on the role of foster sisters and brothers, can be both involved in, and informed about, the issues and the process and the value of their own contributions to our knowledge of how best to help children, should not be overlooked.

Ultimately, we believe that providing substitute family care can be a positive, helpful and rewarding experience for young people and carers but only if all concerned are realistic about what can be achieved. As there is acceptance about the criteria that can be applied to 'good enough parenting' maybe we should think about what criteria can be identified for 'good enough fostering,' in all its different forms. Particularly in that little researched area of placement drift which has been the main focus of this introductory chapter. It is our hope that this will be a task that foster carers, children, social workers, academics, and perhaps parents, will work together on in the near future with a view to providing a foster care service that is better able to meet the needs of children and families in the millennium and beyond.

References

Bowlby, J. (1953) *Child Care and the Growth of Love.* Penguin

Farmer, E. and Parker, R. (1991) *Trials and Tribulations: Returning Children from Care to their Families.* HMSO.

Fratter, J. (1989) *Family Placement and Access: Achieving Permanency for Children in Contact with Birth Parents.* Barnados

Goldstein, J., Freud, A., and Solnit, A. (1973) *Beyond the Best Interests of the Child.* Free press.

Heywood, J. (1998) *Children in Care.* Routledge & Kegan Paul

Lindsey, C. (1995) Alternative Caretakers in *Assessment of Parenting* (Eds. Reder, P. and Lucey, C.)

Rowe, J. and Lambert, L. (1973) *Children Who Wait.* ABAFA

Robertson, James and Robertson, Joyce (1969) *Young Children in Brief Separation:* John Concorde Film Council

Tristeliotis, J.P. (1983) Identity and Security in Adoption and Long Term Fostering. *Adoption and Fostering,* 7:1, 22-31.

1.1 The Child - Changing Perceptions of Children and Childhood

Moira Borland

Introduction

It hardly needs saying that we are living in a time of rapid change and that foster care is constantly evolving in response to new legislation, changes in how services are provided and developments in understanding of what constitutes 'good practice'. Twenty five years ago the foster *parents'* role was to care for the child 'as a member of their own family'. Today foster *carers* are asked to take on a whole range of tasks and to adapt the service they offer to cater for individual children. As many of the chapters in this volume will no doubt illustrate, by actively responding to new challenges, foster care continues to provide a relevant service for today's children.

This chapter will argue that in addition to taking on new tasks and roles, present day foster carers are being asked to assimilate new and in some respects competing views about the nature of children, their needs and their relationships with parents or carers. New sociological perspectives on childhood and the children's rights movement have challenged some of the traditional ways of understanding children's lives, yet there has been relatively little explicit consideration of what this means for the day-to-day care of children.

Through changes in private law and general attitudes, these shifts in perspective affect all children and parents. However their impact is brought into much sharper focus in the field of foster care, partly since foster carers work within the framework of local authorities' duties to children. This brings with it a requirement to safeguard and promote children's welfare, to promote contact with parents and to take account of the child's race, religion and cultural and linguistic background. There is also a duty to ascertain the views of the child and to have regard to these views when making decisions which affect the child, in accordance with the child's age and maturity. The views of parents are also to be sought and taken into account. Within this framework, foster carers look after some of the most needy yet challenging children and young people in our society, aiming to care for them in a manner which respects their individuality and maximises their right to self-determination whilst also safeguarding and promoting their welfare.

These considerations give rise to some practical dilemmas. For example, in what circumstances can a desire to safeguard children justify disregarding their views, not respecting privacy or restricting their freedom? Questions such as these have been widely debated in principle but the arguments have not always filtered through to people caring directly for children. This is unfortunate, since this is one of the many subjects on which practitioners and theoreticians have much to learn from each other. While carers can benefit from an understanding of the thoughtful consideration which others have given to these issues, feedback based on practical experience is invaluable in refining the theoretical arguments and furthering our understanding of how best to care for children.

This chapter outlines some aspects of current thinking about children and suggests some ways in which these ideas impact on foster care. Each perspective can be considered only briefly and further reading is suggested in the bibliography.

Changing Lives and Changing Perceptions of Children

Few would deny that the current lives of Britain's children would have been unimaginable to many of the previous generation. Though a minority of children continue to experience poverty and social deprivation, materially most are well provided for, while holidays abroad, satellite television and their ability to 'surf the net' allow many children unprecedented access to the wider world. However with increased opportunity and material prosperity has come a range of concerns about their safety and future security in a changing and unpredictable world (Hill and Tisdall, 1997). High competition in the job market adds to the pressure to succeed at school and an increasing number of children will live through the break-up of their parents' marriage. Fears about dangers from traffic and abusive strangers has resulted in many parents restricting children's scope to explore their local environment and enjoy unsupervised play, while for some children exposure to abuse, neglect and exploitation is a depressing reality. Children are seen as knowledgeable and privileged yet at the same time vulnerable and under pressure (Borland et al., 1998).

Children can also be considered a threat. Some media reports portray young people as all-powerful, asserting their right to challenge parental actions and ignore adult guidance, while using their child status to protect them from the full consequences of their own behaviour, for example if they break the law. Accounts of classroom indiscipline and child crime fuel fears that children are out of control, which in turn is often attributed to the eroding of adult authority. At the same time a relentless catalogue of child sexual abuse continues to be uncovered. Children have been abused within families, the church and care homes, providing compelling evidence that they are more vulnerable when adults have too much control and that empowering children is a key means of protecting them. Thus contemporary views about 'problem' children, how to best care for them and how to manage their relationship with adults are complex and in some respects contradictory.

There is of course nothing new about society holding conflicting or complex views about the nature of children or how they should be treated. Throughout history two essential images of children recur: that of the unruly child, needing to be guided, controlled or even tamed and the innocent child, requiring protection from corruption and the adult world. The prevailing view has shifted at different points in history, reflecting the social and economic conditions of the time. For example at the start of the 19th century child-labour was viewed as an acceptable practice through which children were taught important

economic, social and moral principles, while by the end of the century it was seen as subjecting 'innocent' children to brutalising conditions and denying them their childhood (Hendrick, 1997).

Thus it might be argued that our present pre-occupations about child crime and sexual abuse are modern day versions of long-standing concerns. However ideas about the 'empowerment' of children are new and add a distinctive dimension to today's debate. Children are no longer seen simply as 'objects' of adult concern but as individuals who actively shape their own lives and who have a right to be protected, to develop their potential and to be consulted in matters which affect their lives.

Two important theoretical perspectives have contributed to this rethinking of how we understand and care for children. The 'new sociology of childhood' has invited us to reconsider our view of childhood and children's experiences, while the children's rights movement has re-evaluated the relationship between children and adults.

The New Sociology of Childhood

Several elements of the 'new' sociological thinking about children are likely to strike a chord with 'child-centred' foster carers. This approach argues that adults do children a disservice by organising and controlling their lives from an adult point of view, rather than seeking to understand and being guided by children's own perspectives. As a consequence, it is argued, adults fail to recognise children's capability, diversity and the ways in which they actively shape their lives. Instead they are depicted as developing along predetermined pathways, passively responding to life events, a view which misrepresents the significant contributions children make in life and implies that childhood's only value is as a preparation for adulthood. It is argued that most research into children has encouraged this viewpoint by treating them as 'objects of study', observing and analysing separate aspects of their behaviour and circumstances, rather than talking with children, exploring the *meaning* of significant events and experiences with them and recognising that childhood is a different but equally valid stage of life (James and Prout, 1997).

Expressed in these broad terms, the new sociological analysis seems uncontroversially child-centred. However it does constitute a challenge to some traditional perspectives, notably those derived from developmental psychology which have been very influential since the start of this century. Based on the study of specific behaviours at different ages, these traditional theories assert that children develop progressively through clearly defined stages. Although differences in individual circumstances and personality are recognised as important influences on how individual children negotiate each stage, all children are expected to progress along broadly similar pathways. The theories of Freud (sexual development), Erikson (psychosocial development), Kohlberg (moral development) and Piaget (cognitive development) would all come into this category, as would attachment theory (Bowlby).

The sociological critique questions two key aspects of developmental approaches, namely the focus on 'normal' development and the ways in which children's needs are defined.

The focus on 'normal' development is criticised on several grounds. Firstly it is argued that the developmental perspective overstates the importance of innate biological development, while underestimating the diverse ways in which social circumstances shape the experience of individual children. Thus, for example, while a developmental psychologist would be interested in the typical reaction of two year olds when separated from familiar carers, the sociologist would argue that the experience of any individual child will be shaped as much by their gender, class, race culture and family circumstances as by the innate characteristics of all two year old children.

A second objection to the psychologist's pre-occupation with normality is that any divergence from the norm is seen as a deficit, so that, for example, the developmental progress of a child with disabilities would be seen as inferior to rather than different from most children. It is further claimed that what is considered 'normal' often reflects western, middle class standards, thus implying the inferiority of other cultures (Woodhead, 1997). Developmental psychology is accused of

pathologising the diversity which the new sociologists wish to celebrate.

Developmental psychology itself has not remained immune from these criticisms. There has been recognition of the powerful ways in which factors such as race, class and gender determine how growing up is experienced and contemporary psychological theory now seeks to understand how the biological and the social interact (Burman, 1994).

Criticism of how children's needs are defined reflect similar arguments, namely that needs are 'socially constructed' rather than biologically determined and as such reflect the values and social and economic conditions of society at any one time.

A Norwegian study provides a useful illustration of how ideas about children's needs change. During the 1980s changes in the work pattern of mothers and children's reluctance to attend after school care contributed to a shift in views about children's need for adult supervision. It became accepted practice for quite young children to remain at home alone after school so that only 15 per cent of 7-9 year olds and 10 per cent of 8-9 year olds were having any day care arrangement after school (Solberg, 1997). Within Britain, leaving an eight year old alone every day might well be seen as constituting neglect, perhaps in part reflecting the fact that most Norwegian children live in small towns and villages which are considered safer.

Thus, it is argued, ideas about what children need result from a complex interplay of social circumstances, traditional assumptions about children and the actions of children themselves. It follows that in order to fully understand children, we need to become aware of the underlying assumptions which influence current perceptions and attitudes.

The New Sociology of Childhood and Foster Care

So, what relevance has this sociological approach for foster carers? Firstly it is important to say that the insights gained from developmental psychology have served child care practice well and should be rethought and refined rather than rejected. It is useful to know that a two year old and a six year old can be expected to respond differently to being separated from their known carers, even if each individual child's reaction will be shaped by their own previous experience and the meaning they and others attach to the separation. In the same way as psychologists are refining developmental theory, foster carers are in a good position to ensure that its use in practice reflects children's lives as they are lived, rather than imposes standards to which they are expected to conform.

Some of the discussion around the introduction of the Assessment and Action Records from the Looking After Children Materials has reflected the tensions between a developmental and sociological perspective on children. The materials themselves are based on a developmental approach, their purpose being to chart children's progress and identify what services or support are needed in order to achieve desirable outcomes in relation to health, education, behavioural and emotional difficulties, family and social relationships, self-care skills, identity and self-presentation. The records aim to adopt the standards most parents expect for children in Britain to-day (Ward, 1995), though their purpose is to highlight individual needs and take into account fundamental aspects of children's social context, including family circumstances, race, religion and culture.

While widely accepted as useful in ensuring reasonable standards of care, critics have claimed that the records' developmental framework marginalises the importance of social context and reflects middle class values. Knight and Caveney (1998) argue that a child's needs and problems cannot be understood through the use of checklists or comparison against standard norms. Rather they argue, social workers need to take time to get to know children as individuals in order to understand the *meaning* of specific behaviours in the context of their lives. For example a willingness to readily share with other children may indicate a degree of self confidence, kindness or a wish to buy friendship. They also object to the fact that some of the questions and expectations reflect middle class values

In replying to these criticisms, Jackson (1998) explains that the purpose of the records is not simply to assess but to prompt discussion of the child's wider situation, encourage more pro-active involvement by social workers and to help ensure that looked after children can expect the same standard of care as children living with their parents. Jackson further claims that, far from valuing individuality, reluctance to set standards for children in care reflects Poor Law notions that children in public care do not merit equal opportunities. As she points out, working class as well as middle class parents want their children to do well. Carefully monitoring children's progress against the standards expected by most parents are an important means of promoting best outcomes and enabling children to fulfil their potential.

This exchange highlights the ways in which different and sometimes opposing ideas underpin current foster care practice. We aim to value children's diversity, while trying to ensure this does not mean they have to settle for a lower standard, and seek to replicate the personal care of a concerned parent through a complex combination of care arrangements, reviews and forms. Given their close knowledge and relationship with the children they care for, foster carers are key players in ensuring that the result is the best possible outcome for the child. Adherents of the new sociology argue that children's lives have been studied, described and understood from an adult perspective, leading to a view of children which does not reflect or give due attention to their actual experience. Foster carers have a key role in ensuring that this does not happen within social work practice.

Children's Rights

The children's rights perspective has much in common with the new sociology of childhood. Both view children as active participants in society and claim that their competence is often underestimated by adults. They also share the belief that the interests of children and adults may be different and that adults cannot always be relied on to effectively represent children's interests.

However interest in Children's Rights is not new, dating at least from the nineteenth century, and the rights claimed for children are not only about challenging adults or asserting independence. The first Declaration on the Rights of the Child, adopted by the League of Nations in 1924, was concerned with children's survival and protection, largely in response to the effects of the First World War.

Protection and welfare rights are no less important in the modern-day UN Convention on the Rights of the Child. By far the majority of the Convention's 54 articles are to do with rights to survival and development through health care, education, food, clean water and appropriate environment. Several articles deal with children's rights when their safety requires removal from their family environment and the state becomes responsible for their care and protection (for example Articles 20 and 25).

In addition children are accorded participation rights, which, as explained in the *Background to the Convention*, are based on 'the concept of the child as an active and contributing participant in society and not merely as a passive recipient of good or bad treatment'. It is this notion of children's entitlement to actively shape their lives which is new. Article 12 accords any child who is capable of forming a view the right to express that view in all matters which affect them and requires that the views of the child be given due weight, in accordance with their age and maturity. In addition children are entitled to freedom of thought (Article 14) and expression (Article 13), free association (Article 15) and to privacy (Article 16).

Britain ratified the convention in 1991 but its provisions are not fully incorporated into UK legislation. However its principles are reflected in the Children Acts which govern each part of the United Kingdom (The Children Act (1989), The Children (Scotland) Act (1995), The Children (Northern Ireland) Order (1995)). Child welfare has thus incorporated a rights perspective into services which have traditionally operated on the basis of meeting needs.

Though the rights rhetoric is powerful, not everyone is convinced that children's interests are best served by giving children rights (Cooper,1998). As part of a study into parents' roles and tasks during middle childhood, colleagues and myself had an opportunity to talk with parents and foster carers about their views of children's rights. Though much more informed than other parents about what adopting a children's rights perspective entailed, foster carers expressed similar reservations to parents. Whilst there was general agreement that children were entitled to protection and to good physical and emotional care, there were doubts as to whether this was best guaranteed through giving children rights. Their preference was to think in terms of adults having a responsibility to meet children's needs rather than to conjure up the somewhat adversarial image of children claiming their right to be provided for and protected. However foster carers were very aware that not all children could rely on their own parents to protect their interests.

When it came to participation and autonomy rights, a similar stance was adopted. While it was acknowledged that 'good' parents and carers would involve children in decisions which affected them, dangers were foreseen if children were given too much say. These included the possibility that their immaturity would result in decisions which were not in their best interests and that adults might put them under pressure to express a particular point of view. Some foster carers thought that conferring rights burdened children with too much responsibility. There was a general view that adopting a 'rights' approach put at risk both children's 'right to be a child' and adults' authority to guide and control them appropriately (Borland et al., 1998).

These arguments put forward by parents and carers reflect many of the objections to the more radical proponents of children's rights. During the 1970s the child liberationists challenged the protectionist stance which had hitherto been adopted (Holt, 1975). They claimed that restrictions on children were discriminatory rather than protective and that, from an early age, children should be accorded the same rights as adults, for example to choose where to live, to vote, work and be sexually active. This perspective was widely criticised for failing to acknowledge the differences between children and adults and the reality of young children's dependence on adult care and protection (Fox- Harding, 1991). A more moderate view now prevails, namely that children do have rights but not the same rights as adults. Children's rights must take into account their best interests so that some adult rights are restricted, while welfare and protective rights are enhanced. Thus there are restrictions on children's right to work but they are entitled to education and to special treatment if they break the law.

One of the key considerations behind this moderate standpoint is that children's capacities to make rational choices develop with age, just as their dependence on adults decreases. According to Ochaita and Espinoza (1997), a rights perspective demands that children's opportunities to be involved in decisions which affect them should be maximised from an early age, starting with giving them a say about everyday matters such as choice of activities in nursery or how to spend leisure time at home. In order to help children learn to form and express a view about their situation, adults need to understand how children think and to communicate in a manner to which children can respond. These authors contend that this requires more rather than less recognition of the differences between adults and children and how patterns of thought and communication develop with age.

In a similar vein, Freeman (1983) argued that self-determination was a capacity to be developed, not a right bestowed. Since children are entitled to develop the ability to be rational and make decisions on their own behalf, adult actions which are consistent with that aim may be justified in terms of children's rights, even if they disregard the child's wishes in the short term. The test is whether the child would be likely to make that choice if capable of rational thought and whether the reasoning behind the decision can be explained to the child in adult life. Requiring children to go to school, for example, can be justified in these terms.

Consistent with the UN Convention, child welfare legislation in the United Kingdom recognises that children's capacity for rational decision making increases with age and seeks to achieve a balance between according children rights to be self-determining and allowing adults to retain enough control to ensure their welfare. Courts, children's panels and local authorities have a duty to ascertain and take into account children's views before making decisions which affect them but their over-riding duty is to act in the children's best interests, not necessarily in accordance with their views. Children's capacity to understand and make an informed decision also determines whether they are able to exercise rights to refuse medical or psychiatric assessment or to give or withhold consent to treatment. Similarly young people are able to initiate their own application to a court but the court will only allow the application to be heard if it considers that the child has 'sufficient understanding' to make an application. Thus, in most respects, adults reserve the right to regulate children's capacity to decide for themselves about important matters.

The rights of children to act independently of their parents are similarly circumscribed. Only 16 and 17 year olds can be accommodated without their parents' consent. Under the Children (Scotland) Act 1995, local authorities can provide 'refuge' to younger children at their request but this will usually last for only seven days (though it can be extended to 14 days) at which point parental consent or grounds for statutory measure are required. Similarly the Scottish Act gives children the right to put their point of view to a children's panel without their parents being present, though the parents are to be given a summary of the main points of the discussion when they rejoin the hearing.

From this perspective it might be argued that far from being a 'children's charter' current UK legislation continues to allow parents, carers and adults in authority considerable discretion in determining the extent to which children's views influence decisions which affect them. Yet it would be wrong to suggest that the relationship between children and adults is unchanged. The language of rights does indicate that children are *entitled* to be cared for and protected by adults and that, in some situations, there will be divergence between children's interests and the wishes of those who care for them. Acknowledging a child's 'right' to be consulted or to be educated puts the onus on adults to take appropriate action and (at least in principle) allows the child to seek redress if they do not do so. Adults now need justification for not respecting children's rights.

Children's Rights and Foster Care

In many respects the foster carer's role within a rights framework is already well developed. Within the foster home, carers have the opportunity to involve children in decisions about every day matters so that they can begin to learn to make choices from a young age. Outwith the foster home, carers may argue for the provision of services to which young people are entitled or help children and young people express their views on particular issues. For example, young people making a decision about whether to have contact with an estranged parent might be helped by ensuring they have relevant information, helping them think through the options, rehearsing how best to convey their own wishes or agreeing how the carer should express the child's views on their behalf.

There may however be scope for the foster carers' role to be extended. As Marshall (1997) points out, there can be several barriers to children exercising their fundamental right to express a view and have that view taken into account, in accordance with age and understanding. Firstly someone has to decide whether the child is capable of forming a view and then to assess their maturity in order to determine how much weight their view should carry. These are crucial decisions, yet at present we lack clarity about who should make them. While the views of experts such as psychologists are extremely useful, it is unrealistic to expect that their services can be engaged in every case. Instead social workers, carers and others who work with children are needing to develop skills in carrying out these tasks. The involvement of carers may be especially important when children have special needs or use idiosyncratic means of communicating.

A second barrier to children's views being accorded due weight in formal decision making procedures is that most people charged with representing their views, for example social workers, safeguarders, guardians ad litem, are required to base decisions on what they consider to be in the child's best interests. The child's view is an important consideration but is nevertheless one of several to be taken into account. In some instances it may be appropriate for foster carers to directly represent the young person's views or to argue that the child's wishes should prevail. This may sometimes result in carers opposing the decisions of social workers in their employing authority but if children's rights are to be taken seriously, this may be a tension which has to be managed.

Most debate about promoting children's rights has focused on children's involvement in formal decision making systems, understandably since the concept and language of rights is well established in legal procedures. Yet working within a rights framework also poses challenges and dilemmas in the day to day management of children. For example, a carer may want to restrict a young girl's wish to receive phone-calls in private or mix in the company she chooses, if there is evidence that her associates are encouraging her to earn money through sex. Not only have they to decide whether it is right to impose limits on her rights to privacy and free association, but to determine the type and level of restraint which would be acceptable in order to protect her. Carers and social work staff would no doubt take into account her age, maturity and level of perceived risk but would still face the difficult task of reconciling competing rights.

However, discussions to resolve matters of this kind would not necessarily be conducted simply in terms of rights. Child care has traditionally operated within a 'needs' rather than 'rights' framework. Drawing on psychological theories, carers are accustomed to think in terms of recognising and finding ways of meeting children's needs, for example for care, affection, praise, boundaries and protection. As indicated by some of the carers and parents who took part in our study referred to above, many prefer this to the more legalistic language of rights, especially when talking about children's well-being. As a result, dilemmas of the kind outlined can be seen as a conflict between meeting (welfare and protection) *needs* and respecting (participation and autonomy) *rights*, rather than reconciling competing needs and rights.

It might be argued that how these dilemmas are conceptualised matters very little in practice. Rights and needs are closely interlinked, both implicitly demanding a response from adults. Indeed rights can be considered an entitlement to have needs met, so that the need to be kept safe becomes a right to protection, whilst participation and autonomy rights derive from the need to become a self-determining individual, capable of making independent decisions. However the two approaches convey different connotations of the adult-child relationship, the language of 'rights' conveying a stronger and more impersonal claim on adults, if necessary backed up by legal powers, whilst 'needs' implies more benign adults who can be relied on to determine and cater for children's needs.

Foster care is required to accommodate both perspectives, as indeed are all parents, though, as noted earlier, rights issues are necessarily far more prominent in foster care. Not clarifying the nature of protection/self -determination dilemmas can result in the perception that giving children rights prevents adults from protecting them. In addition the powerful language of rights can accord self-determination claims more weight than is appropriate and suggest that there is little scope for negotiation or discretion on these issues. In the example given above, this kind of thinking might result in the belief that the right to free association and privacy prevented any restrictions being imposed. Care about terminology will not necessarily make these decisions easier nor help find ways of persuading young people away from dangerous life-styles, but may allow key issues to emerge more clearly.

Consideration of rights issues thus further illustrates the complexity of the foster care task, as carers seek to assimilate a range of views about children, their relationship with adults and how to best promote their interests. There is much to be learned from foster carers' extensive experience about how competing demands are managed and resolved and about the practical consequences for individual children.

Concluding Remarks

This chapter has highlighted a range of competing perspectives which foster carers seek to accommodate as they care for some of the most troubled children in our society. Some of these children will be seen by the outside world as victims, others as a threat. Foster carers know these simplistic distinctions seldom reflect an individual child's complex experience and may find themselves challenging stereotypes held by neighbours, school staff or potential employers.

Though based on clearly articulated principles and duties, the child welfare system also incorporates different perspectives.

Traditional developmental approaches now encompass respect for children's rights and increased attention to how social context shapes children's experience. These developments are to be welcomed since they help ensure that children are cared for and understood within frameworks which take account of the risks, complexity and diversity in their lives.

Of course foster carers do not take on the caring task alone. They are part of a wider network, working in partnership with young people, parents, social workers and a range of other professionals. It is likely that each of these partners will hold somewhat different ideas about the nature of childhood, children and their relationship with adults and will have their own understanding of what is meant by 'respecting rights', 'meeting needs' and 'promoting welfare'. Further discussion about how such phrases have been interpreted in theory and in practice can only enhance effective collaboration and help ensure that the caring task is understood in all its complexity.

References

Borland, M., Laybourn, A., Hill, M., Brown, J. (1998) *Middle Childhood: The Perspectives of Children and Parents,* Jessica Kingsley, London

Burman, E (1994) *Deconstructing Developmental Psychology* Routledge, London

Cooper, D.M.(1998) More Law and more rights: will children benefit? in *Child and Family Social Work* Vol 3. 3 pp77-86

Fox Harding, L. (1991) *Perspectives in Child Care Policy* Longman, London

Freeman, M. (1983) *Rights and Wrongs of Children* Pinter, London

Hendrick, H. (1997) Constructions and Reconstructions of British Childhood: An Interpretive Survey,1800 to the Present in James, A. and Prout, A. (Eds.)(1997) *Constructing and Reconstructing Childhood* Falmer Press, London

*Hill, M. and Tisdall, K. (1997) *Children and Society,* Longman, London

Jackson, S. (1998) Looking After Children: a New Approach or Just an Exercise in Formfilling? A Response to Knight and Caveney *British Journal of Social Work* 28, pp45-56

*James, A. and Prout, A. (1997) *Constructing and Reconstructing Childhood* Falmer Press, London

Holt, J. (1975) *Escape from Childhood: The Needs and Rights of Children* Penguin, Harmondsworth

Knight, T. and Caveney, S. (1998) Assessment and Action Records: Will they Promote Good Parenting? *British Journal of Social Work* 28, pp29-43

Marshall, K. (1997) *Children's Rights in the Balance. The Participation-Protection Debate* The Stationery Office, Edinburgh

Ochaita, E. and Espinoza, M.A. (1997) Children's Participation in Family and School Life: A Psychological and Development Approach *The International Journal of Children's Rights* 5, pp279-297

Solberg, A. (1997) Negotiating Childhood: Changing Constructions of Age for Norwegian Children in James, A. and Prout, A. (Eds.) (1997) *Constructing and Reconstructing Childhood* Falmer Press, London

Ward, H. (1995) *Looking After Children: Research into Practice* HMSO, London

Woodhead, M. (1997) Psychology and the Cultural Construction of Children's Needs in James, A. and Prout, A. (Eds.) (1997) *Constructing and Reconstructing Childhood* Falmer Press, London

* Recommended further reading

1.2 Education - For Children and Young People in Public Care

Peter Sandiford and Mari Piper

In 1998 the Government introduced, amongst other initiatives, new funding structures for further and higher education, literacy and numeracy schemes, pupil restraint guidance and behaviour support plans. The newly formed Social Exclusion Unit has issued specific targets for pupils in the public care, and The Children's Society in *No Lessons Learnt* (1998) and others have raised the issue of rising exclusion rates. We have also heard how boys, and particularly Afro-Caribbean boys (Children's Society 1998) are more likely to fail educationally. We see that employment is, increasingly, more dependent on academic qualification, whilst reports have been published relating education failure to a future life of crime (Audit Commission 1994).

The needs of children and young people in public care are also high on the social policy and political agendas. In November 1997 Sir William Utting published a report on the safeguards for children living away from home - *People Like Us*. This report led to the establishment of the Ministerial Task Force that is looking at the care and safety of looked after children and young people. A United Kingdom Joint Working Party on Foster Care was established in September 1997 with the aims:

- To seek to improve the quality of foster care through the development of national standards, following wide consultation with both users of foster care services and those responsible for delivering them.

- To promote the widest possible use of the resultant good practice guide to encourage consistency of foster care service provision nation wide.

In addition the Department for Education and Employment has established an inter-agency forum promoting the education and attainment of looked after children and within Parliament a number of members have formed an all party interest group on the needs of looked after children and young people. To quote Sir William:

The importance of health and education services for looked after children has been emphasised in a sequence of reports. The Review received vigorous representations about the inadequacies of both..... Whatever the cause, it produces a scandalous situation in which the life prospects of these young people may be irretrievably damaged and their immediate safety put at greater risk. A corporate approach is needed by education and social services to resolve it. **2.16**

Other areas in which children's interests are not adequately safeguarded at the moment are education and health. The low expectations of educational achievement from fostered children (and those looked after generally) and higher rates of exclusion mean they are not given the help and encouragement they need to succeed, with all the implications that follow for employment and life in general thereafter. Health concerns also may not be adequately addressed, particularly where there are several moves. Public services need to act corporately and each play their part in the successful parenting of children who are looked after. The education and health services should be active in helping the foster carer to provide the best care for the child and to ensure that the carer has some positive help in rectifying problems and difficulties rather than feeling unsupported. **3.52**

Sir William Utting - *People Like Us* (1997)

The responsibility for meeting the needs of what Utting (1997) describes as *this most disadvantaged of groups* lies with the local authority as corporate parent. Research studies have highlighted that looked after children and young people make up 33 per cent of all secondary school exclusions and 66 per cent of all primary school exclusions (DfEE unpublished). In addition research studies have indicated that, 75 per cent leave school with no qualifications (Biehal et al., 1995), more than 50 per cent of young people leaving care after 16 years of age are unemployed (Sinclair et al., 1996), and 23 per cent of adults and 38 per cent of young prisoners, under the age of 21 years, have been in public care (National Prison Survey 1991). Angela Devlin in 1995 estimated that 90 per cent plus of all prisoners have experienced educational failure. We must ask the question 'are these children and young people being educated?'

The Three Princesses is a fairy story written by Mari Piper, a young woman who spent five years in public care, moving home a total of twenty five times. In 1997 she started studying for an English degree at Leeds University and in 1998 she became a member of the Ministerial Task Force created to respond to the Utting Report - *People Like Us*. This chapter will go on to look at some of the practices that could have influenced the lives of the three 'princesses' before Mari concludes with her observations about how these practices would have influenced both herself and others with whom she was in care.

The Three Princesses

Once-upon-a-time a king and queen were blessed by three beautiful daughters. All three were clever and talented, and won the admiration of a dull old wizard named Disillusion. He was very ugly, very old and very boring, but he knew one very powerful spell. Anyone he cast a spell on had to wear glasses which made them see things only one way. The person wearing these glasses would believe that the way they saw things was the only way anything could be seen, and would not know they were wearing the glasses.

Disillusion thought the princesses were the most beautiful girls in the land, and asked the king if he would give one of them to him in marriage. The princesses hated the old wizard, and the king refused the wizards request. The wizard became very annoyed at this and threatened to curse the princesses if the king did not change his mind. The king and queen were very upset and arranged for the princesses to be taken away and hidden.

The princesses were taken away in a carriage secretly one night, and on the way a fairy appeared. She told the princesses that they could each have a wish.

'Oh!' said the first princess, 'I wish to go to lots of parties and have great fun' (she was very outgoing). 'Alacazam!' cried the fairy, and the princess was at a party.

'I wish to go to a university and get a good career' said the second princess (who was rather serious). 'Alacazam!' cried the fairy, and the princess was at a university.

The third princess missed her mum and dad a great deal and so she said 'I wish for a family to love'. 'Alacazam!' cried the fairy and there she was, with two lovely daughters.

The fairy also gave each princess a set of foster parents. All the foster parents were loving and kind, but in time wicked old Disillusion found the

princesses and put his cursed spectacles on all the foster parents.

The foster parents still loved the princesses, and tried to do their best for them, but they couldn't listen to the princesses anymore.

Years went by, and the first princess got lonely. She still went to lots of parties, but she couldn't get to university, and she had no one to love, foster parents couldn't listen to her because of Disillusion and one day she walked to the top of a cliff called despair and threw herself off it to be dashed to pieces on the rocks of depression.

The second princess enjoyed her university, but felt unloved, and her foster parents wouldn't let her go to parties and have fun because of the curse laid upon them by Disillusion. So she wandered about the world amongst the lonely people who never talk to anyone.

The third princess loved her daughters, but she could not go to university, or parties. So she took her children to a small island called Benefits System. It was very crowded but at least nobody there was having fun or going to university.

Like all good stories this one contains a moral, and the moral of this story is that Disillusion is a wicked old wizard, who must be defeated at all costs And the way to defeat him is to always keep your eyes and mind open.

Open Eyes and Open Minds - Practices that Will Make a Difference

Mari wrote this story to highlight the many issues that face both children and young people who are in public care and those charged with that most important of tasks, to care for them. In addition it relates to many aspects of the quality of care young people should have a right to expect. This book looks at many of the issues affecting the provision of good quality foster care and this chapter looks at those particularly related to education.

Success in society is nearly always tied to educational success, one of the areas in which children in public care are recognised as being particularly disadvantaged. Are the lives of the three princesses therefore surprising? All three seemed to be looking for their carer to care and be their champion but because of Disillusion and the cursed spectacles they lost the support they should have had. Sonia Jackson said in 1995:

It is through school that children earn passports to different kinds of futures - that is one of the reasons why parents care about it so passionately, why they move house and take out insurance and even risk political suicide to send their child to the school of their choice.

What is it that foster carers in particular can do to influence the educational outcomes of the children and young people they are caring for?

A quick answer would be very little in view of the difficulties placed in their way and the impact of self-fulfilling prophecies of low achievement, unless of course, they receive a great deal of support and training from others within the local authority, from both the education and social service departments. Is the enemy Disillusion or is it more that foster carers are not aware of the need to champion education or even that they are allowed to do so? How often will the carers role in education be identified in a placement agreement and be a feature of the carers supervision?

Felicity Fletcher-Campbell (1997) quotes a foster carer as saying:

> *When people start fostering there is in no part a package which says "are you a suitable foster parent" that covers education - nothing. You're taught about all the other issues but you don't cover education. You come into it and I didn't even know about statementing kids...if your own kid hasn't had problems or been to that sort of school where there are kids with problems you haven't a clue...I looked through the foster parent fact file and, again, very little on the education side.*

It has been estimated that less than 25 per cent of foster carers across two local authorities had received training in how to meet the educational needs of children and young people they were caring for (NCB 1998 unpublished).

Increasingly, training material for carers is becoming available through such organisations as NCB, Leeds Social Services, First Key and Who Cares? Trust. But in what ways, once trained, might a foster carer influence the educational success of the child or young person they are caring for?

Before a quality educational service can be delivered by carers it needs to be strategically planned by the local education and the social services departments working together to initiate jointly supported initiatives and

planning that recognise the needs of this most vulnerable of groups. This might include the following nine broad areas:

1. Education and social service departments to demonstrate a commitment to joint planning for each child in public care.

2. Recruitment and selection should ensure that all new foster carers are willing and capable of promoting and advocating on educational issues for the children and young people they will be caring for. To quote Sonia Jackson (1995):

   > *Foster carers and residential workers should see themselves as partners in the educational process and educational qualifications should count for a lot more than they do at present in the selection of carers*

3. All those involved in the care of the child or young person (parents, carers and the social worker) should have clearly defined roles in promoting educational success. These should be recorded in the placement agreement.

4. The setting of achievement benchmarks for children and young people in public care that are monitored and reported to elected members.

5. Clear policies on funding all aspects of education for children and young people in public care. This should include such areas as national and international school trips, music lessons, and further and higher education.

6. There should be a policy in every school of reporting absence from school on the first day and within one hour of school commencing.

7. Each school to include in their whole school policy, their anti-discriminatory policy and their behaviour and discipline policy explicit references relevant to children and young people in public care. These should be made public through such documents as the school brochure.

8. No child should move school for any reason during a critical educational period e.g., exams. All decisions on the home placement for a child should be linked to meeting their educational needs e.g., access to the most appropriate school or maintaining their existing school place.

9. The school exclusion policy should require that if a child in public care is at risk of exclusion or is expressing behaviour management problems a discussion between the teacher and the child and their carer should take place well in advance of action being taken by the school to exclude (there may be negotiable exceptions such as serious violent behaviour - currently 1.2 per cent of the excluded population as a whole). Where a child is permanently excluded they should receive a suitable full time education package within three weeks of exclusion.

If there are policies, jointly agreed by education and social service departments, on each of these there can then be high expectations regarding the practice and responsibility of foster carers. These might include the following four areas:

Educational Ethos

It is important that carers recognise the importance of educational endeavour and achievement and contribute to the development of an ethos within the home that promotes this. This may be achieved by:

- Recognising the need for regular school attendance and finding strategies that achieve this, eg prompt interventions at the onset of non attendance together with routines for bedtime and getting up in the morning.

- Encouraging and promoting homework by ensuring that time, space and necessary materials are available.

- Encouraging young people to read and make use of libraries.

- Using and creating opportunities to counsel, explain, educate and discuss discriminatory topics and utilise all available resources such as books, magazines, newspapers and TV.

- Showing interest in what they are doing in school, including looking at and discussing school work, and offering appropriate help and support.

- Discussing with them the educational choices they face such as subject options, further education and career plans.

- Ensuring that natural parents are involved as much as possible.

Values

Sonia Jackson (1997) found that adults coming from a care background who had gone on to succeed all had somebody who had championed their education and encouraged them to achieve their full potential.

If carers are to have ambition and high expectations for the children and young people they are caring for, they must rid themselves of self-fulfilling prophesies of failure and low achievement. The second report to the Department of Health on *Assessing Outcomes in Child Care* (1995) evaluated how the Looking After Children (LAC) materials were seen by social workers and carers, compared to a community group of parents of non-looked after children from across social divides. The study found the most controversy to be about questions relating to the amount of reading being undertaken and whether children were learning to play musical instruments.

> *even in these families, parents regarded this as a genuine issue, although they did not always have the wherewithal to engineer a change: it was only nine per cent of children in the community group had limited access to books: only the children in the looked after group whose carers thought the question irrelevant.*

and

> *The question about whether looked after children were learning to play musical instruments also attracted the criticism that it reflected a middle class aspiration that was irrelevant to the families of children in care or accommodated. The evidence from our data demonstrates the fallacy of this assumption.*
> Department of Health on Assessing
> Outcomes in Child Care (1995)

If expectations held by carers for those they are caring for are below those held by natural parents for their own children it is unlikely that children and young people in public care will feel that they have somebody championing their education and encouraging them to achieve their ambitions.

Literacy

It is widely acknowledged that success in achieving literacy is fundamental to all other aspects of educational achievement. For many years it has also been acknowledged that parental support has been central to pupil's educational life chances. For children and young people in public care this is even more the case and taking an interest in reading with them is one way of becoming involved and showing an interest. In the *NCB Education Audit* (Unpublished - 1998) fewer than 30 per cent of carers said they regularly read with or to the 5 - 14 year old for whom they were charged with caring. Following a project conducted by the Who Cares? Trust (1995) where looked after young people purchased a book and then read it with their carer (adult supported) the following was noted:

- When asked if they ever read with an adult, at the start of the project 20 out of 68 young people responding said they did.
- Adult supporters felt that young people below the age of 14 were the most enthusiastic about the project. Nearly half of all participants were described as 'very enthusiastic'.
- Information about the young person's educational attainment was not readily available to adult supporters.
- The majority of young people said they had enjoyed having an adult to read to.
- The majority of adult supporters noted a positive attitude to reading among the young people, and that their reading ability had improved during the project.
- Some supporters had bad memories of school and felt inhibited about providing educational support.
- The process of buying books and the support given with reading helped the relationship between the young person and their supporter to improve.

The supporters had undertaken what amounted to paired reading which is a proven way to help with a young person's reading. It can range from reading out loud together, to the young person reading the passage to themselves and then talking about it with the supporter demonstrating their understanding of what they have read. When a mistake is made Cynthia Fletcher (unpublished 1996) identified that there are two ways of helping that are sometimes hard for carers to get used to:

1. Where they get a word wrong you just tell them what the word is, then they say it after you. You do not make them struggle and struggle, or 'break it up' or 'sound it out'.

2. When they get the word right, you smile and show you are pleased. You do not nag and fuss about the words they got wrong.

Above all Fletcher says

> *show interest in the book they have chosen, talk about what is happening in it and listen and do not do all the talking. Reading can be a warm experience so get close.*

Accountability, Including Monitoring and Evaluation

Providing foster carers have been selected on the basis that they have the ability to promote the education of the children and young people in their care, it is appropriate that their supervising social worker ensures they are complying with the stated standards, policies and guidelines of that local authority and that they hold ambitions as regards the achievements for those children and young people for whom they are caring. This might include the support given by the carer to the undertaking of homework, time spent reading with them or their attendance at school meetings such as parents evenings or school plays. It is likely that many social workers will need specific training in order to meet this requirement.

The arrival and adoption of National Standards in Foster Care will ensure that there is greater accountability expected of carers and perhaps greater expectations of new carers being able to promote the education of those for whom they are caring. Given the importance of education to future life chances can we continue to allow children and young people, already so disadvantaged, to be placed in families where education is not seen as being so important or where the carers themselves do not have the ability to promote it?

Mari finishes her fairy story by identifying some of the practices that helped and some that were missing and might have made a difference to the lives of the real life princesses:

In fairy stories the greatest power is the power of naming, so I shall name the princesses for you. The first princess is called Lisa. She didn't do very well at school, as she was often excluded because she was 'trouble'. No-one appealed these exclusions. Because she did not do well at school no one encouraged her to go to college, or to do re-sits. She couldn't find a job, so she started going out a lot. Her foster parents were pleased to see her looking so happy so they did not stop her. In time Lisa started using drugs very heavily and was eventually admitted to a psychiatric hospital where she remains today.

The second princess is me. I got support from my foster parents to go to university. But before that I was moved lots of times. I have been to five different senior schools as well as college. Now I am at university I am getting financial support but no practical or emotional support. In the holidays I often have to remain at university because I have nowhere to stay. When I was applying for university my social worker couldn't help me because they did not know how to apply. They did not understand the points system (grades are converted into points, and you have to score a certain amount of points to go to different universities). No-one in social services knew how to apply for an education grant, even though education and social services are part of the same organisation.

The third princess is called Shelly. She also got some encouragement to go to school. Shelly had many different foster homes, but never felt that anyone really cared about her. So when she had her first daughter at just 15 years of age she felt she had found someone to care. Shelly's foster parents assumed that education was no longer a priority and all that support stopped. Several years later Shelly cannot get a job because she has no qualifications. Neither can she go back to college because she no longer has the support, or anyone to look after her two children.

All three of us needed support from our foster parents at different times. Lisa needed help to fight continual exclusions; other children were behaving much worse than her, but when they were excluded their parents complained. She needed support to go to college. Shelly needed to feel loved and helped in balancing education and child care. She still needs someone to arrange free childcare for her so that she can return to college. I needed someone to fight for me, someone to tell social services that it was wrong to keep moving me around the country. I needed a champion to ensure that I got support when I went to university. Foster parents who will support, help and fight for the children they care for are essential for educational success. Above all, you must be prepared to see things in many different ways and not be Disillusioned.

Let me retell the story the way we would have wanted it to be...

...The fairy also gave each princess a set of foster parents. All the foster parents were loving and kind, but in time wicked old Disillusion found the princesses and tried to put his cursed spectacles on all the foster parents. However, the foster parents had been armed by the fairy with two mighty weapons; the 'sword of knowledge', and the 'shield of understanding'. They battled mightily with Disillusion, and finally hurt him so much that he ran, or rather limped, back to his miserable, draughty castle. The foster parents then sealed him up in the dungeon, where he remains to this day.

The first princess went to her parties and had lots of fun, but the foster parents made sure that she did not go to parties on school-nights. Sometimes she thought they were unfair, but she knew that they loved her and wanted her to succeed. She went to a university in a far away, exotic place, and became a brilliant doctor. She developed cures for almost every disease known to man (and even cured diseases that no-one knew about!).

The second princess worked very hard, but her foster parents also made her see that people and having fun were important too. In fact, she found that she got on with other people so well that when she had finished university she became an ambassador and because of her work there was world peace.

The third princess loved her daughters very much, but she loved her foster parents too, and so she felt safe leaving her daughters with them every day whilst she went to school. When she had finished university she became an economist, and worked out a way of sharing all the world's resources amongst all the people so that no-one was ever in need again.

Perhaps these things seem a little bit ambitious for three girls from care, but the most important job that a true champion must do is believe in the person they are championing. Knowledge and understanding helped the foster parents fight off Disillusion, but they also had to believe in the princesses enough to fight for them.

The recommendations above are the tools that can help foster carers to fight Disillusion, so that they can then be free to help the children they are fostering. Without these tools, how could a foster parent appeal an exclusion for Lisa? How could they know that social services shouldn't be moving me so often? How could they insist that childcare is provided for Shelly's children whilst she finishes her education? You do not send a champion to fight a wizard without giving them weapons, and you shouldn't expect foster carers to fight the world without telling them how to do it.

Education is for children and young people in public care.

References

Smith, R. (1998) *No Lessons Learnt - A survey of School Exclusions.* The Children's Society

Audit Commission (1994) *Seen But Not Heard.* HMSO

Utting Report The (1997) *People Like Us.* HMSO

Biehal, N., Clayden, J., Stein, M., and Wade, J. (1995) *Moving On.* HMSO

Sinclair, R., and Gibbs, I. (1996) *Quality of Care in Children's Homes.* University of York

National Prison Survey (1991) HMSO

Devlin, A. (1995) *Criminal Classes.* Waterside Press

Jackson, S. (1995) *Transforming Lives: The Crucial Role of Education for Young People in the Care System.* Royal Society of Arts - First Tory Laughland Memorial Lecture

Fletcher-Campbell, F. (1997) *The Education of Children Who are Looked-After.* NFER

Ward, H. ed. (1995) *Looking After Children: Research into Practice. The Second Report.* HMSO

Bald, J., Bean, J., Meegan, F. (1995) *A Book Of My Own.* The Who Cares? Trust

1.3 Leaving Care Work - Young People's Rights and Participation

Dr Bob Broad

Introduction

Participation in leaving care work by young people who are, or have been fostered, should be developed through local focus groups, planning forums, and regional groupings, with social services departments and others. Leaving care projects have made a start at bringing forward ideas about young people's participation in the monitoring and, less so, the management of leaving care projects and leaving care policies.

This chapter will look at young people's rights and participation and is based around empirical research findings on the work of leaving care projects (Broad 1998). Much of the work of these projects should be complementary to the existing work of foster carers. Where such projects do not exist at present greater responsibility will fall to the foster carer. Preparation for leaving care should begin early in a young person's life and support networks should be available long after the young person has left the care system.

Background — Children's Rights and Participation: the Legislative Context

The Children Act 1989, The Children Act (Scotland) 1995 and the Children's Order (Northern Ireland) 1995 give support for greater participation by users about the style and substance of service delivery and can be seen as being complemented and reinforced by the children's rights movements, with the **United Nation Convention on the Rights of the Child** being its flag-bearer. This convention was adopted by the United Nations in 1989 and ratified by the United Kingdom Government in 1991 subject to some important reservations. The convention sets out in a number of statements about the rights which all children and young people up to the age of 18 should have. The convention covers three main sets of rights: the child's right to protection from abuse and exploitation, the right to the provision of services, and the right to participate in decision making.

United Nations Convention on the Rights of the Child - summary of the relevant sections that apply to young people leaving care up to 18 years of age:

- Any child being looked after away from home in a boarding school, long stay institution or hospital must also receive proper care (Article 3).

- Children should be separated against their will only if it is in the child's best interests. If this has to happen, the child, their parents and anyone else entitled to have an interest has the right to go to court and ask to have their case heard (Article 9).

- The right to privacy (Article 16) and to freedom from exploitation (Article 36).

- The child to be provided with the opportunity to be heard at any judicial or administrative hearing affecting the child, confirming the *child's right to participate in decision making affecting them* (Article 12) (emphasis added).

- If separated from their parents, the child has the right to keep in touch regularly with the parents, unless this would be harmful to the child (Article 9).

- Children have the right to be as healthy as possible (Article 24).

- Disabled children must be helped to be as independent as possible (Article 24).

- Children have the right to live in a safe, ...healthy environment (Article 24).

- Every child has the right to an adequate standard of living. This is, in the main, for parents to provide, but in cases of need the government should help parents reach this standard (Article 27).

– State parties recognise the right of every child to a standard of living adequate for the child's physical, mental, spiritual, moral and social development (Article 27).

– The parent's or others responsible for the child have a primary responsibility to secure, within their abilities and financial capacities, the conditions of living necessary for the child's development (Article 27).

– Every child has the right to benefit from social security taking account of the …circumstances of the child and those responsible for the child (Article 26).

– Children should be cared for properly… This is mainly for the child's parents to do but the government is expected to give suitable help to parents (Article 18).

– If children cannot live with their family, they must be properly looked after by another family or in a children's home. The child's race, religion, culture and language must all be considered when a new home is being chosen (Article 20).

– A child temporarily or permanently deprived of his or her family environment, or in whose best interests cannot be allowed to remain in that environment, shall be entitled to special protection and assistance provided by the state (Article 20).

– Different kinds of secondary school should be available for children. In addition for those with the ability, higher education should also be provided (Article 28).

– The government must protect children from: doing work which could be dangerous or which could harm their health or interfere with their education (Article 32), dangerous drugs (Article 33), being abducted or sold (Article 35) and sexual abuse (Article 34).

According to the Children's Rights Development Unit report (CRDU, 1994) the government has still not fully carried out its responsibilities under the Convention in respect of young people leaving care. In 1994 it concluded (CRDU, 1994:39):

Unless policies are developed at local authority level, backed up with the necessary resources these obligations under the Convention are being breached. There are models of good after-care provision which have been developed and which, if disseminated, could be widely adopted.

Planning for Leaving Care

Subsequent to the UN Convention of the Rights of the Child (1991) the Association of Metropolitan Authorities (AMA) produced a checklist for supporting care leavers up to 18 years under Articles 1 and Article 3.2. After posing the question about how authorities can ensure there are sufficient resources available and make 'real' choices possible, the AMA makes a comprehensive statement about leaving care (1995:47).

*A Checklist for Supporting Care Leavers up to 18 Years -**The Association of Metropolitan Authorities (1995).***
Local authorities could consider the following for young people leaving care:

● Conducting an assessment with the young person about whether or not they feel ready for independent living.

● Support, information and training over an extended period to ensure that the young care leaver is confident and ready for independent living.

● Material assistance and housing to young people leaving care to ensure they are able to achieve an adequate standard of living and to protect them from drug abuse and sexual exploitation.

● Reviewing policies and practice on early preparation for independence and making sure these reviews are carried out with young people allowing flexibility in the system which allows for the varying needs of different children and young people to be met.

● Allowing young people to experiment with independence and with the option of returning to accommodation or care, or getting different levels of support if they wish to do so.

● That planning is done at corporate level so that all services on which young people depend are provided in a co-ordinated and consistent manner including, for example, social services, housing, education and welfare rights services.

In the foster care field the issue of children's rights would seem not one, that any organisation has strongly articulated, if at all. This seems to be for a range of reasons, including the fundamental ethical/legal one, namely what is meant by children's rights and how and why should this apply to foster care. Other issues include the absence of a group representing the rights of foster children, (as opposed to the needs of foster carers), the dominance of social services influence pre-placement, the individual nature of foster care and the foster carer's work with a foster child or children, and not least of all, the reported shortage of foster placements (see, NFCA, 1997).

However, in respect, not of rights, but of consultation with, and participation by, young people who are fostered, the NFCA advise that there are two important initiatives involving that organisation. First there is a questionnaire survey which was sent to 13,000 foster homes by the NFCA to obtain the views of young people in foster care about foster care services. These views have been used to inform the production of the National Standards in Foster Care and will also be used as a basis for participation in the development of the foster care service. Also in a Who Cares? Trust research study, which recorded the views of 2,000 children in public care, it was found that children and young people in foster care tended to have more say on the whole than those in other types of placements (Who Cares? Trust, 1998: 33) but, it must be stressed this 'say' is about current placement, and not broader policy, issues. 'Participation in decision making' is a very limited definition of consultation, and derives from discretionary professional practice rather than participation as legal rights and secure entitlements.

If 'planning for leaving home' was a 'good practice' exercise for birth parents about what it would be desirable (though not necessarily attainable) for young people to have in order to leave home to live elsewhere there would probably be a range of qualities suggested. These would be based around a set of values which would vary from one family to another. These might well begin with the young person wanting to leave home and being and feeling prepared to do so, as far as is possible. A good educational attainment level (with anticipated enhanced employment prospects), good health, the 'right' timing. It would also be important to try to reach some sort of understanding about where to move to, and if relevant, with whom. Critically, and unless there are reasons to the contrary, there would probably be an assumption that the young person could return home if needed or wanted, though subject perhaps to further discussion. Young care leavers should be provided with similar 'good practice'.

Young People in Transition

There is evidence that in the population as a whole the length of the transition from childhood to adulthood, i.e. the period of youth, is increasing (Jones,1995) with the transition to training and education becoming more complex (for example, see COYPSS, 1995). Jones describes youth as an extended period

> in which a gradual transition is effected between childhood and citizenship, mediated by the family and the state (Jones, 1995:1).

It can be argued that in order to successfully make the transition from being 'at home,' however that is defined, to living away from home, requires the young person to have the following essentials: financial support, somewhere to live, a desire to leave home, a resilient personality and lastly, a friendship and family network which is supportive. Being a young person aged between 16 and 21 seeking to leave home involves a range of financial, emotional, developmental, psycho-social and physical transitions, too complex to do other than outline here. Furthermore the responsibility for carrying the costs involved in making this drawn out transition, from a dependent child to an independent young adult have shifted (back) onto families, as state funding has fallen away.

Governments have introduced fundamental changes to the role of the state, placing more emphasis on the family to provide for its members. It is not intended to reproduce here the evidence and arguments ably presented elsewhere. (see Coleman and Warren-Adamson, 1992, in connection with social policies and young people). According to the British Youth Council (1996) and in comparison with former times, across a series of financial and social indicators the position of young people in the United Kingdom is undergoing steady and ongoing changes. These changes significantly impact on young people seeking to make the transition from home or foster care to more independent living because these changes affect the capacity of young people to gain economic independence and therefore to pay for and live in separate accommodation. This is the critical point - the capacity to be financially independent. This then raises further questions namely:

- At what age is this independence expected?

- How will it take place?

- Who will pay to support the young person making this transition?

- What will such payments cover?

- What happens if insufficient supports are available?

- Are other options, i.e. ways of leaving home, available?

Within this difficult social policy context for young people in transition to adulthood Wheal's practical and positive book on working with young people shows just what can be done by foster carers and other child care workers (and indeed parents) with young people when using imaginative ideas and good communication underpinned by principles of partnership and empowerment (Wheal, 1998).

Difficulties about making the transition to adulthood are widespread, and are summed up bluntly in a Coalition on Young People and Social Security (or COYPSS) report which specifically examined the options and opportunities available to young people from the age of 16 in their transition from school to the labour market. The report states (1995:4):

- The transition from school to the labour market has become unacceptably dificult and complex, with young people facing a series of obstacles to gaining employment, education and training.

- There is a lack of support for young people making this transition.

- There is a lack of coherence and co-ordination between bodies responsible for aspects of the transition.

- The options on offer to young people leaving school are limited.

- Many of the training schemes for young people offer poor quality and fail to prepare young people for employment or to lead to jobs.

For young people leaving foster care, usually by 18 years of age, who are planning or expected or prepared to enter either the world of employment, further and higher education, or youth training of some sort, a high level of support and care must be provided.

According to the National Foster Care Association (NFCA, 1997:8) up to 40, 000 children and young people are living in foster homes in the UK on any one day which represents about two thirds of all children looked after by local authorities. From research in the young people leaving care field it is predominantly in the 16-17 age group, possibly stretching into the 18-19 age group where transitional supports are most needed, and where financial entitlements are either unclear, under considerable pressure, inadequate, or not available. Up to two thirds of young people leave care at 16 or 17 (Biehal et al., 1992). This is in stark contrast to the age at which the general population leave home which is 23 or 24 years.

Nationally young people leaving care have called for a charter of rights on at least two occasions in the 1990s. In 1992 the London and South East Leaving Care Support Group produced its leaving care charter, which was published by RPS Rainer. Another charter with aspirations for national implementation, was launched by young people in the North West of England, and handed into Downing Street and the Department of Health in London (Community Care, 1992). What both these charters had in common is their commitment to clearly specified and legally enforceable rights associated with leaving care which go some way to explaining their non implementation to date.

The emphasis throughout this debate, about rights and services, is on developing and building on good practice. In many cases it appears to be a question of 'there is good practice in leaving care work out there - you just have to find it'. Yet in the leaving care field, as it applies to work by, and with, young people attending specialist leaving care projects there has been something of a culture which has embraced the notion of children's rights or something akin to it, namely participation of young people in leaving care practice and leaving care policies. It is to these findings in response to the specific question about young people's participation that attention is turned.

Young People's Participation in Leaving Care Work

In the Social Services Inspectorate's inspection of leaving care (1997) there was, (unsurprisingly) nothing specifically on young people's 'participation', or children's or young people's rights, but there was a short section on consultation which contained examples from six local authorities. These examples cover much of the 'support young people' type of participation covered in this chapter. The comment part of the consultation section was:

> We found that regular consultation was more likely to take place where an established support group met regularly or where groups were easily identified e.g. in residential care...

and

> Although they had never met each other before they said they would like to meet up again for social reasons and to contribute some ideas about how services might be developed in the future *as far as foster care was concerned* (emphasis added)

(Social Services Inspectorate, 1997:11)

The data presented here is taken and adapted from *Young People Leaving Care: Life After the Children Act 1989* (Broad, 1998). The empirical research findings in the book are based on a questionnaire survey of 46 projects working with 3,308 young people leaving care. The 46 projects were chosen from a listing of 106 leaving care projects, that is projects working with young people leaving care, and receiving services under Section 24 of the Children Act 1989. They consisted of three types of projects:

local authority projects (30 per cent of the sample), joint local authority/voluntary organisation projects (33 per cent), and voluntary organisation projects (37 per cent). Ten of the projects were based in the South East (outside London), nine were in London boroughs, six were in the South West of England, five were in Wales, seven were in the North West, four in the North East of England, and five were in the Midlands.

It is important to answer the question 'What does **participation** mean in the leaving care context and how can it be categorised?' The *five categories of participation* mainly used here are :

- participation as a means of quality control (project monitoring)
- participation as influencing local policy development (policy development)
- participation as support for other young people (supporting young people)
- participation as contributing to project development (project development)
- participation as a voice on national policies (campaigning/lobbying)

Participation should be for all young people including black young people, those with disabilities or HIV/AIDS or anyone else who can be regarded as being discriminated against and may sometimes not be given, or allowed, the opportunity to fully participate. It is important to place anti-discriminatory practice which has full participation and the challenging of structural oppression at its centre, within a policy context. In system terms what is most probably needed is a systematic policy, planning, action, review, cycle in place in which anti-discriminatory practice is systematically regarded as good practice, and where its absence is regarded as bad practice and critically reviewed. Anti-discriminatory work is normally evaluated on impact and not on intentions. In the leaving care research what is not known from the policy statements, which concern intent and procedure, is the extent to which the reported encouragement to specific groups of young people was sustained, supported, and effective over time. In relation to foster care and anti-discriminatory participation there needs to be more input into policy issues such as placement choice/selection and a policy on same race placements. Other issues including the location of the foster carer, access and support networks should also be seen as critical.

The issue of young people's participation in leaving care work, sometimes presented as a straightforward issue, is in fact a complex one in which a number of concerns and ideologies derived from different agendas, all converge. The first one to consider is what, if anything, the Law states about this issue. One of the five basic principles of part 3 of the Law (others being to safeguard the well being of the child, the promotion of partnerships with parents, the restating of the importance of families, corporate responsibilities), is of local authorities having a duty placed on them to ascertain and take due account, if they are deemed to be sufficiently mature, of young peoples', as well as parents', wishes and feelings. The Law also places a clear statutory duty on social services and the courts to ascertain the wishes and feelings of the child and to take these into account when making decisions. In addition the Guidance and Regulations (paragraph 7.18) states that:

> *young people should be fully involved in discussions and plans for their future. Well before a young person leaves care, a continuing care plan should be formulated with him. This should specify the type of help the young person will be receiving and from whom.*

Foster carers and parents should be involved in devising the plan. Local authorities are also advised to ensure that the written statements on their policies and practices, and their leaving care guides, should be informed by the views of young people who are or have been in care, and those of parents and foster carers. It is suggested that one way of obtaining the views of young people is to encourage groups of young people to meet and discuss such matters. The idea of establishing a newsletter was also presented in the guidance (para 7.22).

A detailed reading of the primary legislation about young people's participation suggests that it means young people being involved in discussions about what has already happened regarding the existing services they are receiving, **as well as** involvement in producing, or at the very least, modifying, leaving care policies. Underpinning these statements about greater participation by young people in the services they receive is the assumption that

prior to the legislation, such listening to children and young people about these matters was **not** everyday practice and could **not** be taken for granted (in respect of residential care for children see Berridge in Hill and Aldgate, 1996). Other wider changes in local government also produced a move away from the old ethos of passive clients simply receiving what the local authority provided like the old bulk purchasing policies in residential child care. In the new world of 'customer care' the shifts from procedures to outcomes, from provider to consumer orientation, from quantity to quality, from uniformity to diversity, and not least of all, from hierarchy to delegation and personal responsibility are heralded as the new currencies in care.

Research Findings

There were a total of 88 examples of participation by young people in local leaving care work, as provided by the 28 projects which stated that young people participated 'other than as a client' in their leaving care project. Of these 28 projects, 19 (or 68 per cent) were from voluntary organisations and the remaining 9 (or 32 per cent) were local authority or joint local authority/voluntary sector teams. The findings on the participation of young people attending the leaving care projects are now produced in rank order.

Projects responded well and creatively to the invitation to record the extent and nature of young people's participation in the projects, as well as to prioritise, generally, their main achievements and problems between 1994 and 1996. The rationale for exploring these areas was simply that it was seen as essential for projects to be given every opportunity to give their views about local practice:

1. **Participation as quality control or checkers of service delivery: 24 examples given including**

   - contributed to setting/achieving charter mark for the project

   - working on staff selection/interview panels - there were several examples given

   - users survey for service feedback

    – participation in evaluation of services

    – regular evaluation questionnaire

2. **Participation as influencing local policy development work: 23 examples given including**

    – member of projects' committees (virtually all voluntary organisation or joint projects)

    – helped with production of local policies

    – young people provide representation/consultation to local authority social services policy working group (forum of councillors and officers from different agencies)

    – group feeds into area community care planning forum

    – asked to contribute in QA statement

    – contribute to social services leaving care policies

    – consultation plus interviews in the development of new ideas and initiatives

    – involvement in development of policies to monitor and influence policies around work with young people

    – joint consultative group

3. **Participation as support for the young people: 16 examples given including**

    – young people invited to return to project to talk to others

    – offer a support service to young people using scheme/tenant support and consultation group

    – helping to run active drop in group

    – furniture for project

    – acting as volunteers

    – helping with the drop in

    – members of peer education group

    – help produce policy guidelines for/with the local authority

4. **Participation in shaping the project's identity and administration: 15 examples given including**

    – member of project committee

    – serving as committee members

    – young people help to contribute to project leaflets/administration feedback forms for the project

    – some clients took part in competition to design team logo - two cash prizes awarded

    – contribute to the writing of the team's leaving care pack

    – staff selection

    – employment of young people under employment services agency scheme

    – helping make an ecology garden

    – on interview panel

    – contributing to the production of a project brochure

    – promotion and publicity work

    – help to produce a (irregular) project newsletter

5. **Participation as expressing a voice on social policy: 10 examples given including**

    – helped set up and participate at conferences run by the project's parent voluntary organisation body

    – commenting on youth homelessness generally

    – contribute to 16+ forum in the area

    – helping with women's health day

    – consultancy re national and local policy/development

    – a young people users forum

    – contribute to local and national forums (in some cases through voluntary organisation's regional and/or national structure)

Voluntary organisations appear to lead the way in developing participatory projects. Whether this is because local authority leaving care teams had already developed ways for the young people to become more involved in the running of projects; whether the voluntary organisations had been slower to start their participation initiatives; whether certain projects gave a higher priority to participation by young people; whether local authority teams did not rate the participation of young people as highly as the other project types or had not pursued or succeeded with it to the same extent is not clear. It should also be recognised that voluntary organisations usually have a greater flexibility in terms of project management committees and structures than local authorities, and therefore greater scope for young people's participation in them if they so choose.

The 11 projects, all voluntary or joint projects, were amongst the more creative of the examples as shown by the increased participation of young people in the running and day to day life of the project (young people involved in joint consultative group and staff selection)

> *enabling and empowering young people to have a greater voice in service delivery (young people form an established consumer group, representatives at local and national voluntary organisation's leaving care committees)*

In terms of the more general management and ethical issues of representativeness and greater user involvement at the more strategic levels, and beyond participation at the service delivery level, Stone (1990:90-92) makes the point that those local authorities and voluntary organisations which are already unrepresentative in terms of race, gender and class are not well placed to encourage clients to take a more active role in terms of user involvement in service or organisational development. Although the depth and permanence of such user involvement would need further exploration, what these young people and projects have achieved is important, desirable and of great worth.

Participation and Anti-discrimination

Another, complementary, way of understanding participation, in addition to direct answers from leaving care projects about participation by young people, is in terms of anti-discriminatory practices and policies i.e. in what way does leaving care work actively encourage participation of **all** the young people attending the projects, and especially when these are black, disabled, gay, lesbian, or single parents.

Of the 3319 young people whose ethnic origin was described in the survey, 78 per cent (or 2579) were described as white, 13 per cent (or 449) described as black, and 3 per cent (or 100) were described as Asian (and 5 per cent as 'other'). 8 per cent (or 245) young people were described as having learning difficulties and 1.4 per cent (or 44) as having physical disabilities. Questions about anti-discrimination were put to all the leaving care teams.

The term anti-discriminatory, literally means 'against discrimination' (like anti-apartheid or anti-vivisection), indicates **actively** working for change, here against all forms of discrimination and oppression. It is its active ingredient and messages which are crucial. The main themes of anti-discriminatory practice (adapted from Thompson, 1994) are:

- A recognition that discrimination occurs, usually systematically and structurally, within organisations, as well as at the practice level, for a range of groups.
- The recognition that social work is a political activity in terms of legislative powers but also sets of power relations.
- Traditional social work relates primarily to the level of the 'case' and not wider issues, or the three levels of the personal, the structural and cultural.
- A recognition that work with young people needs to take place at the personal, and cultural and structural levels to be fully integrated and anti-discriminatory.
- At the personal level the emphasis will be on personal empowerment and political and social education.
- If they do not already do so, staff require anti-discriminatory training to fully understand what constitutes discrimination and anti-discriminatory practice and policies.
- The actions of staff, project teams and organisations will either challenge or support discrimination.

The following are five examples of ways in which leaving care projects took anti-discriminatory interests forward:

- Undertaking work with housing associations to the point where contractors need to be 'approved'.

- Young black people supported in choosing housing in boroughs and areas where they feel safe.

- Address gender issues in placement.

- Staff selection to be based on anti-discriminatory policies.

- Interviewing (staff) to include black as well as female young people.

Particular attention was also highlighted on the needs of young women with children and pregnant young women, such as understanding their need to create space in which they can develop their own awareness and confidence; develop their understanding of what young women's needs are, what resources are relevant to them, and develop plans that work; how young women relate to other young women and to young men; supporting young women's confidence in articulating their own needs; being understanding, responsive, unbiased and informative

Conclusion

Despite the United Nations Convention and the Children Act, the issue of legally enforceable, not just social, rights for children, including those leaving care remains deeply complex and unsatisfactory. Research about how these relate to leaving care, including foster care, practices are concerned, is incomplete.

Participation derived from:

- social justice principles

- emphasis on legal entitlements

- anti-discriminatory principles

- children's rights

- forms of user control

have had limited expression and remain more elusive than those where there has been emphasis on social welfare forms of participation. It is time for this to change to ensure you people who are leaving or who have left the care system get the help and support to which they are entitled and are enabled to participate in the decision making process that affects their lives.

References

Association of Metropolitan Authorities, (1995) *Checklist for Children: Local Authorities and the UN Convention on the Rights of the Child*, London: AMA

Berridge, D. (1996), Residential Child Care in England and Wales: the Inquiries and After, in Hill, M., and Aldgate, J. op. cit. 180-95

Berridge, D. and Brodie, I. (1998), Children's Homes Revisited, London: Jessica Kingsley

Biehal, N., Clayden, J., Stein, M. and Wade, J. (1992) *Prepared for Living? A Survey of Young People Leaving the Care of Three Local Authorities*, London: NCB

British Youth Council, (1996) *Never Had it so Good? The Truth About Being Young in 1990s Britain*, London BYC

Broad, B. (1994), *Leaving Care in the 1990s*, on behalf of the After Care Consortium, Kent: RPS Rainer .

Broad, B. and Denney, D. (1996), Users' rights and the probation service: some opportunities and obstacles in the *Howard Journal of Criminal Justice*, 35 (1), 61-77

Broad, B (1997), The inadequate child care legislation governing work with young people leaving care: a research based review, *Childright*, September 1997, (139), 17-18

Broad, B. and Saunders, L. (1998), Involving young people leaving care as peer researchers in a health research project: a learning experience, *Research, Policy and Planning*, 16, (1) 1-9

Broad, B. (1998), *Young People Leaving Care: Life After the Children Act 1989*, London: Jessica Kingsley

Cliffe, D. and Berridge, D. (1991), *Closing Children's Homes: an End to Residential Care?* London: National Children's Homes

Coalition of Young People and Social Security (COYPSS) (1995), *Taking Their Chances Education, Training, and Employment Opportunities for Young People*, London: The Children's Society.

Coleman, J. and Warren-Adamson, Eds. (1992) *Youth Policy in the 1990s -The Way Forward*, London: Routledge

Community Care (1992), Care Leavers' Charter highlights deficiencies, *Community Care* article, 3 December, Sutton: Community Care

Community Care, (1995) *Leaving Care Checklist*, London: Reed Publishing.

CRDU (1994), *Children's Rights Development Unit Report*, London: CRDU

Croft, S. and Beresford, P. (1993), *Getting Involved - a Practical Manual*, London: Open Services Project.

Department of Health (1997), *...When Leaving Home is Also Leaving Care...* An Inspection of Services for Young People Leaving Care, London: Department of Health

First Key, (1996) *Standards in Leaving Care, Report of the National Working Group*, Leeds: First Key

Fry, E. (1992) *After Care. Making the Most of Fostercare*, London National Foster Care Association

Hammersmith and Fulham Social Services Department, (1995) *Leaving Care Policy*, London: London Borough of Hammersmith and Fulham

Hill, M. and Aldgate, J., Eds. (1996), *Child Welfare Services*, London: Jessica Kingsley.

Jones, G. (1995), *Leaving Home*, Buckingham: Open University Press.

Killeen, D. (1992) *Housing and Income-Social Policy on Leaving Home*, in Coleman, J. and Warren-Adamson, op. cit. 189-202

National Foster Care Association (1997), *Foster Care in Crisis*, London: NFCA

Scottish Office, (1998), *Fostering and Adoption Disruption Research Project: the Temporary Placements*, Edinburgh: Scottish Office

Shaw, C. (1998), *Remember My Messages*, London: The Who Cares? Trust

Social Services Inspectorate and the Office for Standards in Education (OFSTED), (1995) *The Education of Children Who are Looked After by Local Authorities*, London: Department of Health

Stone, M. (1990) *Young People Leaving Care*, Kent: RPS Rainer

Thompson, N. (1993) *Anti-discriminatory Practice*, London: Macmillan

Wheal, A. (1998), *Adolescence Positive Approaches for Working with Young People*, Dorset, Russell House

1.4 Identity Issues

Roger Greeff and Vivien Stuart

For all of us the question 'Who am I?' is a complex one. It consists of a series of more specific questions - What are my origins and history? Who do I belong with? What am I good at? There are also more subtle questions about our relationships with other people - Does anyone love me? Who can I love? Am I respected and valued? In these areas, we need feedback from other people - they need to show, and perhaps tell us explicitly, that they care about us, value what we do and so on.

Identity is about both **change and continuity**. As we move through life, so our sense of who we are alters and develops - a twenty-year old who still sees themselves as they were at twelve has failed to notice that adolescence changes us! We develop new abilities, take on new roles, and build new relationships. We also lose some important elements - relationships end, we move to a new area and have only the memories. It is perhaps important to note that identity is in part a collection of memories - a theme to which we will return.

Alongside change, identity is also about **continuity** - although there is so much change, our sense is that we go on being essentially the same person. Psychologists have suggested that one significant threat to mental health is the impact of too much change - if our world is in turmoil, particularly if the changes seem out of our own control, then any sense of personal stability is difficult or impossible to hold onto. This links with the third key characteristic of identity: identity needs to be built around a sense of **security** - that significant parts of our world are stable and reliable.

What we have said so far is applicable to all of us as human beings. We want to argue that the task for foster children in building or holding on to a positive sense of self is just the same as for anyone else, but with some very important additional challenges. It is also important to remember the diversity of situations which fostering covers. Some children will come from backgrounds which have offered them a lot of positives, others from profoundly damaging ones. Some children are in fostering on a short-term respite basis, while for others their entire family life is changing permanently.

Who Cares?

Interestingly, this was the title chosen by one of the first groups of young people in care to convene in this country: they produced a booklet about their experiences and views which is still worth reading. Are these foster carers looking after me just because they are paid to do it, or do they care about me? Does my social worker care enough to keep appointments and visit me often enough to get to know me well? These are the questions in the present, but there are also haunting questions about the past: surely my mum did really care for me, even though she let me down? What was it about me that led my dad to desert me? Foster carers are often startled to discover that children in their care still hold very idealised views of their parents - perhaps very unrealistic ones - and dream of the parent who will one day return and take them back. This is surely a reflection of a very basic human need to believe that we have a parent who cares about us.

A fundamental difficulty for children in foster care can be the uncertainty about who is my parent? Birth parents are distanced, and although the social services department is in one sense a 'corporate parent, even the social worker is far from playing the role of a parent. It is here that the foster carer, even in short-term placements, will inevitably go some way towards filling the role of 'parent' - though with great care not to usurp the birth parents.

Knowing who cares about us is a part of a wider layer of identity - of **connectedness, belonging and shared history**. Keith White calls this a sense of '**community**'. Much of our sense of identity is not so much about individual characteristics and achievements, as about the **groupings** of people we belong to - the football team, vegetarians, and so on. Of all the groups to which we belong, much the most significant for most of us is the **family**.

Family

For many children coming into foster care, their family life will already have been complicated and perhaps fragmented. We know from research that many children will have seen members of the family leave, and new members arrive, and that their families will be characterised by instability and unexpected change (Fisher, Packman Bebbington and Miles). For instance, a foster child's step father may be the only father she remembers.

It is in this area that the **continuity** of identity of children and young people entering foster care is at risk. If foster care is short-term or respite, then the risk is less, but the studies by the Robertsons indicated many years ago how important - and how difficult - it is to maintain a clear memory of key figures in very small children during even a short period of separation. In a variety of ways it is the foster carer's role to keep alive the child's sense that those people are still out there. The Children Act makes it clear that **contact** is to be a priority for all children in foster care, and broadens our concept of 'contact' in two important ways. Contact is not just with parents, but with brothers and sisters, other relatives, friends and other people important to the child; and contact is not just about visiting: it is also about telephone conversations, letters and cards. This point is reinforced by research: Jane Rowe (1984) found that 'contact with grandparents was almost always very positive. Friction between foster parents and grandparents seemed minimal and children gained a lot'. Whenever a child is admitted to foster care, the social worker should do the research to provide a 'map' of the whole range of people with whom the child needs to maintain contact - and then the social worker, with the foster carers and parents, needs to plan in some detail how this will be achieved.

It will also be important to the child in foster care that contact happens in a reliable, reassuring way. Part of this will be the quality of relationships between the foster carers and the family. As with parents who live apart, so in this situation, it will be important to the child that the different people who all matter to them are able to offer them the reassurance that they negotiate rather than battle - that important parts of their world, and therefore themselves, are integrated not disintegrated. The child's sense of self will benefit if carers are able to build positive relationships with the family members with whom the child is in contact.

Belonging to a Group - Class, Religion and Race

As well as belonging to a family, our sense of who we are is related to a whole set of groupings we belong to - other people with whom we identify and with whom we share important characteristics. The Law makes clear that plans for foster care must recognise a child's race, religion, culture, and the languages they are used to speaking. Whilst these factors are especially crucial for black children, they apply in varying ways to all children. In all these areas, a good foster home will recognise and respect these aspects of who a child is, and will nurture, rather than ignore, them.

Religion can either be a relatively isolated element of identity - attending mass once a month - or can be a central part of a culture and way of life. For many Muslims, Islam is a way of life, not just a religion, and parents may question whether a foster home could possibly provide adequately for their child unless the carers are themselves practising Muslims. As well as religious observance as such, dress, etiquette, morality, and food will all be involved. We need to know just how religion figures in the life of the child and their family, and to offer the maximum continuity possible.

Shama Ahmed suggests that 'One consequence of the racial prejudice that persists and accumulates in our society is what amounts to a psychic assault on Black people'. (in Morgan and Righton: 217) Black children (African-Caribbean, Asian and African, for example) face a great deal of racial prejudice in their everyday life and will regularly see negative images of black people in inferior positions. Lena Robinson describes this as 'an environment that is unsupportive, denigrating, oppressive and even hostile' (1995: 105 referring to Baldwin 1985). The danger is that black children may then take on board this sense that black is second best, and integrate this into a negative sense of themselves as black.

Writers such as John Small (1986) have argued that black children need to learn 'survival strategies' - ways of dealing with the negatives of racism in everyday life, and that it is as they do this that they will be able to develop a sense that being black is valuable and something of which to be proud. Jocelyn Maxime (1986: 101) similarly speaks of 'the survival skills necessary for the development of a positive racial identity.' black children need positive black role models, a sense of the achievements in black history, a positive view of their own cultural background, open discussion of racism and how to deal with it, and to hear appreciation for 'black' aspects of their physical appearance. They need, too, to feel that they belong to a black community.

Ideally, placement finding will place a child in a foster home from the same background, but not infrequently children are placed in a different 'group'. The adjustments can make real demands on the child. The stressful process a child may go through in discovering how this new family lives has been nicely captured by Alice Winter in *Only People Cry*.

One of the boundaries that children often cross when they move from home into foster care, but one that is seldom acknowledged, is social class. Even if children are not moving from working class homes to middle class foster care, they are almost certain to be moving to a home which is better off. One of the dilemmas of foster care is how far foster carers should try to provide continuity for the child in terms of daily routine, food and so on, and to what extent to introduce new patterns: these might involve manners, clothing, or accent.

Mary was fostering four year-old David. Walking down the street one day, David ran back to her, saying ' I've stood in some shit.' Mary corrected him, telling him that ' we call it dog dirt, not shit.' A few days later David was playing out with Mary's grandchildren, and came running in to tell Mary that two year-old Freddie had 'done a dog-dirt in the sandpit.'

Oppression

In discussing social class, religion and race, we have begun to touch on aspects of a child's identity which may already be undervalued. Society tends to regard certain groups as inherently 'second class': in one way or another you will experience this if you are working class, black, Muslim, a woman, disabled, gay or lesbian. These messages percolate into the consciousness of our children even at a very early age: one of our daughters, at the age of three or four was discussing growing up. She said that she did not want to grow up to be a woman because 'the world is for men'.

Much more seriously, many young women entering foster care will have experienced violence or sexual abuse by men on women, either at first hand or by watching their parents. It is crucial that foster homes try to re-balance this pattern, and offer the foster child positive messages about their gender, sexual orientation, abilities, race or class. They may also need to hear from their carers clear messages that this mis-treatment is **wrong**.

Labels

Other sources of stigma for some children in foster care include a range of **labels** which may have been applied to them. Their behaviour, their feelings, and their ability to learn may all have been seen as difficult, disturbed, or failing. The Who Cares? group asked for the right 'to be as much a part of society as the next person and not to be labelled.' In order to help and support the children they look after, foster carers and social workers need all the information available about a child, and need to make sense of it: knowing whether this is a lively child who is unused to boundaries on his behaviour, or whether he has Attention Deficit Disorder may be very important in knowing how to respond. Equally, we need to be aware how labels can 'stick' - if we believe, as all foster carers and social workers must, in the capacity of young people to heal, to grow and to change, then we must also believe that any label, however correct, is only valid now, not necessarily for the future. The Looked After Children (LAC) materials should help us to hold on to an understanding of continuous and complex developments going on within every child, and so help to ensure that children are not permanently blighted by labels which may (or may not) have been true years ago, but are certainly no longer valid.

Abilities and Disability

We have been thinking about negative labels, but a sense of self esteem draws heavily on the opposite - the **positive feedback** we receive about how we behave. This is especially evident in the primary school years, when identity is very much caught up with what we can do - climb trees, dance, do well in school or at sport and so on. Not least because their education has often been disrupted, many children and young people in foster care will have had very restricted success in school. Part of the art of foster care is to note the achievements of the child across the whole range of their activities, and to offer them praise and appreciation.

Sue, a foster carer, expressed her delight when her 12 year old foster child, Anna, achieved success in her music-making. Not only was Sue able to let Anna know how pleased she was with her achievement, but she was also able to link it with wider themes for Anna: 'I bet you get that from your Dad - he's musical: he played the guitar.'

A significant number of young people in foster care have either physical or learning **disabilities**: for them, the label of disability is powerful, and some of the routes to achievement are restricted. Philippa Russell refers to research by Brimblecombe, Kuh and others which shows that two thirds of disabled school leavers have nothing to do during the day outside the home, and limited opportunity for social life. They are three times more likely than their non-disabled peer group to feel isolated and lonely, and Russell (p. 180) comments that 'lack of social confidence and poor self esteem were conspicuous' in this group. Two thirds of the young people also felt they had insufficient information about their medical condition and its implications. Foster carers will want to ensure as far as they can that disabled foster children receive the information and explanation they need, that they have stimulation, activity and the chance to succeed, and that they have social contacts and opportunity to develop social skills.

One label which can easily carry stigma is that of being '**In Care**' (Who Cares?). People at school and out in the local community easily assume that being in foster care must be in some way the child's fault. Equally, the reasons for being in foster care may be difficult and painful for the child, as she may only gradually be developing a full understanding and coming to terms with the questions 'why am I in foster care?' and 'why can't my own family look after me?'

> *You have the micky taken out of you at school - or fear they might find out and take the micky . . . It's mostly a joke - they don't mean to hurt, they only think it's a game.*
>
> ('Robert' in Thorpe in Triseliotis 1980: 95)

This raises the need for a '**cover story**' to be worked out. This is the idea that the foster carers, the child and the social worker may need to talk together to anticipate the questions that may be asked by people in the foster family's environment, and to agree how much they need to be told - enough to quench their curiosity, but little enough to avoid the child feeling that their personal history is open house for anyone and everyone. This discussion will need to be very child-centred - how much do they know so far; how much do they understand; how much are they reasonably comfortable with; how much do they want other people to know? One thing for child and carers to remember in this process is that once information is released, it cannot be recalled: perhaps it is best to be cautious, and to ask how much do we **need** to tell this person? There may be different groups of people, some of whom *need* to know more, some very little.

Sexual Abuse

Experiences of abuse seriously affect identity and self esteem, not least in the case of **sexual abuse**. Sexual abuse has sadly been part of the experience of many of the children now coming into foster care, and that experience will often have 'spoiled' the child's sense of themselves. The abuse can leave a child with feelings of having been damaged, of somehow being responsible for the fact that the abuse happened, of guilt, of shame and so on. All of this will of course have a major impact on their sense of their own value and worth.

Most children who have been sexually abused have received very powerful messages about their own lack of worth. It is common for them to have been told that it is them or something about them that caused the abuse to happen. Not only can this leave questions about identity as a whole but more specifically their sexual identity. They may feel there is something inherently dangerous about them which is beyond their control that makes others behave sexually towards them. They are likely to have learned that this is what adults expect, at least in private. It may also be the only way they have learned to receive physical affection. They may also have learned at some level about sexual pleasure which is likely to reinforce the message that they are responsible for the whole thing anyway. Not surprisingly, this can leave young people with a very confused and destructive sense of who they are and with very strong needs to have those received messages challenged if they are to move on and rebuild a positive sense of who they are.

First and foremost they need to be told, and probably told over and over again, that they were not responsible for the abuse and that it is the adults who are responsible. Talking of a whole range of aspects of their earlier lives where children may harbour a sense that it must have been their fault, Claudia Jewett says that

> the clear message that you must give to children ...is: "It was not your fault. It was not because you were bad in any way, or because you were unlovable. There is nothing you could have done - or can do - to make things different.

It is also common for children to believe they have been damaged internally in some way during the abuse.

One adult survivor had watched her perpetrator kill and gut chickens: in her four year old mind she thought that her abuse was something similar to this.

So clear explanations need to be given to try to enable children to move on from these distorted impressions and experiences. Also to try and sort out the muddle of feelings about the possibility that the abuse may in part have given physical pleasure as well as pain, fear and secrecy. It is easy to make assumptions that children who have been sexually abused know about sex, but it is essential that they are given good sex education and ideas about safe physical contact. This is to help them make sense of what has happened and what sex is and can be about.

Control is also likely to be an issue for children who have been sexually abused. Control and choice have been taken away in a quite fundamental way for these young people. Jewett suggests that the experience of loss can also leave children feeling they have no real control over important aspects of their own lives. She suggests (p. 119) that carers try to find ways of 'letting the child experience being in charge, being included in decision making, and exercising control over some areas of [their] life'. Both groups can otherwise be left with a profound feeling of helplessness.

Security

June Thoburn (1994) suggests that children need both a sense of identity and a sense of 'permanence'. Identity involves knowing about their birth family and past relationships, appropriate contact with important people, fitting together the past and the present, and being valued as the person you are. By permanence she means security, belonging, a base in family life, loving and being loved. In a similar vein, Clare Winnicott commented that 'So many of the children we meet have no sense of the past and therefore no sense of the present and of the future.' (in Morgan and Righton: 1994). The Who Cares? Group asked that young people in the care system be given

> the right to know who we are...to have factual information about our family origins and background ...Make sure every young person really understands [their] situation and why [they] cannot live with [their] family

Information and Explanation

> When you know as little as I do about your parents, you do wonder. Your own father could have been a murderer - it's very doubtful, but you wonder "Will this run in the family?"
>
> ('Andrew' quoted by Thorpe in Triseliotis: 95)

For children in the care system, much of the information about their lives before admission is missing, and this gap can leave the child uncertain, confused and preoccupied. In this context, the requirement that the agency shares information with the foster carer is crucial - essential information for the carer and the child should be in the Foster Placement Agreement. However it is unlikely that this basic information will be sufficient if the young person is to spend an extensive period of their childhood in care. This means that the social workers and foster carers involved at the start need to make every effort to gather and store background information. The social worker should routinely produce a 'social history' - the history of the child and their family, and should have ensured that the child understands, as far as their age allows, why they are moving.

The carer will need to check out with the child how they feel about all this, and how far they really understand. Children may, for instance, harbour quite unfounded feelings that somehow they must have been responsible for whatever went wrong in the family. Birth parents and other relations are likely to know most about the child's history and so may be in a position to help in reassuring them that the problems were not their fault. It may be a task for the social worker and foster carer to maintain the relationships which will enable the child to continue tapping into this source of knowledge about themselves. The process of explanation and understanding will be a continuing one, in which the carer will almost certainly play a key role. Vera Fahlberg comments that if a child's personal history becomes fragmented 'it becomes more difficult for them to develop a strong sense of self and for them to understand how the past influences present behaviours'. (1991: 353)

Life story work is a way of sharing and exploring with a child the information we have about their history and background, helping them to record those events and sometimes their feelings about them. Life story work is a live and ongoing process as a child's perception and understanding changes as they grow older. The information they are able to handle and their feelings about it may also change, creating the need to return to the material and check out whether they are ready for a more complex and sophisticated level of understanding, or perhaps has misinterpreted or forgotten previous information. Recording the information in written form allows the child to return to it in their own time. If a further move occurs they will be able to take

this with them, maintaining in a tangible way some continuity in a time of further change. Ryan and Walker, whose book Making Life Story Books is especially useful, suggest that children can discover the 'various people, places and concerns which form part of [their] life…and so gain further understanding of their life as a whole and why they are where they are' (see also ch. 2.13).

Part of helping to maintain identity when a child has to move is about ensuring that their **possessions**, clothes, photos, toys and larger items like their bike, go with them. It is also crucial that we are very cautious about discarding any of the child's possessions until we have fully checked out their significance for them. Even very 'tatty', smelly clothes or toys may have significance - it's a matter of who gave them, the moments they remind them of, and simply the fact that they have had them for a long time in a rapidly changing life. Some of the items with the most memories and associations attached may be stored in a 'Life Story Box'. Need we say, it does not help to develop positive identity if these possessions are moved in plastic rubbish bags, with a clear message about you and your belongings!

Weinstein has suggested that personal identity hinges on the answers to three questions - Who am I? To whom do I belong? and What is going to happen to me? The third question is an important one, and links to Thoburn's suggestion that children need a sense of identity linked with a sense of permanence. Triseliotis, Sellick and Short comment that finding a foster home does not necessarily resolve all the fears and anxieties a child may harbour. 'A child's world can still be populated with apprehensions. To a child, what happened before can also happen again.' (1995: 117) It is perhaps surprising, but some children in foster care can still be unclear about the fostering plan for them.

> I think you're only out in a certain place for a certain length of time, say two or three years and then you're supposed to be moved. I don't know why - perhaps people get fed up with you.
>
> ('Derek' in Thorpe : 91)

So foster carers need to ensure that foster children are as clear as they can be about the future as well as the past. For many of the children there will inevitably be an element of uncertainty, but at least we can be clear and honest about what the uncertainty is, and what we hope will happen.

Fitting it all Together

Like continuity, another important aspect of identity is a sense of **wholeness** - that all the various parts of our self are integrated and linked together. There is a great sense of sadness when we realise that somehow we have left behind for ever a particular relationship, a significant stage of life, or even a specially loved possession. This is one of the major costs to children in foster care: they have left behind a great many important aspects of themselves as they move from home to home. One crucial piece of information that foster carers need is some indication of the range of moves and changes that this child has experienced - and the **losses** involved.

The critical area is the loss of relationships - of people. Rejection is the direct opposite of love: in the same way that love affirms our value, if we feel rejected, we also doubt our worth. At some level the child will probably feel that if important people, perhaps parents, have deserted them, this must prove that they have little worth and should not expect that anyone will value or care about them in the future (Jewett 1991: 107). Losses can also leave the child feeling very much alone and isolated. Children may also have learned that it seems best not to trust in relationships and other people, or they will let you down. This may well lead to suspicion when new relationships are offered, and to a need to **test out** the commitment of the new foster carers - if I show them the very worst side of myself, will they still want me? Claudia Jewett observes that 'many children react to a loss…by provoking negative exchanges, constantly pushing and testing…limits' (p. 111). If foster carers can survive the testing out, and show that they can accept the whole child as they are, affectionate and hostile, happy and distressed, they will have made a major contribution to their sense of wholeness and integration.

One fact that we can easily ignore is the way that the foster home can quite rapidly become part of the child's sense of who they are. As positive relationships develop, so attachment will grow. Vera Fahlberg suggests that there are two key processes in which a child will build an attachment to carers. First, as the child learns that the carers are sensitive to their needs, and will respond when they begin to feel distressed, they will learn that it is safe to trust them and to rely on them - they regularly meet their basic needs in a reliable way. Secondly, children need stimulation and enjoyable new experiences: as carers regularly invite them to join in appropriate shared activity and to introduce them to new interests, sharing the experience and valuing their achievements, another important level of their needs is being met and a relationship being built. In these ways, the foster carers will be countering the effects of earlier losses by 'helping enhance the child's sense of belonging, competence and self worth' (Jewett p. 112).

This leads on to the fact that perhaps the most important factor contributing to anyone's sense of self-worth is the experience of **an unconditional commitment from another human being**. 'It seems probable that this irrational acceptance, this sense of being loved as a whole without reservation, is the basis of adult confidence in oneself as a person, and of satisfying relationships with others' (Storr 1960: 48) This sense of unconditional love and acceptance is arguably the crucial element that most parents give to their children. Here we face the contradiction spelled out in the Foster Care Agreement that all foster carers should sign. They agree 'to care for the child…as if [they] were a member of the foster parent's family' - but also to allow the child to be removed at any time that social services decide that is best: foster carers are trying to offer a committed, secure relationship within an uncertain time frame.

It is important, too, that love is a two-way process. Children and young people need to receive love, but they also need to be able to give it. Fairbairn suggests that adult mental illness may result from situations where ' the child feels that [they] are not really loved as a person, and that [their] own love is not accepted'. We referred earlier to Thoburn's suggestion that loving and being loved are elements of the 'permanence' that children need.

Conclusion

In summary, if foster carers are to nurture a positive sense of identity and self-worth in the children for whom they care, they will need **to listen to them, give real attention to them, value them, respect them** - and ideally offer them love. This will not be easy, and goes beyond the demands of parenting our own children. Foster children have been through profoundly damaging experiences, and may need us to revisit those experiences with them. As Clare Winnicott said, our aim must be

> *to get in touch with the children's real selves, what they are feeling about themselves and their lives at [this] moment...We want to help children to... maintain a sense of their own unique identity and worth... As all children who come our way have been through painful experiences of one kind or another, we need to seek contact with the suffering part of each child, because locked up in the suffering is each child's potential for living and for feeling love as well as for feeling fear, anxiety and hostility... The greatest re-assurance we can give to children is the feeling that they are understood and accepted right down to the painful sad bit in the middle. If we do not deny this painful bit of themselves, they need not do so, and their natural resilience can take them on into life again.*

References

Ahmed, S. Children in Care: The Racial Dimension in Social Work Assessment in Morgan. S and Righton P (Eds.) (1989) *Child Care: Concerns and Conflicts*, London: Open University

Baldwin, J.A. (1985) *African Self-consciousness: an Afrocentric Questionnaire, Western Journal of Black Studies*

Bebbington, A. and Miles, J. (1989) The Background of Children Who Enter Local Authority Care, *British Journal of Social Work*

Fahlberg, V. (1991) *A Child's Journey Through Placement* London: BAAF

Fairburn, W. (1952) *Psychoanalytical Studies of Personality*, London, Tavistock

Fisher, M., Marsh and Phillips, D. (1986) *In and Out of Care: The Experiences of Childen, Parents and Social Workers* London: Batsford

Foster Placement *(Children) Regulations 1991*, schedule 3:1

Health, Dept. of (1998) *Quality Protects*

Jewett, C. (1982) *Helping Children Cope With Separation and Loss* London: BAAF

Maxime, J. Some Psychological Models of Black Self-Concept in Ahmen, S., Cheetham, J., and Small, J. (Eds.) (1986) *Social Work with Black People and Their Families* London: BAAF

Packman, J. (1986) *Who Needs Care? Social Work Decisions About Children* Oxford: Basil, B.

Page, R. and Clark, G. (Eds.) (1977) *Who Cares? Young People in Care Speak Out* London: National Childrens Bureau

Robertson, J. and Robertson, J. (1971) *Young Children in Brief Separation: a Fresh Look, Psychoanalytic Study of the Child*

Robinson, L. (1995) *Psychology for Social Workers - Black Perspectives* London: Routledge

Rowe, J., Caine, H., Hundleby, M. and Keane, A. (1984) *Long Term Foster Care* London: BAAF

Russell, P. Handicapped Children in Kahan, B. (Ed.) (1989) *Child Care Research, Policy and Practice* London: Open University

Small, J. Transracial Placement: Conflicts and Contradictions in Ahmed, S., Cheetham, J. and Small, J. (Eds.) (1986) *Social Work with Black Children and Their Families* London: BAAF

Storr, A. *The Integrity of the Personality* London: Pelican

Thoburn, J. (1994) *Child Placement: Principles and Practice* Aldershot: Arena

Thorpe, R. The Experience of Children and Parents Living Apart in Triseliotis, J. (Ed.) (1980) *New Developments in Fostering and Adoption* London: RKP

Triseliotis, J., Sellick, C. and Short, R. (1995) *Foster Care Theory and Practice* London: BAAF

White, K. (1983) *Welfare of the Child, Social Work Today*

Winnicott, C. Communicating With Children in Morgan, S. and Righton, P. (Eds.) (1989) *Childcare: Concerns and Conflicts* London: Open University

Winnicott, C. (1964) *Communicating with Children, Child Care Quarterly Review.*

Winter, A. (1997) in *Working with Children who are Joining New Families*, Bath

1.5 The International Perspective of Foster Care

Clive Sellick

Introduction

This chapter has two main aims. Firstly it seeks to bring together the relevant international foster care literature including international instruments, conference publications, government statistics, recent research studies and practice accounts. Secondly it sets out to provide the readership with an overview of contemporary foster care policy and practice through a two point framework designed to make sense of the complexity and diversity of foster care in an international context.

A considerable amount of recent literature has sought to achieve a world view of foster care policy and practice. Yet all accounts in spite of their rigour have encountered enormous difficulties in constructing definitions, comparisons or frameworks for shaping foster care on a world stage. Most point to the importance of foster care for children separated from their own families. Many identify the potential of foster care to reach and meet the physical, psychological and social needs of such children. Some document the roles and needs of other participants such as parents, foster carers and the staff of fostering agencies. All describe very different circumstances surrounding the provision of foster care throughout the world and taken together this literature illustrates the diverse nature of fostering. Foster care policy and practice reflects and responds to national and regional events including wars and famines as well as domestic adversity associated with parental ill health, imprisonment, addiction and abuse. Foster care may be provided by public, private or independent agencies. In parts of the world fostering is an informal response shaped by tradition rather than by regulation.

In short there is no one single international perspective on foster care but rather a collection of different and changing perspectives. Amongst these however a number of trends and developments have emerged within the world of foster care which this chapter sets out to explore. It begins by summarising some major instruments established by international agencies which set the scene for contemporary foster care policy and practice.

International Instruments and Guidance: Practice Implications

The first place to start a journey through fostering is Article 20 of the United Nations Convention on the Rights of the Child. Since its adoption in 1989 the Convention has been ratified almost universally. By the start of 1997, 68 countries or State Parties had submitted initial implementation reports to the monitoring Committee on the Rights of the Child (UNICEF, 1998.) Article 20 states:

1. A child temporarily or permanently deprived of his or her family environment, or in whose own best interests cannot be allowed to remain in that environment, shall be entitled to special protection and assistance provided by the State.

2. State Parties shall in accordance with their national laws ensure alternative care for such a child.

3. Such care should include, *inter alia*, foster placement, *kafalah* of Islamic law, adoption, or if necessary, placement in suitable institutions for the care of children. When considering solutions, due regard shall be paid to the desirability of continuity in a child's upbringing and to the child's ethnic, religious, cultural and linguistic background.

This Article suggests a hierarchy of placement options for a child separated from family and neighbourhood placing foster care before adoption and residential care. The earlier Declaration on Social and Legal

Principles relating to the Protection and Welfare of Children (UN, 1986) contains specific guidance on foster care and adoption. For example it states that:

- workers responsible for foster placement should have appropriate professional training
- the placement of children should be regulated by law
- foster care should not preclude either family reunification or adoption
- in all matters foster carers and as appropriate the child and parents should be properly involved
- the placement should be supervised by a competent authority or agency to ensure the child's welfare.

The participation of all the parties, the child, parents, foster carers and social work staff of the fostering agency is further highlighted by the International Foster Care Organisation (IFCO). Indeed its published guidelines for foster family care are defined in relation to each of these participants (IFCO, 1996). These guidelines add further detail to the foster care task. They establish for example a range of responsibilities for carers including the provision of physical care, nurture and emotional support to children. They also set out a continuum of foster care comprising pre-adoption care, weekend care, respite care, the care of siblings and long term care for children as an alternative to adoption. The IFCO guidelines are also underpinned by an injunction to 'reduce the risk of out of home placement by building the strength of Foster Care Agencies and Foster Families to protect the health, safety, ethnic heritage and dignity of children placed in their care' (IFCO,1996:5). Many of these guidelines have been included in the domestic legislation of a growing number of countries as far apart as the United Kingdom and Uganda and Romania and Belize.

A recent publication which profiles foster care systems in 21 different countries of Europe, Asia, Africa, Australasia and North and South America shows how despite these international guidelines, in practice foster care looks very different across the world (Colton and Williams, 1997a). Although there is no one overarching framework which gives universal

meaning to fostering the editors elsewhere offer a definition which illustrates the diverse nature of foster care. They write

> 'Foster Care' is care provided in the carers' home, on a temporary or permanent basis, through the mediation of a recognised authority, by specific carers, who may be relatives or not, to a child who may or may not be officially resident with the foster carers
>
> (Colton and Williams, 1997b:48).

Colton and Williams have constructed five main criteria against which a country's foster care system may be measured. They write that foster care may or may not:

- include care by relatives
- include only those placements which are mediated by a recognised authority
- include only temporary placements
- mean round the clock care
- involve a private home.

These criteria can be seen in operation in different parts of the world. In some sub-Saharan African countries children displaced by conflict or orphaned by AIDS may either be taken in spontaneously by strangers or be placed by village elders in their role as a competent and recognised authority (SCF,1997). In Islamic countries across the Middle East and South East Asia adoption is considered to be incompatible with religious doctrine. The concept of *kafalah* referred to in Article 20 of the UN Convention from the arabic word meaning guarantor or attorney provides a permanent form of fostering. In countries in transition in Central and Eastern Europe (CEE) western style temporary foster care is considerably underdeveloped. The provision of small family group homes may be viewed either as foster care in countries such as the United States of America or Finland whilst commentators from other western countries would be as likely to define these as small scale residential care provision. The picture then is one of considerable diversity and complexity.

There appears to be two major approaches to analysing foster care in an international context. One looks at particular countries or groups of countries and examines how foster care operates according to national or regional demands and realities. The other seeks to extract major themes or trends within the foster care service itself and to measure these against domestic priorities. This chapter will take the second of these two approaches partly because the first is already well documented in the available literature (see for example, Colton and Hellinck, 1993; Madge, 1994; Ruxton, 1996; Colton and Williams, 1997a and b; and Pringle, 1998) but partly because this approach also lends itself to a simple two part framework familiar to those involved in foster care.

This model views foster care as being either principally a service which supplements birth family care or one which substitutes for that care. Supplementary foster care is generally a short term service for families and children to assist them in overcoming a temporary crisis often related to parental absence through illness or brief imprisonment or where the child has been or is likely to be harmed. Substitute foster care implies a longer period of alternative care for children who cannot be cared for by their parents because of death, loss, maltreatment, or long term illness. The two paradigms are not however entirely separate or self-contained. Both have to incorporate new developments such as kinship care, foster care for children in emergencies and the professionalisation of foster care. For convenience discussion here about the professionalisation of the service is considered in connection with supplementary foster care particularly since practice developments have been led by specialist foster care schemes most of which are temporary in nature. By the same token discussion about kinship care and emergency care will be placed within the section which considers substitute care since in practice many children live for longer periods of time in these care situations.

Foster Care as a Means of Supplementing and Supporting Family Care

There is an established tradition in the UK which emphasizes foster care as a temporary service to help families over periods of stress or to perform specific tasks for young people in need of assistance and accommodation. Legislative change in the 1970s gave additional legal rights to children and foster carers and made it more possible to terminate parental contact and place children for adoption without parental consent. The emphasis on working with families and the development of skills by both social workers and foster carers to do so therefore diminished. The 1989 Children Act in England and Wales brought back more of a balance. So whilst some children continue to be maltreated by their parents and to suffer significant harm, in practice most children in the UK spend very short periods of time in public care and return safely to their families. An extensive study of placements in several British local authorities over two years found that 'the day to day, bread and butter work of fostering is still the placement of younger children needing care for a brief period during a family crisis or to give relief to hard pressed parents' (Rowe et al., 1989:79). Recent government figures continue to support this finding (Department of Health, 1997). One study which examined all temporary foster care placements in a northern English city over a 12 months period found that foster care was predominantly a short term service for younger children and that the majority of all children aged under ten years returned to their families within three months (Stone, 1995). Other research indicates a more recent trend of children remaining in foster care for rather longer periods (Waterhouse, 1997). However there is still an emphasis in the UK on frequent family contact, the notion of foster care as a voluntary service and the importance of social workers, parents and foster carers working together collaboratively, flexibly and sensitively.

British Government figures show how foster care has become the principle placement of choice for children separated from their families, 64 per cent of whom are fostered compared to 12 per cent who are living in residential homes (Department of Health, 1997). Elsewhere in western Europe the provision of residential and foster care services is more balanced. Countries such as France and Denmark for example have almost equal proportions of children in foster and residential care (Madge, 1994). Whilst there are many regional variations within western Europe foster care and family maintenance programmes have developed at a faster pace in northern Europe where child welfare services are more likely to be found in the public sector (Ruxton, 1996). In Sweden for example legislative changes which provided family support services, including supplementary foster care, led to a significant fall in the numbers of children placed in out of home care through court action (Baddredine and Idstrom, 1995). Also in northern Europe but across the Baltic Sea in the former soviet republic of Lithuania the evaluation of a pilot fostering project has also pointed to the need for an integrated range of child welfare services including foster care much in the way that experience has taught practitioners in the West. This project has had a wider influence than its staff initially imagined. Its success in finding foster families for institutionalised children has hastened the development of more appropriate legislation and policy (Cox, 1998).

Southern European countries especially those with a relatively recent history of totalitarian government such as Greece, Portugal and Spain and where the Catholic and Orthodox Churches maintain a significant position in the provision of child welfare services tend to invest less in foster care schemes. However, here as elsewhere in western Europe the overall balance of care continues to shift towards less costly and more humane foster care services. Although there is neither a uniform transfer from residential to foster care across western Europe nor a shift from child protection to family support programmes 'behind both these trends there remains the crucial issue of cost and the relative expense of residential care' (Pringle, 1998:83).

The Professionalisation of Foster Care

The position of foster carers in the provision of child welfare services has changed considerably over the past two decades, particularly in the West. The professionalisation of foster care associated initially with the specialist schemes which provided alternative placement programmes for adolescents has also influenced mainstream foster care provision. Service conditions and support services to foster carers have developed considerably particularly over the past twenty years. These include the payment

of fees, the provision of regular training, respite facilities and specialist advice as well as a greater recognition paid to carers by fostering agencies as fellow colleagues. These have elevated the role of foster carers both in the public and independent foster care sectors. In some places such as Romania (Government of Romania, 1997) and Denmark (Southon, 1986) foster carers are paid salaries similar to those of social workers. The development of regular training programmes for approved foster carers is particularly evident in North America (Pasztor and Wynne, 1995). Canadian and American foster carers are likely to have twice the amount of training as their British peers. They are also more likely to be exposed to training with a clear theoretical and methodological base (Hill et al., 1993).

Foster Care as a Form of Substitute Family Care

Temporary or supplementary foster care which provides placements for children and support to their families is widely underdeveloped outside of the West. One recent report estimated that there are 700,000 children living in institutions throughout the countries of the CEE, the former Soviet Union Commonwealth of Independent States (CIS) and the Baltic States (Black and Smith, 1997). As Harwin found in her study of Russian children in public care 'no one should underestimate the legacy of socialism on child care' (Harwin, 1996:2). In the first half of this century foster care was more developed in some parts of the CEE than in the West. For example in Hungary 87 per cent of children in public care were fostered in 1938. However this figure had fallen to 20 per cent by 1955 as child welfare services and budgets were centralised, private and independent initiatives supressed and children's institutions expanded. (Herczog, 1998) The legacy of communism also means that disabled children and those from the Roma or gypsy communities are still significantly over represented in the institutions of countries such as Romania and Bulgaria (Dickens and Watts, 1996; UNICEF, 1997).

The continuing lack of family support including supplementary foster care schemes means that for impoverished families across the region the only available form of support is the children's institutions. Once admitted most children will remain in these throughout their childhoods (The Children's Health Care Collaborative Study Group, 1994). Where foster care exists at all it is likely to be substitute or permanent care for children who have lost touch with their families. These are the social orphans of the region. In countries such as Hungary and Poland changes have occurred more quickly than elsewhere because there were remnants of earlier systems upon which to build. In Hungary there is evidence of foster care programmes targeted at gypsy children (Diosi, 1994) and in Poland foster carers have been recruited to care for children transferred from the institutions (Stelmasjuk, 1994). Elsewhere in the region foster families have been providing permanent placements for children for many years. In Serbia for example evidence exists of a foster care village where for more than 50 years children have been placed both from families and institutions across the country with villagers who foster them until they reach adulthood (Nestorovie, 1996). Here as in Poland policy and practice were cemented by a combination of religious and political imperatives in spite of apparent contradictions.

Foster Care with Relatives

Kinship foster care is well established in many parts of the world. In CEE countries in transition and in developing countries in sub-Saharan Africa it is the principle form of foster family care. In countries across the CEE region such as Romania, Poland and Hungary the numbers of fostered children have remained small both in absolute and relative terms. Of these as many as 70 per cent are in kinship foster care living with often elderly grandparents or other relatives without adequate financial support (UNICEF, 1997). In Poland such relatives were compelled to foster young relatives by the courts, even without their consent, and this legacy still influences policy and practice (Stelmaszuk, 1995). In non Western countries where the rearing of children is not considered to be the sole responsibility of parents 'it is not surprising to find various forms of indigenous fostering in which responsibility for children's care,

socialisation and education are shared, on a more extended basis, by various people within the family network.' (Tolfree, 1995:185).

Elsewhere in the world even where there are formal and very well developed child welfare systems kinship foster care is on the increase. In the USA for example it is the fastest growing service of the child welfare system and provides up to 44 per cent of foster carers approved by authorised authorities in some states (Gleeson and Craig, 1994). This is used especially for African American children to provide culturally appropriate placements. Likewise in New Zealand kinship foster care is being developed to meet the needs of both white pakeha and Maori children (Read, 1998). A recent study of the organisation of fostering services in England found that 12 per cent of approved foster placements across the country were with family members and that in some local authorities this rose to 30 per cent (Waterhouse, 1997). Kinship foster care is likely to offer additional placement choice, better reflect a child's cultural background and brings less risk of breakdown.

Foster Care in Emergencies

During the conflict in the Great Lakes region of Africa in 1994 over 10,000 unaccompanied refugee children from Rwanda were taken in by families in Zaire. (SCF, 1997). Many were received spontaneously by local families and others were placed by non governmental organisations (NGOs). Many of these children have been repatriated especially when their families were traced but others have remained with their foster families and have developed new attachments. There is evidence however that unknown numbers of children who remain with the new families are being exploited as child labourers or are subject to physical and sexual abuse. Elsewhere in the world such as Thailand, Uganda and the former Yugoslavia, Save the Children (SCF) is concerned that separated children are also being used in armed conflicts. The international NGO sector and some governments are attempting to use international instruments such as Article 20 of the UN Convention to regulate foster placement and to avoid widescale abuses in emergency situations.

Conclusion

Foster care as a tool of social policy is used throughout the world according to local circumstances and demands within countries and regions. Its particular usage therefore varies considerably. It is however a universal care service for children separated from their families which generally provides a more humane, responsive and cost effective alternative to placing children in residential institutions. It is used when children have been harmed within their own families as well as when they have been separated by armed conflict or disease. In developed countries foster care is more likely to be a supplementary and usually temporary service as a part of a wider programme of family support. Developing countries and those in transition are slowly using foster care as an alternative to institutional care which is more likely to be a form of long term substitute care. In these countries children tend to be fostered within their wider families. There is however a two way traffic of ideas so that countries with sophisticated child welfare services are expanding kinship foster care as a positive placement option.

The role of the non-governmental sector is particularly important in transferring ideas and practice from developed, especially western European, countries. International NGO initiatives are usually aimed at encouraging governments and indigenous agencies to implement programmes of their own by training and employing staff to undertake work with children and families and with recruiting and supporting foster carers. However, progress remains slow due to a combination of past legacies and current financial crises. The continued use of large institutions and the underdevelopment of professional social work training mitigate against sustainable foster care schemes in many areas of the world.

The diverse nature of contemporary foster care offers little clear direction for future developments. The West faces increasing difficulties in recruiting sufficient numbers of foster carers for children presenting behavioural and emotional difficulties whilst simultaneously reducing residential provision for these children. Other countries, especially those in the CEE, are using the NGO sector to introduce a Western style of foster care whilst retaining a very large institutional sector. The international perspective is likely to remain diverse and although this chapter has attempted to describe different trends and developments these do not offer a clear view of the future. Foster care is therefore in need of further ongoing review and analysis by commentators across the world.

References

Baddredine, K., and Idstrom, U. (1995). Alternative Options provided for Children in Foster Care: Different Forms of Placement in Sweden. In Thelen, H. (Ed.) *Foster Children in a Changing World*. European IFCO Conference, Berlin 1994

Black, M., and Smith, C. (1997). *Rights of Institutionalised Children*. European Conference Report 6-8 May 1997. Bucharest. UNICEF. Save The Children

Colton, M., and Hellinck, W. (1993). *Child Care in the EC: A Country-Specific Guide to Foster and Residential Care*. Aldershot. Arena

Colton, M., and Williams, M. (1997a). (Eds.). *The World of Foster Care*. Aldershot. Arena

Colton, M., and Williams, M. (1997b). *The Nature of Foster Care: International Trends. Adoption and Fostering*, 21,1,44-49

Cox, J. (1998). Developing Fostering Services in Lithuania. *Adoption and Fostering*, 21, 4

Dickens, J., and Watts, J. (1996). Developing Alternatives to Residential Care in Romania. *Adoption and Fostering*, 20, 3, 8-13

Diosi, A. (1994). Learning From Each Other: Professional Gypsy Foster Parents in Hungary. *Adoption and Fostering* 18, 4, 38-42

Gleeson, J., and Craig, L. (1994). Kinship Care in Child Welfare: An Analysis of States' Policies. *Children and Youth Services Review* 16, 2, 7-31

Government of Romania, (1997). *The Emergency Order Concerning the Protection of the Child in Difficulty*. Article 23 (3)

Harwin, J. (1996). *Children of the Russian State*. Aldershot. Avebury

Health, Department of (1997). *Children Looked After by Local Authorities. Year Ending 31 March 1996. England*. London. HMSO

Herczog, M. (1998). Assessing Child Welfare Outcomes in Central and Eastern Europe *Children and Society*, 12, 223-227

Hill, M., Nutter, R., Giltinan, D., Hudson, J., and Galaway, B. (1993). A Comparative Study of Specialist Fostering in the UK and North America. *Adoption and Fostering*, 17, 2, 17-22

International Foster Care Organisation, (1996). *International Guidelines for Foster Family Care*. IFCO.

Madge, N. (1994). *Children and Residential Care in Europe*. London. National Children's Bureau

Nestovovic, M. (1996). *Towards a life: foster home centre. Milosevac 1931-1996*. VFC Video. Zastava Film Belgrade

Pasztor, E., and Wynne, S. (1995). *Foster Parent Retention and Recruitment: the State of the Art in Practice and Policy*. Washington. Child Welfare League of America

Pringle, K. (1998). *Children and Social Welfare in Europe*. Buckingham. Open University Press

Read, L. (1998). *Implementing a Fostering Programme in New Zealand*. Unpublished. University of East Anglia, Norwich

Rowe, J., Hundleby, M., and Garnett, L. (1989). *Child Care Now: a Survey of Placement Patterns* London BAAF

Ruxton, S. (1996). *Children in Europe*. London. NCH Action For Children

SCF, (1997). *Keeping Children With Families in Emergencies* Nairobi Save The Children Fund

Southon, V. (1986). *Children in Care: Paying Their New Families* London HMSO

Stelmaszuk, Z. (1994). Fostering in Poland. *Social Work in Europe*, 1,2,39-41

Stelmaszuk, Z. (1995). Foster Care in Times of Socio-economic Change: Expectations and Perspectives In Thelan H (Ed.) *Foster Children in a Changing World* Berlin International Foster Care Organisation

Stone, J. (1995). *Making Positive Moves: Developing Short Term Fostering Services* London BAAF

The Children's Health Care Collaborative Study Group. (1994). The Causes of Children's Institutionalization in Romania. *Childcare, Health and Development*, 20, 77-88

Tolfree, D. (1995). *Roofs and Roots: The Care of Separated Children in the Developing World*. Aldershot. Arena

UNICEF, (1986). *Declaration on Social and Legal Principles Relating to the Protection and Welfare of children*. New York UNICEF

UNICEF, (1997). *Children At Risk in Central and Eastern Europe:Perils and Promises*. Economies in Transition Studies Regional Monitoring Report No.4.Florence. UNICEF

UNICEF, (1998). *Implementation Handbook for the Convention on the Rights of the Child*. New York UNICEF

Waterhouse, S. (1997). *The Organisation of Fostering Services: a Study of the Arrangements for Delivery of Fostering Services in England*. London. National Foster Care Association

2.1 National Standards in Foster Care

Derek Warren

The need for more consistent — and higher — standards in the provision of foster care services throughout the UK sparked a debate that gained momentum from late 1996. This was fuelled by a series of critical reports highlighting inconsistencies and shortcomings in the quality of care available for children and young people. Resultant discussions led to the formation of a ground-breaking national working party. By late 1998, following the most comprehensive consultation exercise ever undertaken on the quality of foster care services in the UK, a set of new National Standards for Foster Care was nearing completion. With the support of the Department of Health and the Northern Ireland, Scottish and Welsh Offices, publication was set for mid 1999.

Critical Reports

When the Social Services Inspectorate (SSI) published its report on the inspection of local authority fostering services in England, in December 1996, it identified serious failings in the quality of foster care provided by six representative authorities. Perhaps the most worrying aspect of the report was the disclosure that many looked after children had not had a comprehensive assessment of their needs — and only a third had individual care plans. Not one of the six authorities surveyed met the regulatory requirements in this respect.

The SSI drew attention to a lack of standards particularly in the area of recruitment, approval, training and retention of foster carers. The report also bemoaned a general lack of experience and knowledge of foster care among social workers: despite the fact that foster care had become the preferred option for placement of looked after children, most students on the main social work qualification course (Diploma in Social Work) spent a maximum of only two days of a two year course studying foster care.

Hard on the heels of the SSI report came an equally critical publication from the Association of Directors of Social Services for England and Wales (ADSS), launched in January 1997. This echoed many of the findings of the SSI. Based on a survey of more than 500 foster carers, a separate survey of 84 directors of social services and the outcome of a national conference held in July 1996, the report highlighted inconsistencies in practice among local authorities.

The ADSS report found foster care services often structured outside overall planning for looked after children — and greater attention and priority was focused on residential care. This despite the fact that two thirds of all looked after children were placed with foster carers. The lack of placement choice for children, too many placements made away from home and community and high levels of disruptions and placement moves were all areas of concern voiced by the ADSS.

Recommendations in the report included a call for the Department of Health and the ADSS to co-operate in the development of both a national quality framework for all foster care agencies and a national protocol for local authority practice in the delivery of foster care services.

While the recommendations were forthright, the results of the ADSS survey demonstrated a certain complacency among social service directors. Seventy five per cent of those who responded viewed their foster care service as 'basically healthy', despite the fact that 69 per cent said they had insufficient carers to match placement needs and 66 per cent said they had difficulties recruiting new carers. Forty one per cent said they were unable to meet the needs of black children who could benefit from foster care.

In March 1997, a new study published by the National Foster Care Association (NFCA), on the organisation of fostering services, gathered data from 88 per cent of local authorities in England. This revealed considerable variations in the quality of management, supervision and support of foster care services. Less than half the authorities allocated all approved carers to a named family placement worker and 40 per cent of authorities found it difficult to comply with requirements for annual reviews of each foster carer.

The study also found that only 20 per cent of authorities could offer a placement choice for children under ten years of age — and this figure plummeted to just three per cent which could offer a choice to children aged over ten. Lack of placement choice inevitably increases the likelihood of placement breakdown and leads to frequent moves for looked after children; further destabilising already traumatised and vulnerable youngsters.

In May 1997, in the wake of the General Election and assumption of office by the new Government, NFCA launched a second publication, *Foster Care in Crisis: A Call to Professionalise the Forgotten Service*. This was not a research-based study, but a campaigning document containing a clarion call for an upgrading of foster care services, greater professionalism and the introduction of national standards.

Inherent in each of these reports was a view of foster care as an undervalued resource and the 'forgotten facet' of children's services provision. This was borne out by David Berridge's *Foster Care: A Research Review*, also published in 1997. He was able to identify only 13 major studies on foster care over the previous 20 years, while ten studies on residential care for children were under way at the time he was compiling his review. This emphasis disregards the current reality, with more than twice as many children and young people now placed with foster carers rather than in residential facilities.

The UK Joint Working Party on Foster Care

By September of 1998, the UK Joint Working Party on Foster Care had been established, chaired by Tom White CBE, a former director of social services for Coventry, former chief executive of NCH - Action for Children. He is currently Chair of the National Foster Care Association (NFCA) and a Coventry City Councillor. The working party brought together for the first time at a national level, directors of social services and social work, foster carers, researchers, family placement practitioners, and representatives of local government associations and voluntary organisations. They were joined by observers from the Department of Health and the Northern Ireland, Scottish and Welsh Offices, each of which had committed funds to the project to ensure it was a genuinely UK-wide initiative.

Both the Association of Directors of Social Services for England and Wales (ADSS) and its Scottish equivalent, the Association of Directors of Social Work (ADSW), were instrumental in the establishment of the Joint Working Party.

The objectives agreed for the Working Party were:

● to seek to improve the quality of foster care in the UK through the development of national standards, following wide consultation with both users of foster care services and those responsible for delivering them; and

● to promote the widest possible use of the resultant quality standards to encourage consistency in foster care service provision nationwide.

The group began by gathering and considering all available material on standards in foster care, both within the UK and overseas. This included standards and criteria already used by the SSI during inspections of local authority fostering services, a new set of standards introduced by the SSI in Northern Ireland and standards adopted by individual authorities. More specific standards for placing children through independent agencies and those for young people leaving the care system (already adopted by First Key, in association with the Association of Metropolitan Authorities, ADSS and others) were also considered.

Internationally, the group was able to draw on standards produced by the International Foster Care Organisation (IFCO) in addition to those produced in individual countries such as the United States and Canada and in other EC countries.

A comprehensive consultation exercise

A first draft of UK national standards for foster care, incorporating 25 proposed standards and the criteria for determining compliance with them, was agreed by the group in June 1998. This was followed by the most comprehensive consultation exercise ever undertaken on the quality of foster care services throughout the UK.

Five thousand copies of the consultation document were produced and distributed. Recipients included every local authority in England, Scotland and Wales, plus the health boards and trusts responsible for foster care services in Northern Ireland. Copies were sent to government departments, local government associations, regional social service inspectorate staff, local foster care associations, hundreds of individual foster carers, fostering panels, elected local authority members, and independent and voluntary sector fostering and child care agencies.

Approximately a hundred separate meetings, workshops and conferences were convened to consider and respond to the document. More than 15,000 questionnaires were sent to children and young people in foster care and the children of foster carers to draw out their views on the quality of care they receive.

National Standards for Foster Care

A statement of values and principles, agreed by the Joint Working Party, informed the drafting of standards. These were reflected as themes throughout the text. They included advocacy for:

- priority to be given to the needs of the child in deciding on each foster placement
- valuing and promoting diversity in terms of race, culture, religion, language, sexuality and gender and
- a partnership approach to foster care — embracing parents, carers, social services and the children themselves.

The proposed standards themselves included a mix of service, practice and professional standards, and were divided into three sections.

The needs and rights of children

The first section covered the needs and rights of children and young people in foster care,

dealing with issues such as equal opportunities, care planning, child assessments, health, education, information for children and young people, and preparing youngsters for adult life.

One of the key issues raised by SSI inspections — that of lack of adequate child assessments, care planning and reviews — was addressed in two specific standards, one on child assessment and a separate guideline on care planning and reviews. These linked the planning process and monitoring of child care plans to the Looking After Children Materials (LAC) issued by the Department of Health, and in particular with the Assessment and Action Records produced as part of the LAC materials. The standards promoted full involvement of all parties, set time scales for the completion of care plans and defined rights of access to the recorded information.

Concerns raised during the consultation process, particularly by social work and family placement practitioners, centred on the high proportion of 'emergency' placements that, of necessity, could not be pre-planned.

An underlying theme in this area was the concept of placement choice for children. The standards assumed and implied that a decision to place a child in foster care should be taken on the basis of that option being selected, from a range of possible placement options, as being in the best interests of the child, rather than as a resource-led decision — or because of a lack of other available options.

Similarly, a standard on matching carers with children and young people promoted the benefits of authorities recruiting a diverse range of foster carers. This was seen as vital in ensuring appropriate placements, matching the needs of children with both the skills and the environment provided by the carer. Meeting this standard assumed the authority would have access to a greater number of carers than the number of children it sought to place in foster care, allowing for an element of choice. This has implications for recruitment and training strategies, given most authorities currently cite a shortage of carers. As a result, children are frequently placed in the only available placement, often with carers not approved for the specific age group or other category into which the child falls.

Recommendations were also made on the quality of social work support available to children and young people in foster care. This standard stressed the importance of each child being assigned a named social worker with relevant training. Recognised here was the need for that social worker to be allotted time to undertake specific work with the child and the child's family towards goals established in the child's care plan. As with many of the standards, this had clear resource implications in terms of the caseload of social workers — and therefore the number of staff required.

A standard on health and safety within foster homes proposed conditions more on a par with those enforced for childminders than has previously been the case in most authorities. A separate standard on safe caring — covering protection of the child from abuse, neglect, exploitation and deprivation — recommended procedures and monitoring to reflect the increased importance given to this issue. This follows a string of high profile prosecutions of abusive carers and the well-publicised Sir William Utting Report, People Like Us, on the safety of children living away from home.

The working party made a number of recommendations within a standard recognising the importance of education for the future of fostered children. These related to the value placed on continuity in the child's schooling, more careful monitoring by authorities of educational progress and a closer partnership between social services, foster carers and education departments in planning for the education of looked after children. Looked after children are ten times more likely to be excluded from school than their contemporaries — and an estimated 75 per cent of looked after children leave school with no recognised qualifications. Significant emphasis was placed on the authority's role as a corporate parent in valuing and promoting the looked after child's education.

The health of children in foster care was dealt with similarly as a separate standard. This again stressed the need for authorities to monitor the health of all children they are looking after, to plan for improved health care and to improve the quality of information collected and provided to carers on the child's health history. Specific criteria proposed that the relevant health authority should appoint a medical advisor for children in foster care and that each child should have a health assessment before any placement in foster care.

The role of the foster carer

Section two covered the quality of care provided by foster carers, examining areas such as assessment and approval, training, payments, supervision and support.

The standard on assessment and approval set out guidelines on the participation of potential carers in their own assessment. It also highlighted the need for provision of clear information on the foster carer's task and the expectations of carers, obtaining verified personal and professional references and a desirable time frame for completion of the assessment process.

Debate on this standard during the consultation process revolved around problems for smaller (unitary) or more rural authorities in running regular assessment groups — and therefore being able to process all applications, including assessment visits, within the prescribed time frame. This has to be balanced against the likelihood of carers losing interest and drifting away if the assessment process becomes too protracted — a common complaint from potential carers.

The standard on supervision, support, information and advice for carers set out a clear supervisory role and line management relationship between a named, qualified supervising social worker and each carer. This reflects a general theme within the standards of a more professional approach to the foster care task. The 1996 research showed that less than half the authorities in England were meeting this standard of allocating all approved carers to a named family placement worker. Concerns were also raised about the clarity of the relationship between foster carer and supervising social worker.

The standard also stipulated levels of information and support which carers should be entitled to expect, both from social services and other disciplines, to ensure they could meet the needs of each child. Specific criteria in this area covered the need for clear information on insurance and legal liability cover for carers, opportunities for carers to share experiences and concerns with other carers, identification of training needs for carers and access to emergency (out-of-hours) support.

A major concern for carers in the current climate of high profile court cases is what procedures are followed if allegations of abuse are made against them. The standard proposes provision of specific written information for each carer on procedures to be followed, including full details of support available to the carer.

A separate standard on annual reviews for carers — which 40 per cent of English authorities were failing to carry out systematically — set out formats for both review meetings and reports. A proposal that each annual review, which constitutes effective re-approval of the carer, should go to the authority's fostering panel, caused some concern among social service managers. Fears were raised that the workload for voluntary panel members would become excessive and unmanageable. Linked with annual reviews was the standard on training for carers, with reviews seen as including an appraisal of future training needs. The training standard was consistent with the theme of a more professional approach to the foster carer's task, focusing on skills development and assessment of competencies, linked with the new (S)NVQs course in foster care. Recommendations were for basic pre- and post-approval training to be mandatory for all approved carers, and for carers to have the opportunity to be trained jointly with social workers.

Main concerns voiced by carers about the provision of training related to the need for courses to be staged at times more convenient to them and for provision of the necessary support to enable them to attend, particularly in terms of childcare and reimbursement of travel expenses.

A standard covering the role of carers in facilitating contact between children and young people and their families while they are in foster care raised discussion about the demands currently placed on carers by court orders and local authority decisions on contact. This was of particular concern where a carer might be caring for two or three children from different families; meeting the demands for contact for each child could place unreasonable demands on the carers time and on their own family, especially if contact was arranged in the carer's home. Both family placement workers and carers felt the onus should be on social services to manage the contact arrangements, but this should be always in close consultation with the carer and should consider the

implications for the carer, in addition to the best interests of the child.

Perhaps the most contentious of the issues raised in the standards consultation document was that of payments to carers. This reflects a wider debate about the future of foster care and whether it can survive as a volunteer-based service. There was broad agreement with a proposed standard on payment of allowances to carers at a level to cover their costs in caring for a foster child and reimbursement of agreed expenses such as travel, extra furniture or meeting special needs of a fostered child.

However, divisions arose within the Joint Working Party itself over a proposed standard on reward payments to carers. Some members felt the resource implications of proposing reward payments for all carers were so great that the inclusion of such a standard would threaten the credibility of the entire standards exercise and so could jeopardise their implementation as a package. A further concern was that such a recommendation implied a change in the fundamental nature of foster care and ignored the altruistic motivation of most carers.

Since no consensus view was achievable, the consultation document went out for circulation without a specific standard on reward payments, but included — as an appendix — a discussion paper entitled What cost foster care? This raised the problems faced by local authorities in trying to recruit and retain foster carers in a changing social climate, with more women in paid employment, fewer 'traditional' two parent families with one parent not working and more alternatives — such as child-minding — where people could be rewarded for taking on a caring role. The paper also detailed changes in the law and in social work practice which have made fostering a much more demanding task for carers.

Authorities already face competition for carers from a growth in new independent fostering agencies, with most authorities now buying in part of their foster care service provision from such agencies. Carers cite not just the greater financial rewards of working for these agencies, but also the increase in support and improved conditions provided to them, as reasons for moving away from local authority fostering services.

Most authorities already offer increased incentives for some carers, through enhanced allowance payments or specialist fee-paying schemes for those providing care for particular categories of young people, such as those on remand or with behavioural problems.

The discussion paper concluded with three options on the future financial basis of the foster care service for debate and comment:

1. A service based as far as possible on a purely altruistic, voluntary approach to foster care.

2. Continue with, and extend, the present arrangements of allowances for the child, enhanced payment schemes, fee paid schemes and contracting out services with the independent sector.

3. Move towards a paid, skill-based service. The working party recognised that authorities will be unable to implement this within existing resources.

However, if there is sufficient support for option 3, which many see as the only practical way forward, the working party would need to make strong recommendations to government for additional 'ringfenced' money to be made available to local authorities for the fostering service.

The role of the corporate parent

The third section of the consultation document dealt with proposed standards on the duties of authorities responsible for the public care of children and young people. This included policy, management structures, professional qualifications and training, recruitment of carers, representation and complaints procedures and the delegation of responsibility for the provision of foster care to other (independent or voluntary) agencies.

The inclusion of policies and plans for foster care services within each authority's child care policy and children's services plans was a key criteria for meeting the standard on effective policies. This addressed the findings of the ADSS survey in 1996, which found foster care services were structured often outside overall planning for looked after children.

The theme of greater professionalism in the approach to foster care services — and recognition of the professional role of foster carers — appeared once more in the standard on management structures. This proposed a clear line management structure throughout the service, with clearly defined lines of authority and responsibility at every level, including foster carers.

Another key element of effective management identified was the need for management information systems which disaggregated data on looked after children to provide specific information on foster care. This should include details of the number and types of foster placements available, levels of unmet need, outcomes for children and young people who are fostered and the effectiveness of the foster care service.

The standard on professional qualifications and training for social work staff proposed changes in national training schemes to include mandatory training in family placement work, including significant focus on foster care. Anything other than rudimentary coverage of foster care has been previously only an optional element of the main Diploma in Social Work course, for instance, despite the growth in importance of foster care within children's services.

With every local authority constantly trying to increase their available pool of foster carers, a separate standard on recruitment of carers recognised the value of greater placement choice for children. The consultation process confirmed that many children are placed in the only available foster home, regardless of assessed need or any care planning for a matched placement. This is borne out by research on levels of disruption of placements and frequent moves for children.

The standard proposed more carefully defined recruitment strategies, aimed at providing a pool of skilled and experienced carers who reflect the needs of the local community. Inherent in this approach is a management information system that monitors recruitment initiatives, records what is successful and unsuccessful in attracting appropriate carers and what must be offered to retain their services. There are obvious overlaps here with the 'payment for skills' debate on financial rewards for carers.

This section also included standards on the role of local authority fostering panels and the criteria for establishing effective representation and complaints procedures for fostering services.

The standard on delegation of responsibility for a foster care placement to an independent or voluntary fostering agency made it clear that this did not reduce the responsibility of the placing authority for ensuring that all quality standards for the care of the child were met. In essence, the standard proposed that — where an authority contracts out the provision of foster care for a child or young person — it must ensure that all legal requirements, and the quality standards and policy requirements applied to its own fostering services, are met by the external agency.

In its final form, the national standards document will include sources of evidence for the achievement of each standard, plus relevant research findings and statutory references, in addition to the criteria for determining compliance included in the consultation document.

National Focus on Foster Care

The work on drafting national standards was taking place at a time of considerable national focus on the future of social services in general and children's services in particular. In November of 1997, *The Utting Report*, on the safety of children living away from home, raised numerous child protection issues, several of which related to foster care. In presenting that report to the House of Commons, Secretary of State, Frank Dobson announced the formation of a ministerial task force to define a government response to the report's recommendations.

One immediate consequence of the deliberations of the task force was a request from the Department of Health for the UK Joint Working Party to take on an extra piece of work developing a new code of practice on the recruitment, selection, training and support of foster carers. This was to be published simultaneously with the national standards in mid 1999.

The White Paper on Social Services, in the autumn of 1998, proposed introduction of mandatory regulation and inspection of all foster care agencies, bringing the plethora of new independent fostering agencies into the regulatory fold for the first time.

The second report of the Health Select Committee on children looked after, published in the summer of 1998, echoed this call for regulation and inspection of agencies. The all-party committee supported the recommendation of the Utting Report for a new code of practice on recruitment and selection of carers, and called for 'a coherent and costed national strategy for the future development of foster care.' The recommendations of their report continued: 'This is a task which the Government may wish to entrust to the newly appointed UK Joint Working Party on Foster Care, the setting up of which we welcome.'

All this suggests the national standards were to be introduced at a time when the foster care service was at something of a crossroads. Almost every authority faces problems in recruiting and retaining sufficient foster carers to meet the needs of children and young people in their care. This calls in to question the future viability of a service based on the traditional voluntary, vocational role of foster carers. The Health Select Committee made a specific and forthright recommendation in this area 'that the Government, in consultation with local government, the NFCA and other interested bodies, should as a matter of urgency draw up proposals for establishing a national framework of payments' (rewarding carers for their levels of skills and experience).

This debate on the future of the foster care service reflects the all-encompassing discussions generated within the working party and explains the group's commitment to making recommendations beyond the proposed national standards, as part of a final report.

However, the introduction and implementation of consistent national standards remained the primary focus of the group throughout 1998. Considerable wider interest in the foster care service, as outlined above, could only enhance the chances of the standards being widely adopted and implemented by local authorities.

In the end, the best chance of the standards becoming genuine benchmarks for effective, high quality foster care services lies in two key areas. The first involves each authority carrying out an audit of their foster care services against the national standards, identifying shortfalls in the quality of care and developing plans to address these. The second lies in encouraging local authorities' own internal registration and inspection departments and the independent Social Services Inspectorate to inspect foster care services against the national standards.

References

Association of Directors of Social Services (1997). *The Foster Carer Market: A National Perspective*, ADSS

Berridge, D. (1997). *Foster Care: A Research Review*, HMSO

Social Services Inspectorate (1996). *Inspection of Local Authority Fostering*, SSI

Utting, Sir W. (1997). *People Like Us: A Report on the Safety of Children Living Away from Home*, DOH

Warren, D. (1997). *Foster Care in Crisis: A Call to Professionalise the Forgotten Service*, National Foster Care Association

Waterhouse, S. (1997). *The Organisation of Fostering Services: A Study of the Arrangements for the Delivery of Fostering Services in England*, National Foster Care Association

2.2 The Professionalisation of Foster Care

Hilary Corrick

The issues surrounding the professionalisation of foster care are complex and controversial, involving questions of finance and quality standards, and our feelings about people who care for children not their own. The motivation of people who choose to become foster carers is frequently questioned, and the basest or most saintly motives ascribed to them. These issues are not new and debates have raged since Victorian times.

Since the last war the perception of foster care by social workers and politicians has changed. It used to be thought of as, (and indeed very largely was), an occupation undertaken as an extension of parenting by mothers using only their 'maternal instincts', and receiving only the perceived costs, because they did it for love and their rewards came from seeing the children thrive. Nowadays the recruitment base of foster carers is much broader and the demand for carers has risen to the point where there is now said to be a national, indeed international crisis in recruitment, even though numbers remain remarkably stable. Many people have begun to consider fostering to be a skilled profession requiring training and deserving of reasonable reward. This shift in perception has not been consistent and many still consider that fostering is a form of community service, rather than a proper job, let alone a professional task. In truth, few would argue that anyone would foster for financial reward alone.

The care system has become increasingly reliant on foster carers in the last few decades. Foster care is seen by many as more effective than residential care, better able to meet the individual needs of children, and as a less stigmatising, more 'normal' experience for a child away from its family. Foster care has not suffered from the spate of scandals and public enquiries arising from institutionalised abuse in many children's homes. For these reasons, many local authorities have established policies that no child should be placed in residential care below 10 or 12 years, except in very unusual circumstances. And finally, although unit costing is complicated, many believe that fostering is significantly cheaper than residential care although Tresiliotes et al. (1995) disputed this.

At the same time there are fewer children in the care system than in the past. This is partly a result of legislation underlining local authorities' duty to prevent children coming into the care system and partly because of a decline in the population of children in the UK. The 1971 Children and Young Person's Act gave this as the first duty of the local authority, and allowed local authorities to allocate resources to enable families to care for their children. Furthermore, the local authority had a responsibility to place a child in, or return a child to, the wider family if at all possible. The tension between focusing resources on prevention or the care system itself, which may reflect a fundamental tension between supporting the family of origin, or caring for the 'rescued' child, has been around a long time. The current laws also underline the duty to promote the welfare of the child within his or her own family and community by providing appropriate services.

In addition to this legislation, initiatives developed by individual local authorities during the 1980s emphasised the development of integrated and positive child care strategies in order to improve preventative services and keep children within their families of origin. For instance, the care population of one large local authority fell from around 2,500 in 1986 to below a thousand in 1991, largely as a result of their integrated, locally based child care strategy which involved families receiving help in the provision of packages of services to prevent the need for care.

The emphasis on preventing children coming into the care system, or staying within it for any length of time, has meant that although homelessness or poverty continue to feature significantly in families who have multiple difficulties and whose children enter the care system, no child should enter public care purely because of these problems.

Whilst the numbers of children in the care system have decreased, however, the challenges posed by developing appropriate ways of providing care for these children have increased. Children in the care system now tend to be the most troubled and challenging children. Working in partnership with parents, exploring ways to support parental care has resulted in some significant delays in court processes for children. It may take several years until it is possible to achieve stability in a child's life; during these years the child is likely to have had many moves. A recent BAAF publication: *Children Adopted from Care* (1998) found the mean length of time in care between admission and adoption was over three years. In these circumstances a child who is not troubled at the start of their care career is likely to be very disturbed by the time a long term placement is sought.

In summary, although the percentage of children in all forms of alternative care is about the same as in the past, a higher proportion are in foster care, and most of these are children with considerable needs.

Despite the shift in emphasis within the care system towards foster care, the number of carers has not risen significantly, although many authorities have tried to recruit carers from a wide range of backgrounds. This may be due in part to the decline in birth rate between 1945 and 1955, so the number of over 35s has dropped: 35 plus is the normal target age group for foster carers. Family placement social workers have put considerable effort into developing initiatives to train carers in the skills they need to help the more challenging children who are now most likely to spend time in foster care. Many foster carers undertake skilled therapeutic work with the children in their care, ensuring that life story work in its widest sense is an integral part of the child's experience. They use the Department of Health Assessment and Action Records with the child, their parents, teachers, health professionals and the social worker to consider the child's developmental needs in the broadest sense.

Foster carers have had to learn to manage challenging and disturbed behaviour in ways which enhance the child's self esteem whilst maintaining ordinary family life. In our culture many parents use some form of corporal punishment with their children on some occasions: for obvious reasons this strategy is not available to those who care for other people's children. Foster carers have now to behave towards their foster children not as if they were their own but as if they were a professional responsibility, allowing themselves a sense of distance and objectivity, while at the same time offering them the individual care and concern of a parent. And many carers have to offer the same level of understanding and generosity to the damaged and sometimes damaging parents of the children, usually in their own home during contact visits.

As a result, what social workers expect of foster carers has become much more complex. We know that it's not enough to be kind and loving. Foster carers are expected to:

- help the child to change his or her behaviour where necessary
- help the child to move on to the next placement
- assess the child's developmental needs across a range of circumstances
- maximise the child's potential
- undertake an LAC assessment by holding the myriad conversations with the child which ensure that the full range of developmental tasks are tackled individually by the child (see *SSI/OFSTED Inspection of the Education of Children who are Looked After by Local Authorities* (1995))

Carers are also required to be adept in:

- writing reports for reviews
- attending court
- acting as Appropriate Adult
- making themselves and their home available for social worker visits
- attending reviews and planning meetings when requested
- sometimes making their own home available for meetings of up to twenty people

- talking the social worker's language whilst not threatening the social worker by being too expert at so doing.

Furthermore there has been a significant increase in the administrative work required of foster carers: keeping diaries, records, report writing, attendance at court. They may be expected to complete Accident Reports and Violent Incident Reports which are modelled on the local authority's forms for their staff, and which appear to take no account of the circumstances of fostering, asking for witnesses for example. Not to mention framing the complexity of family life into a description of the child's behaviour for the social worker.

The foster carer must meet all these expectations (and others specific to the needs of the child they are looking after) whilst maintaining their own family life and ensuring that the needs of their own children are not neglected. And they must do all this without any sense of being part of a professional team, or full professional recognition.

Ideally, the placement of each child with a foster carer is based on a clear care plan for the child and on a contract with the carer; it is time limited. The tasks to be carried out by the carer are clearly specified and reviewed regularly. Respite care, in the form of regular alternative brief placements for the child, may be built into the contract, and high levels of support are provided. Foster carers are expected to maintain their competencies by continued training and by attending regular support meetings with other carers.

Teenage care schemes, pioneered in Kent, were intended to give foster carers the skills and support they need to look after particularly challenging teenagers, mostly for limited periods of time. As well as requiring a particular commitment and level of expertise from the carers, the schemes place particular duties on the local authority: a higher level of professional and peer group support, out of hours contact, task-focused work by the child's social worker, and payment for the foster carers in addition to maintenance payments. By the late 1980s it was obvious that there were other groups of children who needed carers with these skills: severely disabled children, children not yet teenage who had had multiple moves, or needed an assessment or help to understand their history and move on to new attachments,

or were acting out in ways that made them very hard to manage, or children who had been excluded from school. These children were seen as likely to need carers with a high level of skill, for a significant period and possibly throughout their time in the care system.

Thomas and Pierson, in *The Dictionary of Social Work* (1995) define a profession as involving expertise, autonomy and a common value base. Clearly the autonomy of foster carers is limited: they often feel entirely dependent on the whims of other people - social workers, parents, guardians ad litem (safeguarders and curators ad litem in Scotland). The recent expansion of independent fostering agencies, however, provides opportunities for foster carers to offer themselves in the wider market place, resulting in an increase in power. *The National Foster Care Association Charter* (1987) provides a clear ethical code to which all foster carers would subscribe. The question of expertise is where the greatest ambivalence lies, but the new National Foster Care Standards will set agreed minimum national criteria for foster carers.

If expertise, autonomy and a common value base are the key defining characteristics of a profession, for foster carers any acknowledgement of these characteristics appears to be dependent on social workers and local authority social service departments. Since social workers themselves have only a shaky hold on the professional status to which they consider themselves entitled, it is perhaps unsurprising that their relationship with foster carers suggests a reluctance to admit carers to a full partnership of professional equals. The local authority control of the budget, and foster carers' commitment to caring for children combined with lack of confidence in their professional status, mean that foster carers feel powerless within the working relationship.

The 'professional foster carer' is generally thought of as someone who has more skills than the basic expectations listed above, and is paid for having these extra skills, which are designed to meet the needs of the most challenging children. They often belong to specialist schemes which developed from the 1980s teenage care projects, and they are sometimes managed by independent agencies.

These foster carers are able to show evidence of their additional skills; in marketing terms they have a portfolio of appropriate skills. The children placed with them are intended to be those who most need the mix of skills the carer can offer, but the carers' pay theoretically reflects the skills of the carer rather than the level of challenge presented by the child. In practice, there are at present no nationally recognised scales of fees, of skills, or of behavioural criteria which require paid carers; there are varying rates of and criteria for payment both from agency to agency and within any one agency. This results in inequalities and the failure to recognise or reward some carers' achievements; many unpaid carers offer the same quality of care to children placed with them as that provided by paid carers.

The present set-up of 'professional carers' presupposes that a child will be able to move to another placement once his or her behaviour has become easier to deal with. In reality an established affection may mean that the child will remain in the placement although no longer needing the specialist help provided by a professional carer; this prevents another child who needs a carer with additional skills being placed with that carer. Of course, if moved on as 'cured' the child might well regress and then again need specialist skills.

If the child remains with the carer for continuity and stability, there is an issue as to whether the carer should still be paid, given that their portfolio of skills are not considered essential for the work with that child: removing the fee seems unfair and may have negative consequences for the continuing success of the placement.

Debate continues over whether fees should attach to the child, based on the difficulties they present and how 'hard to place' they are, or to the level of skill exhibited by the carer: this may be fundamental to the professional status of carers. No other occupation has its pay dependant on the behaviour of their clients. And 'hard to place' may be for reasons not connected to the child's behaviour but to do with the agency's failure to recruit carers sufficiently widely.

Current budgetary pressures within social services departments expose fostering budgets as 'soft' targets compared to staffing commitments, and a system in which some foster carers are fee paid and comparable carers are not, raises the possibility of ceasing to fee pay any carers. Although salaried themselves

some social workers feel that carers ought to foster 'for love'; this feeling explains their ambivalence to carers' allowances and fees, and the fact that local authorities may change the criteria for, or level of, payment almost on a whim. On the other hand, the availability of an alternative 'employer' in the independent sector gives the carer more bargaining power. The development of Best Value within local authorities explains why up to a quarter of local authorities are considering the adoption of the NFCA three tiered fully fee paid fostering service. Any mixed system with fee paid and non- fee paid is bound to give rise to ambiguities and injustices: carers who are paid to care for a child who is easy to manage, or unpaid carers successfully managing a much more challenging child. Local authorities seem happier to pay foster carers when they have been recruited and trained by independent agencies; in this situation local authorities may merely pay the bills and fail to scrutinise the quality of care or the justice of the fee levels.

Despite these issues around payment of foster carers, it may no longer be appropriate to rely on a largely voluntary and unpaid system of carers. The culture of public service became eroded during the 1980s, the population is ageing, and women are choosing to return to work when their children go to school; many families can no longer live on one (usually male) income alone. Job security has also eroded the feelings of reliance on one person's wage. Indeed, women in receipt of benefit are under increased pressure to return to work. The Association of Directors of Social Services (1997) enquired into whether local authorities should consider introducing 'a fully professionalised foster care service', and found that most carers (65 per cent) questioned thought fostering should be paid; this is in line with other surveys. In theory paying all foster carers might help to resolve some of the problems identified by Colton and Williams (1997); the shortage of carers and the unrealistic expectations of many foster carers of the sort of children available (most carers want healthy babies, whilst most children needing placements are older and have challenging behaviour).

Such a move towards the professionalisation of foster care raises issues about how to treat kin carers, people who are looking after a child from their extended family and who don't want to be part of the general pool of carers, available for all children. Historically and internationally, informal care by relatives is an integral part of the cultural framework of many societies. The Law has increased the proportion of these carers to significant levels in some authorities; they enable children to be placed within their own communities with families who share their heritage (see chapter 2.8).

It might seem that it is logical for kin carers to be paid in circumstances when conventional foster carers would be paid; the Ombudsman in 1989 ruled that a woman approved as a local authority foster carer should be paid an additional fee whilst caring for her grandson, who had Down's Syndrome, in the same way that a non-related, stranger carer would be paid in the same situation. Many social workers feel uncomfortable about payments to people caring for children from the extended family, as other people may do the same thing without payment or recognition. They feel concerned that local authorities may be financing placements that would happen anyway, and becoming income maintenance agencies rather than social work agencies.

It is possible that paying all foster carers might enable people caring for children to whom they are related to achieve higher levels of skill; involving them more closely in foster care support networks might also encourage them to make themselves available as foster carers for other, non-related, children who need placements. Payment, with the consequent labelling of the child as in the care system, is known to be stigmatising for the child, and there have to be some clear gains for the child in being looked after - regular checks on their welfare, clear controls on levels of contact, and so on. Alternatively, if we only reward stranger carers, on the basis that families ought to care without pay for the children of the extended family or that payment could and should operate through other channels, we should look at different criteria for assessing carers for children who need to be in the care system but are most appropriately placed within the extended family.

Colton and Williams (1997) identify a slow and fragmented move away from a system in which well-meaning and largely untrained people volunteer to take children in need to specialist schemes involving highly trained professional carers, supported by other highly trained professionals, who care for disturbed children and young people. If this trend continues, professional foster carer could eventually be a realistic career option. To make this statement, however, is to define 'professional' in quite limited ways. The definition used by Thomas and Pierson (1995) focuses on autonomy, and foster carers are bound to be primarily accountable to social services as the monopoly employer rather than to any carers' association, even though it is possible to envisage such a carers' association coming to have a significant role in the defining and maintaining of care standards.

Other constraints on the professionalisation of foster care range from matters of detail and organisation to emotive issues. Questions outstanding include:

- what levels of pay and other benefits would be appropriate?

- how would these fit with the minimum wage legislation?

- how are competencies decided?

- what are adequate levels of training and supervision?

- what number of hours should be worked in a week?

There are also problems about how the transition period between amateur and professional foster care might be managed; a situation could arise (and indeed has already done so to some extent) in which different levels of pay and paid schemes co-exist with unpaid, which can lead to conflict. Foster carers who are also childminders are especially aware of these ambiguities. It is also important to avoid inefficient fragmentation of foster care into specialist schemes with different structures and criteria.

If foster carers had a greater sense of group identity and an occupational structure, their relationship with local authorities would change. Much research shows carers not feeling that they are treated as partners, often excluded from the decision making even when they have to carry out the decisions, as with levels of contact. A sense of identity as carers, and a professional body with the power to negotiate with social services, might make the relationship between carers and social workers more equal and ultimately more beneficial for all, - children, carers and social workers, - improving communication and reducing ambivalence. Payment of all foster carers might also reduce the sense of guilt which many social workers feel about the fact that they are paid whilst the carers are not, and which contributes to the difficulties in the carer-social worker relationship.

Any move towards the professionalisation of foster care would, however, make social workers uneasy in the short term. *The SSI Inspection of Local Authority Fostering* 1995-6 suggested that many field workers were negative about the growing role of foster carers as professional partners in a service for families rather than merely substitute parents. The Inspection suggests that experienced foster carers cause some social workers to feel uneasy and deskilled. Social workers, after all, receive little or no training on working with foster carers. If foster care is to develop social workers and senior managers need to give consideration to the consequences for their practice — training pathways will be needed for practitioners too, focussing on working in partnership. The Best Value approach, requiring local authorities to look at their own services critically in comparison with services provided elsewhere, is leading a number of authorities to commission services from elsewhere. If this trend continues, as seems likely, it will significantly shift the relationship between social workers, managers, and carers.

More abstract issues involve the perceived conflict between love and money - it has in particular to be noted that children in the care system (as well as some social workers and carers) find it hard to believe in the adequacy of care for pay, that is, that good quality family life can be provided for financial reward. A parallel would be that we would have better nurses if we paid them less. Professionals such as lawyers and doctors also find it difficult to accept carers as partners. Finally, there is the problem of how universal fee paid care could be funded.

In 1996 The National Foster Care Association produced a report on the job specification of carers and the development of their professional role. This scheme provides three levels of skill specification for carers, with a parallel fee scale. The NFCA's Foster Care Charter, referred to earlier, sets out a possible ethical base for foster care, a nexus of shared values to which all foster carers would subscribe; a value system like this is essential to any group which wishes to call itself a profession. In combination with the National Standards and the development of (S)NVQs for foster carers these documents could form a strategy for the professionalisation of foster care, focusing both on a material recognition of the different types and levels of skill individual carers have, and on an understanding of carers' shared values.

This is a structural framework for the development of professionalised foster care services. If it is to occur, it will be largely driven by local authority managers on the basis of service level needs for quantity and quality of carers. The tension between professional demands and restricted budgets will mean that if professional developments within foster care are to be coherent and reflect more than economic necessity, foster carers themselves will have to take more control of the process.

Whatever path is taken, the question of the future development of foster care needs to be considered and some attempt made to resolve the difficult ethical and pragmatic problems it raises. Social trends are changing the way the care system operates and the needs of looked after children; it is important to be aware of both the strengths and the weaknesses of foster care, and the implications of possible developments.

References

Association of Directors of Social Services, Children and Families Committee Report (1997) *The Foster Care Market: A National Perspective*

Audit Commission (1994) *Seen But Not Heard* London HMSO

BAAF: (1997) *Securing the Future*

Berridge, D. (1997) *A Research Review*. The Stationery Office

Carrington, L. (1994) *Family Business, Community Care*

Colton, M. and Williams, M. (Eds.) (1997) *The World of Foster Care: An International Sourcebook on Foster Family Care Systems* Arena

Health, Dept. of, Social Services Inspection (1995) *Independent Fostering Agencies Study* London: HMSO

Health, Dept. of, *Inspection of Local Authority Fostering 1994-5*

Health, Dept. of, *Inspectoion of Local Authority Fostering 1995-6*

National Foster Care Association (1987) *Foster Care Charter*

National Foster Care Association (1996) *Foster Carers: Payment for Skills*

Ombudsman Complaint No. 88/C/115 11 December 1989

SSI/OFSTED Joint Report (1995) *The Education of Children Who Are Looked After by Local Authorities* London: HMSO

Thomas, M. and Pierson, J. (Eds.) *Dictionary of Social Work* Collins Educational

Waterhouse, S. How Foster Carers View Contact, *Adoption and Fostering* Vol 16, no 2, pp 42-47

Waterhouse, S. (1997) *The Organisation of Fostering Services* NFCA

2.3 The Health of Children who are Fostered

Dr Marion Miles

There are more than 50,000 children and young people looked after by local authorities; of these 32,000 are placed in foster homes. Under the Arrangements for Placement of Children Regulations of the Child Act a medical examination and written health assessment are required before placement, if possible, or as soon as is practicable afterwards if not. Subsequently, further health and development assessments are required at six monthly intervals for children under the age of two years and at yearly intervals thereafter. All children in foster care must be registered with a general practitioner and receive dental care.

Introduction

This chapter looks at some of the areas that foster carers highlight as concerns for them. It also shows the importance of good health care at all stages in the development of a child. Health of looked after children has received high attention in recent times and this chapter shows the important role carers have to play in improving the health of looked after children. The chapter also shows that there is much to learn both for the carer and social worker which could well form part of further training for both groups.

Later in the chapter there is a discussion about the interpretation and use of health information and consideration is given as to how to make it available to carers and the children and young people concerned. How best to encourage young people to be interested in their own health and in keeping their health records is also covered. The health of carers is also noted as well as strategies for improvement in the health care of looked after children are suggested.

During 1998 many initiatives and reports have been published by the government and government departments all highlighting the need for improvement in the health of looked after children.

Background

The current statutory arrangements recognise the need to establish the health and developmental status of looked after children. These arrangements are highly relevant since past studies have shown that these children have frequently suffered deprivation, the majority of the birth families having experienced problems arising from low incomes and inadequate housing. Although the collection of health data on looked after children has been surprisingly poor there are studies which have shown that they are likely to have developmental and health problems. Sadly, many looked after children have been exposed to abuse or neglect with subsequent and significant adverse effects on health and development.

Child protection issues may be clearly identified. Not infrequently sexual abuse may not be disclosed until months or even years after placement thereby providing the missing piece of the puzzle in a child with behavioural problems or failure to thrive. In a Newcastle study, 60 per cent of children with foster families had experienced abuse or neglect at some time. More conservative figures suggest that about 25 per cent of children entering the care system had been or were at similar risk.

The previous lack of emphasis on health needs of looked after children has largely been re-addressed by implementation of the above regulations. It is, however, still relevant to consider why health needs are often overlooked since lessons remain to be learnt.

Children in stable birth families benefit from the presence of a parent who is familiar with the child's personal family history and who is alert to the development of symptoms and signs of less than satisfactory health. Parents overwhelmed by personal problems or disadvantage, however, are at risk of becoming desensitised to their children's needs. They are less likely to monitor progress and seek appropriate advice and support. Inadequate parenting may be compounded by children suffering repeated changes of carer. Thus health information becomes, at best, fragmented, but more often, lost all together. Social workers understandably give priority to matters other than those related to health. So health information is rarely well documented in interviews with parents and family members.

It is recommended that the required health and developmental reviews are recorded using forms such as those designed for this purpose by the British Agencies for Adoption and Fostering (BAAF). Some local authorities have produced their own versions of these records but the important point is that similar, relevant information is collected on all looked after children so that high standards of supervision can be maintained. Most local authorities now use the Looking After Children (LAC) Assessment and Action records, one section of which relates to health. Regular inclusion of health and developmental status in reviews should ensure that needs are more adequately identified and addressed.

Reflection on these issues serves to highlight the critically important role of foster carers who can act as advocates for good health care for all children. They are also guardians of health information on behalf of the children and probably most importantly, can demonstrate by continuing good example how to promote health and take responsibility for maintaining it.

Specific Health Concerns

As already stated, there is a deplorable lack of information at both national and local level which could provide profiles of the health status of looked after children. However, in the absence of well documented levels of incidence, the following sections include many health issues identified and regularly raised by carers during consultation with looked after children.

Immunisation

Of all the many things done by health professionals to children, the one which can most easily bear scrutiny and be justified is the delivery and completion of an immunisation programme. Despite the recent waves of anxiety about the uncorroborated effects of measles vaccine and similar concerns about other vaccines in the 1970's there is convincing evidence that most routine vaccines can be given with no significant adverse side effects to the individual. They provide impressive community protection against specific infectious disease.

Unfortunately, many looked after children miss out on immunisation because their parents fail to keep appointments, or more worryingly, 'do not believe in injections' and avoid seeking or listening to health advice from professionals. Social workers may not give high priority to completion of an immunisation programme because they, misguidedly, defer to parental choice and do not always pursue the best interest of the child.

Frequently, past information about immunisation is missing or difficult to retrieve. Where there is real doubt that previous immunisations have been given it is better to assume that they have not and commence a new programme. The **worst** that can happen is that the child has a mildly sore arm. The **best** is that adequate protection has been provided.

Foster carers need a well documented agreement with their placing agency so that they can be seen to be acting on behalf of whoever has parental responsibility when presenting a child for immunisation.

Carers should be given adequate information about the health of the child **and** their family as in my experience, carers worry lest they are inadvertently caring for an infected child. Some babies born to mothers infected with hepatitis B need to be protected by immunisation with hepatitis B vaccine. In these cases, it is very important that the babies receive the vaccine at the right time. For this to happen foster carers need to be appropriately advised. It would be extremely good practice for carers receiving a young baby, especially one with a mother who has misused drugs, to ask routinely 'does this baby need hepatitis vaccination or not?' A prompt such as this could set into action a process, often overlooked, due to the stress associated with separation from the mother and the subsequent placement.

When older children and young people are involved, their consent to immunisation should be sought. When refused, which happens rarely if the young person has been advised sympathetically, continuing effort should be made to try to persuade the young person to re-consider giving them valid reasons which are carefully and sensitively explained. This is a very important contribution that carers can make.

Growth

Growth parameters provide a very good indicator of a child's well being. Each child must have a growth record, measurements recorded on a growth chart. In this way the concerns about deviant growth can be identified and investigated. Merely obtaining measurements is not enough. Recordings must be plotted in order to identify whether a child is maintaining an expected growth centile or not whilst remembering that there are seasonal variations in growth.

Heredity has probably the strongest influence on growth. If a child is small it is essential to obtain parental heights in order to interpret the child's growth satisfactorily. A small child may have small parents. This does not necessarily exclude other significant factors but usually explains a child's small size. Conversely when a small child has parents of normal or increased height other reasons for slow growth must not be excluded.

Adequate nutrition is essential for normal growth especially during infancy. Babies who are small at birth usually show 'catch up' growth, however, if there has been prolonged growth impairment during pregnancy, the effects may persist. Maternal alcohol abuse may cause a baby to be born with foetal alcohol syndrome (FAS) or foetal alcohol effects (FAE) a feature of which is growth retardation.

Emotional distress affects the production of growth hormone on which childhood growth is dependent. Naturally occurring growth deficiency is uncommon.

Chronic illness such as heart, respiratory, gastrointestinal, kidney or thyroid problems can adversely affect growth as can genetic chromosomal abnormalities such as Down syndrome and Turner syndrome.

Tall stature

Overfeeding in infancy may result in obesity and tall stature. Occasionally tall stature present as a feature of a specific syndrome or chromosomal abnormality.

Anorexia nervosa

This eating disorder results in severe weight loss. Typically teenage girls are affected. There may be an earlier history of obesity and usually disturbed attitude towards weight and body image. Frequently there are associated psychiatric symptoms.

Asthma

Asthma is the commonest chronic health disorder of childhood. It affects at least 10 per cent of children and appears to be an increasing problem. Eczema and hay-fever may be accompanying conditions which add to the child's discomfort and occasional misery.

The great majority of children with asthma have airways which are hyper reactive to irritants and exercise. Thus asthma can be provoked by infection, exercise and air pollution. The characteristic symptoms are cough, wheeze and breathlessness. When a cough at night or following exercise is the only symptom there is a danger that the diagnosis may be overlooked.

Asthma can have significant adverse social effects which include isolation at school because of repeated absences, impaired activity and, paradoxically, over protectiveness. Happily continuing advances in treatment facilitate the leading of a normal or near normal life for the majority of children. The proper administration of inhaled drugs requires instruction and supervision from an appropriate health professional.

Techniques for rendering bedrooms dust free are helpful. Similarly children should be encouraged to enjoy physical fitness. Removal of pets must be considered with care lest this results in counterproductive emotional distress.

Hearing

Many looked after children have missed out on routine checks on hearing. Any carer concern about a baby's hearing, poor or absent response to household sounds, should be acted upon urgently. Deaf babies can babble. However, when a hearing aid is necessary, it should be fitted as soon as possible, by the age of 12 months at the latest, if the child is to develop speech.

Older children may have experienced frequent colds and ear infections without having had a subsequent hearing review. If the child develops an intermittent hearing loss it can compound possible earlier under-stimulation of language development resulting in a significant communication problem. Such children should be assessed when statutory health reviews take place to ensure that appropriate arrangements are made for comprehensive hearing and speech and language assessments. Assumptions that children are lazy, stubborn or contrary should not be made to account for lack of response to the spoken word. The child may be intermittently deaf and have 'learned' to block out distorted sounds.

Vision

It is important for carers to know about vision in birth parents. Short-sightedness (myopia) runs in families. It develops from the ages of three to four years when the child can be noticed to peer closely at perhaps the television set. School children have regular vision tests but looked after children are at risk of missing these because they often move from school to school. When in doubt the advice of an optician may be sought.

Squints (lazy eyes) also run in families. In young babies the eyes often turn outwards. Turning in is always abnormal and requires specialist advice. Squints do not correct themselves and should always be taken seriously since there may also be a refractive error which, if not corrected, may progress to permanently impaired vision.

One or both of the eyes of young babies may water frequently or even constantly. The duct which drains the tears into the nose may be blocked. In the vast majority of cases the problem resolves by the age of 12 months. If an infection occurs antibiotic drops may be needed.

Infections and infestations

Rarely some children are born with a deficient immune system which leaves them exposed to repeated infections. Protective treatment is required for life.

Other children may be born to mothers with HIV infection. If the infection is transmitted to the baby (this happens less frequently than originally feared) the immune deficiency may cause a rapidly progressive illness. Other babies are more slowly affected with a longer life expectancy. Chest symptoms vary depending on the type of respiratory infection present. Other infants come to attention with failure to thrive, persistent thrush and other infections, delay or regression of developmental milestones and rarely, secondary cancers. Precise diagnosis may be delayed until the age of 18 months. Treatment involves the use of specific drugs from a specialist centre.

Since HIV infection can eventually present in an apparently well infant or older child no guarantees about the absence of infection can be given to carers. All these children deserve to lead as normal a life as possible. They should be fully immunised in the routine manner. If still in contact with infected family members an inactivated polio vaccine should be used to protect the adult.

Hepatitis B infection occurs in some Asian mothers and among those involved in drug misuse. When identified the children should be vaccinated to protect them from infection. However, not all children are recognised and some become carriers and may be placed with carers. Since the child's status cannot be quickly established, some carers involved in emergency placements may be at risk of becoming infected themselves. Observation of usual personal hygiene practice makes infection unlikely but carers are advised to be vaccinated against hepatitis B as a precautionary measure.

Scabies

Scabies is easily passed by contact. It occurs commonly between the fingers and around the wrist. It causes intense itching which can continue after treatment which should involve all family members.

Headlice

Headlice worry everyone except health professionals. Infestation with headlice does not threaten health but does cause considerable anxiety despite repeated reassurances to the contrary. Headlice live happily on clean or dirty hair and are passed from head to head by crawling. When the eggs hatch the empty shells (nits) remain but it is the presence of lice which constitutes a definite infestation.

Until recently, treatment relied on the use of insecticides. Because of concern about possible toxicity of these drugs and the development of resistance, emphasis is now placed on earlier detection by regular hair grooming. This consists of using a detection comb on washed hair to which conditioner has been applied. As each section of hair is combed the comb should be cleaned and the process repeated as necessary. In special circumstances insecticides may have to be purchased or prescribed by a general practitioner.

Epilepsy (fits)

This term describes a broad range of conditions of varying severity.

Epilepsy control is sometimes erratic prior to the child becoming looked after. Observations by carers can draw attention to this.

Fits may occur in association with learning difficulties or other disabilities as part of a neuro-developmental problem. Other children may have poorly recognised, and therefore poorly controlled, epilepsy with significant effects on learning potential. A child may have absences which have not been observed in a dysfunctional family. Other children may experience adverse side effects of medication in which case the observations of the carer about drowsiness or variable concentration are invaluable.

Developmental problems

Many children placed with foster carers have experienced neglect and under stimulation. If infants are not talked to or only when being told to 'stop it' or 'shut up', language development can be delayed. Lack of play experience can impair motor skills so these children may appear to be developing slowly. Foster carers need to provide appropriate play materials and activities for the youngster in their care and will often enjoy seeing a child bloom once praised and rewarded with smiles.

Unfortunately there are sometimes more permanent reasons for slow development either hereditary or due to their past care. Well recorded observations by a carer can contribute greatly to a paediatric assessment which in turn may indicate the need for investigation and multi-disciplinary assessment.

Bedwetting (nocturnal enuresis)

Bedwetting although not a serious medical condition causes considerable distress both to the children involved and their carers. It may be precipitated by anxiety and occur in a child with no previous history or recur, for similar reasons, when it had previously ceased. Bedwetting by looked after children, may appear more resistant to treatment and sympathetic encouragement, than with children who remain in their birth families.

As children mature they become able to control bladder contractions and wake as the contractions begin in order to go to the lavatory. Genetic influences appear to play a role in bedwetting.

Management advice varies. Obviously infection should be excluded and previous, possible punitive, approaches discussed. In children aged 4–7 support and development of a positive attitude is appropriate. Since youngsters tend to rush going to the lavatory, encouragement of efficient bladder emptying is advisable and the use of some form of star chart with the child may prove effective.

After the age of 7, by which time spontaneous cure has often occurred, the use of an alarm can be considered. Correct use of the alarm should be monitored and this role is often successfully filled by a school nurse. Success rates of up to 75 per cent within one to two weeks are usual.

Older children can be involved in a discussion around management, and spontaneous and drug promoted, improvement. Once old enough to understand the aim, children should be encouraged to take responsibility for bed changing and washing of bed linen. This should not be imposed as a punishment and should not be viewed as such by carers.

Various drugs may be used with older children, especially when domestic stress becomes an additional problem but relapse usually occurs when the drugs are stopped.

Since over half a million children in the UK are affected, continuing support is needed for many children and their carers. The Enuresis Resources and Information Centre (ERIC) offers valuable advice and information on a national basis which can complement local services which are often variable.

Teeth

Dental care must be practised. Sugary food and drinks may have been encouraged and have contributed to dental problems. Oral hygiene should be encouraged at all ages. Tooth brushing should start once teeth appear using a baby brush and become the child's own responsibility by the age of six to seven. Attending a dentist should be introduced by the age of three. Yearly reviews are recommended unless shorter intervals are advised by the dentist. Children with disabilities may require special attention.

Thumb sucking presents no real problems unless it persists beyond the age of nine years. Dummies are a greater risk to language development than to teeth unless they are sweetened in which case they encourage the development of caries. Some children may need orthodontic work around the age of 9 years.

Skin care

Although cleanliness and good personal hygiene should be encouraged some children have naturally dry skin and the condition can be exacerbated where the local water is hard and bubble bath used over enthusiastically. The skin of black and Asian children can become dry very easily and may need more regular application of bath oil and moisturiser. Pigmented skin reacts to injury by depigmentation and sometimes overgrowth of scar tissue. The latter may justify specialist intervention.

Many children have warts. They usually disappear spontaneously and do not require treatment other than reassurance.

Verrucae can cause pain and require advice and treatment from a chiropodist (podiatrist).

Acne is usually a problem of adolescence. Treatment has become much more effective usually with satisfactory results.

At national level we are advised to take better, more effective care to avoid sun damage to skin since the development of skin cancer is related to continuing exposure to ultra violet light especially UVB. Fair skinned and red-haired children are at greater risk than others. For all children the sensible use of clothing cover, including a hat, and sunscreen is essential.

Food, nut and other allergy

A severe reaction (anaphylaxis) to a variety of substances can include breathing difficulty, collapse and occasionally death. Less severe allergic reactions include rash and facial swelling.

Foods are the commonest cause of anaphylaxis including nut allergy. Bee and wasp stings are the next most common cause. Peanut oil in food and ointments is safe.

Children with a family history of allergy should avoid peanuts and peanut products until the age of three years.

Any child about whom there is concern should be seen by a specialist in allergy for advice and treatment.

Adolescence

Adolescents have their own specific health problems and needs. They are often overtly worried about weight, diet, acne and exercise. They are usually less willing to discuss other topics such as sexual development and health, sexually transmitted disease and drug misuse. Behavioural problems of looked after children are common and may reflect or be exacerbated by earlier abuse. The challenge to carers and health professionals is to find ways of sharing information, accessing advice and providing sympathetic support without alienating and patronising the young person.

Teenage pregnancy presents health risks to any young mother and her baby. Teenage girls who are looked after face specific disadvantage. Much information and advice about sexual health and safe sex is delivered within the educational system. Since many looked after young people have disrupted schooling they very often miss the appropriate sex education. Although generally speaking adolescents are most likely to see a GP, many looked after children are unable to maintain such a stable relationship and may not be able to take advantage of the contraceptive advice offered. Attendance at a family planning clinic is a preferred option for most girls and those under 16 need to know that confidential contraceptive advice is available even though sexual activity is not encouraged at this age.

Alcohol and tobacco misuse can be part of an addictive family pattern. Understanding family history is important in order to consider the necessity to refer the young person for appropriate counselling.

Adolescence may be a stressful, confusing time even when within a caring and loving family. For those who have been poorly nurtured; have experienced erratic school; face the uncertainties associated with leaving care, the future can look bleak and threatening. One young person summed up the situation succinctly:

> It's not being in care, what matters, is when you've got to leave it. Where are you gonna be? Where you gonna go? What's gonna happen?

Care leavers may become homeless; unemployed; up to one in four girls become pregnant; young men may drift into prostitution; others enter the prison system. Young people leaving care must be given appropriate preparation which should include health care issues.

Health of Carers

The stress of caring for foster children should not be underestimated. A little stress may be helpful, too much stress, however, is counter productive and can result in under-achievement and physical ill health. It is therefore important to consider the health status and health potential of carers to avoid overload and a possible disruption of placement.

Much has been written about the downside of applications from carers who are overweight or who smoke. Being overweight may mean an undesirable eating pattern and set a poor example for the child or the carer's mobility may be impaired. Smoking, including passive smoking, may cause respiratory problems both for the carer and the child. It is also a poor role model for impressionable young people.

Information Sharing

The real challenge is not just to obtain and record health information, but to use it! Too often forms are filled only to be shelved in notes while little or no action is taken about health issues identified.

My personal experience of a review of local authority medical forms revealed that identified gaps in immunisation cover, referrals for specialist health advice and even the absence of registration with a GP were not acted upon either because the significance was not appreciated by a social worker or because there was confusion about who should do what. Most foster carers act as a guardian terriers to the child in their care. They are persistent, effective advocates so long as they know what needs to be done, why and by whom.

So how should health information be shared? Surprisingly, many young people do not want to take responsibility for holding health information themselves. They feel imposed upon enough already and usually prefer carers to take charge. Many young people have learned to be suspicious of records; they doubt that confidentiality is maintained.

The personal health record (PCHR) is widely used for children under five years and records important health information about immunisation, growth and health reviews and is held by parents on behalf of the child. Ideally it should move with the child when the carer changes. Many parents, especially mothers, wish to hang onto PCHR's when children are accommodated. A skilful social worker can usually persuade a mother to share the information, either in the form of the original record or by making a copy which stays with the child. For older children there are several forms of health records. One is supported by, and available from, BAAF. A filofax format is recommended so that additional, relevant pages can be added as appropriate.

Foster carers should know about the common local health problems. Paradoxically, there is no statutory medical adviser for looked after children as there is for children awaiting adoption, although there is a need for an effective health visitor and advocate. In the National Standards in Foster Care, due for publication in mid-1999, it is recommended that every local authority should designate a medical advisor for children in foster care. Increasingly community paediatricians are assuming this role in order to collate health information about looked after children and to advise local authorities accordingly. Local profiles of the health needs of these children are invaluable and can be used to focus training and discussion in foster carer groups. Although BAAF and the National Foster Care Association (NFCA) provide excellent training programmes for foster carers they can expect, and should demand, sessions at local levels where they can meet the medical advisor and identify gaps in resources.

Consumer Views

As already indicated there is a real danger that collection of health information is seen as an end in itself. To be of significant use the information must be useful to the young person and importantly, to the carers and other contributors to the care plan.

It is important to establish a process whereby the expectation of looked after children and carers are identified and considered. Ideally, if the Annual Medical Examination Review (AME) is to be meaningful the young person should be encouraged to consider what, if any, health issues, he or she want to raise. If there are none, and there are no carer concerns, immunisation advice is being followed, vision and dental reviews are being observed, it is reasonable to challenge the need for the AME. If there is confidence that the young person knows how to access health advice, and sexual health advice in particular, a flexible approach should be supported. The statutory review by the social worker should ensure that health issues are considered and acted upon as necessary. Where there is a designated medical advisor written or advice by telephone can be constructive and reassure.

Use of personal health records should encourage the young person to take possession of health information and to participate appropriately. The Who Cares? Trust has produced excellent advisory material for young people. Similarly, publications such as *The Diary of a Teenage Health Freak* often proves to be more use than many official documents.

There is continuing debate about who is best placed to do the statutory medical review. It would seem logical to involve the GP with whom the child or young person is registered. However, if that GP has little child health experience, or no deep interest in looked after children, it may be better to involve a member of the local community paediatric team. If a consultant paediatrician has an overview of the team's work and responsibility for looked after children, advocacy of the needs of local after children is reinforced at policy making level.

Many young people have been conditioned by experience to expect little from routine medical examinations. Understandably they resent being summoned to see a doctor they do not know, to fulfil a purpose they do not understand and sometimes to be asked, with minimal preamble to '*take your clothes off and get on the couch*'.

There are many aspects of health care which need to be identified and considered carefully in order to meet the best interests of each child. A 'healthier nation' is the aim of government. If this is to be achieved for looked after children there needs to be a change of attitude and way of working for many of those concerned and the importance of the role of carers in health care and health promotion must be acknowledged.

References

Bamford, F.(1988) *The Physical Health of Children in Care; Research Needs.* Economic and Social Research Council, London

Bebbington, A., Miles, J. (1989) The Background of Children Who Enter Local Authority Care. *British Journal of Social Work*

Health Committee, Second Report (1998) Children Looked After by Local Authorities: Report and Proceedings of the Committee, Volume 1, London: HMSO

2.4 The Mental Health of Children who are Looked After

Dr Ann Buchanan

Children who are looked after, whether in residential care or foster care are children first, with all the needs and aspirations of children and young people living with their own families and prone to all the problems, including emotional and behavioural difficulties of children and young people generally. In this chapter therefore, I will start by looking at what we know about the mental health of young people, the numbers of young people involved and some of the causes of their difficulties. Then I will consider the growing information about the mental health of young people who have been looked after; and finally I will share with you some of the new findings on 'recovery' or what we can do, without being specialists, to help young people with emotional and behavioural difficulties.

The Problem Children and Young People Can Do Without

For many young people, emotional and behavioural difficulties limit their life opportunities. Such difficulties interfere with family and peer-group relationships, cause problems at school and consequently educational progress, leave young people with less qualifications than they are capable of, and poorer employment prospects. Emotional and behavioural difficulties in childhood can be associated with problematic adult relationships and in some cases a tendency to depression in adult life.

For those who are foster carers or residential workers, it is important to say at the start, that although looked-after young people are a high risk group for a range of psychological difficulties, more than three-quarters of children who are looked after have no more mental health problems than children in the population generally. We also know that around half of all children who have problems at one age 'recover' or get over them. Specialist help is needed for young people who have

educational difficulties and for those rare children with the more serious mental illnesses. For the vast majority of children with emotional and behavioural difficulties, however, the best people to help these young people get over their problems are those who have the day-to-day caring responsibility for them, and this may be their foster carers.

The Mental Health of Young People

Researchers (Rutter and Smith 1995) conclude that the number of children with emotional and behavioural problems has increased in recent years. In any community, the prevalence of children with such disorders will vary depending on their age, whether the children are living in an inner city or rural area, whether they are boys or girls.

Types of disorders

Rates of emotional and behavioural problems will also vary according to the type of disorder (Buchanan and Ten Brinke 1998). Broadly speaking there are two types of disorders. Behavioural disorders are where the child 'acts out' or 'externalises' their distress. *Externalising disorders* are more common amongst boys. These disorders include Attention Deficit Hyperactivity Disorder (ADHD), where the young child seems to be on the go all the time, is unable to wait, and cannot sit still long enough to concentrate on lessons; and Conduct Disorders where the child may be involved in antisocial acts such as stealing. Emotional disorders are more common amongst girls, particularly amongst teenage girls. Children with emotional disorders 'internalise' their distress and may be depressed, moody or very anxious. This group of problems is therefore known as *internalising disorders*. The two groups are not totally separate. Some children with 'externalising' behaviour can internalise their distress and become depressed particularly as they get older.

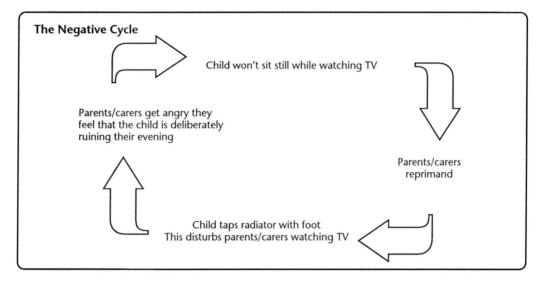

The overactive type of externalising behaviour, which in the extreme may be diagnosed as ADHD, is quite common amongst small boys. It is now generally believed that some children are born with this tendency but how they do as they grow up depends on how well the parents or carers manage them. Because hyperactive behaviour can be very tiring, particularly when parents or carers are under stress themselves, it is easy for the child to become the butt of constant telling-off.

This leads to a destructive cycle whereby the child becomes more anxious, more overactive, and consequently more reprimanded. The dilemma is that children who are constantly told off can become negative about themselves and those around them and are at risk of developing a conduct disorder. In the extreme ADHD may be helped by medication, but for less severe problems there are now a range of proven behavioural strategies to help manage these children (Welster-Stratton 1998). The main strategy is to reverse the negative cycle by keeping the child busy doing positive activities for which they can be praised. The child may also need coping strategies to learn to slow down their behaviour.

With both externalising and internalising behaviour, there is a wide range of normality. Moody behaviour, for example, is quite common in adolescents. Parents are often surprised when their confidant, energetic and out-going twelve year old, becomes a mass of complexes, inertia, up and down moods, tears, and irritability around the onset of puberty.

Most parents and carers, with a bit of compromise, coaxing and negotiation, learn to live through this period. What young people need at this time is a listening ear, sensitive

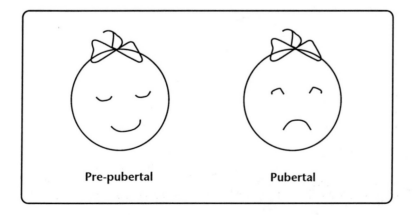

Pre-pubertal   Pubertal

guidance, and adult time. The young person's behaviour only becomes a problem when it interferes with other important activities in their lives such as going to school or schoolwork, or when the depression lasts more than two or three weeks or affects eating or sleeping. If there are school problems it is important to find out whether they have specific difficulties with their work at school or are being bullied. If these strategies fail, children may be helped by being checked out by their GP who may prescribe medication.

Young people with severe depression exhibit their distress, by negative comments about themselves, a demeanour of hopelessness, acts of deliberate self-harm (cutting arms, overdosing), or by indulging in high risk behaviour such as substance abuse, or very promiscuous behaviour. There is considerable evidence that 'internalising' disorders are more 'within' the person but whether this inherent tendency becomes a problem to the young person and interferes with their life prospects will be related to the environment they live in and how they are helped to cope. The hardest task for all young people is to learn to live with themselves and their emotions.

Causes of emotional and behavioural disorders

Although there is now believed to be a strong genetic component to many psychological disorders, research has shown these are not deterministic but simply mean that some children are more vulnerable than others to psychological disorders and less able to cope with life's adversities.

Emotional and behavioural disorders may be sparked off by difficulties in any area of a child's life: tense family relationships, problems at school, peer group pressures, community issues. Physical ill health, diet, allergens and of course, alcohol and drugs may just tip the balance in vulnerable young people towards mental illness. It is important to remember that although there is a movement to legalise 'soft' drugs, all substance abuse can lead to serious mental health problems and is particularly risky for those children who already have emotional or behavioural problems.

Most children, regardless of their vulnerability, cope quite well with single adversities, such as a parent's death, but their vulnerability will increase and their coping ability will decrease when disasters pile up and when these are compounded by other factors such as physical ill-heath. Some children will become stronger, more resilient, through coping with a disaster while other children will become 'sensitized' by a bad experience, so that when they meet a difficulty later in their life, this sparks off a collapse. A breakdown therefore may be related to events that happened many years previously.

Not all children in a family will react the same way. Apart from being treated differently within the family, different children 'perceive' their treatment differently, for example one child may think a parent was unloving because the parent 'allowed' them to be looked after by social services. Whereas a brother or sister, may perceive being taken into care as an opportunity to escape from an impossible situation. A child's perceptions influence how they react. These perceptions may be related to

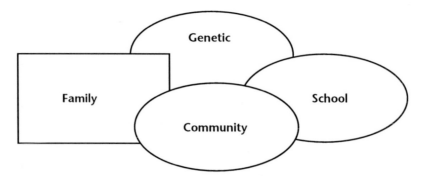

The Interacting Systems - each bringing risk factors and factors that protect a child from emotional and behaviour disorders

early attachment experiences. Whatever causes these different perceptions of the world, when trying to help young people it is important to see the world as they see it.

In research, using the large birth cohort studies such as NCDS, it is possible to track large groups of children from childhood to adult life and to assess what happens to them. Our 1998 study was based on NCDS. We found a wide range of factors that were strongly associated with internalising disorders and another range of factors strongly associated with externalising (Buchanan and Ten Brinke).There was also a range of factors that seemed to 'protect' children.

Finding an association between different factors and emotional and behavioural problems does not say what caused them. For example, we found that children who received specialist treatment were more likely to have emotional and behavioural problems. Hopefully the treatment did not cause the problem! The association was probably linked to the fact that only children with severe problems get any specialist treatment at all

Genetic/biological risk and protective factors

We found risk and protective factors were linked to different aspects of the child's life. First there were factors relating to the *child* themself. Boys for example were more likely to have externalising behaviour than girls. Children with a high IQ were generally less likely to have problems - this might be because they had better problem-solving skills. On the other hand children who were clumsy and may have been the butt of bullying, were more likely than other children to have internalising problems as they grew up.

Family risk and protective factors

The second group of factors were those broadly associated with *the family*. Whether the child was living in an intact family was less important than how the family got on together. We found that children, whose fathers or father-figures read to them when they were small, were less likely to develop externalising behaviour. Parenting styles were strongly linked to externalising behaviours. Parents or carers who 'did enjoyable things together' with their children and who were interested in their children's education seemed to protect their offspring from all sorts of psychological problems. The child who had a father or father-figure who took an interest in them, was a particular bonus. On the other hand, highly critical parenting, family conflict, parents who were involved in criminal activities, poor reading ability in a child, were all strongly linked with externalising problems. Many of these children went on to develop antisocial behaviour.

Family adversities such as parental mental ill health were also linked to psychological problems in their offspring. Here we do not know whether the link is genetic, the consequence of living with an ill parent or a mixture of the two. The strongest link with both internalising and externalising behaviour at all ages and also to long term problems in adult life, was a high level of domestic tension when the child was age seven. On the other hand the family involvement factors, such as father and mother's interest in education, outings with father and a father who was involved in the child management were highly protective.

School factors

The next group of associations were those connected with school. Good reading skills, as measured by standardised tests, was protective against behavioural problems. There was also a suggestion that where a child's reading skills were rated highly by a teacher, indicating some positive teacher/child interaction, the association was stronger. Frequent school moves was a risk factor for internalising and externalising problems in adolescence, while good school attendance was protective.

The strongest findings in this study were linked to young peoples attitudes at age 16. Children who felt school was largely a waste of time, who did not like school, who felt there was no point in planning the future were likely to have problems that carried over in adult life. The children's experiences may, of course, have led to these attitudes, but the young person's negative views then influenced their behaviour. We need to know how a young person perceives themself and their world if we want to help a young person.

Children Who are Looked After

There is now considerable evidence that children, who have been in 'care', to use the previous term, are more likely than other children to have emotional and behavioural problems, and are also more likely to have problems in adult life. Most children who have been in care, do not have major emotional or behavioural problems, but the risk of having psychological problems is significantly greater than, for example, children who have been brought up in severely disadvantaged homes but who have remained with their families (Cheung and Buchanan 1997). In the NCDS (Buchanan and Ten Brinke 1997) using longitudinal data, the author found that 25 per cent of children and young people who had been in care (at any time in their lives, for any period, in any type of placement) had significant emotional and behavioural problems, compared to 8 per cent in the population generally, or 15 per cent of children brought up in severe disadvantage. Similarly 20 per cent of children who had been in care had a measurable tendency to depression in adult life compared to 7 per cent of the population generally.

Causes of distress amongst young people who are looked after

Children who enter care carry many of the person, family, school and community risk factors associated with emotional and behavioural disorders, long before they are ever looked after. Once they enter care, in addition to the trials and tribulations that all children experience while growing up, children who are looked after have the extra burden of the trauma that lead to the separation from their families and the continuing experience of being 'in care'.

This experience was vividly illustrated in an earlier study (Buchanan, Wheal, Walder and McDonald 1993) involving young people who were looked after. Nearly one in three of these young people reported that they had tried to kill themselves. Some of these attempts were unlikely to have been successful:

> I jumped out of the window…but I landed on my feet; I threw myself into the canal but the water was cold so I got out.

It is often thought that acts of deliberate self-harm are simply attention seeking. Contrary to the stereotype many of these attempts had gone unnoticed by parents or carers. As a communication, they were total failures.

Issues around living away from home were often cited as the cause of their distress:

> I was so sick of f------ care and all it involves… I decided to end it all.

Other young people appeared to be particularly vulnerable when they were having key meetings to decide their future. Considerable distress was also related to bullying. Young people were so frightened of 'grassing' when being bullied, that they rarely asked for help.

> There was my little brother on the floor…they were kicking the daylights out of him…I told them to stop but they wouldn't. They hurt him quite badly.

More generally, children and young people who are being looked after complained of the 'stigma' of care.

> People think that just because you are in care you are trash or something.

They also felt disempowered by over-solicitous approaches:

> I just hate it when people feel sorry for you just because you are in care…it makes you feel yuk.

What Can be Done?

The literature on emotional and behavioural disorders in children presents a rather depressing picture of a world where no light dawns. There is talk of 'stability' meaning once a child has a disorder, there is a high risk that the behaviour will remain 'stable' or 'disordered'. There is also talk about 'continuity' of childhood disorders into 'adulthood'.

The 'recovery' study by the author, again using longitudinal data from The National Child Development Study, painted a more positive picture (Buchanan and Ten Brinke 1998). Firstly, if the band of problematic behaviour is widened to include the top 20 per cent of children with such difficulties, emotional and

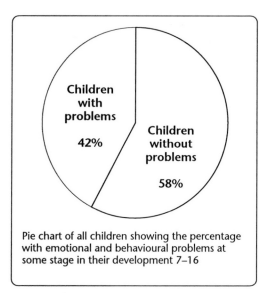

Pie chart of all children showing the percentage with emotional and behavioural problems at some stage in their development 7–16

Children with problems 42%

Children without problems 58%

behavioural problems in children are remarkably common. Nearly *half of all children* between the age of 7 and 16 have at least one difficult patch.

Parents, of course, are well aware of this. They know, for example, that their child may have had a very difficult period when he started school but by the time he entered secondary school, the problems had passed. Between the time the child started primary school and entering secondary school, parents and schoolteachers consciously or subconsciously involved him in a range of activities that helped him overcome the difficulties.

In the above study, only *6 per cent of all children* had problems throughout childhood. The very strong message from this study is that although many children have problems at some stage, most children 'recover'. Indeed around half of the children, who had a problem at one of the time points used in the study 7, 11, or 16, had 'recovered' by the next age. Some of this recovery may relate to the natural processes of their development: the sickly child becomes healthier, the small child grows tall, but biological factors are not all explanatory. Just as the family, school and community may have played a part in causing the problem, it may also play a part in overcoming the difficulties.

Factors associated with recovery

Unfortunately, although the NCDS demonstrated convincingly that there is a substantial 'recovery rate' and found many risk and protective factors associated with emotional and behavioural disorders, it was less successful in finding factors associated with 'recovery'. This was probably because the data collected was not sensitive enough to measure the more subtle nuances about a young person's changing development, family relationships, and school life.

Happily, the study found that most children *with* emotional and behavioural problems but who received specialist treatment were more likely to 'recover'; children who reacted badly during adolescence to a parental divorce and remarriage were also likely to recover. Education bringing both increased self-esteem and qualifications, was a powerful escape route for many children, but children often could not do it all by themselves. Children who had parents who were interested in their education were less likely to have long term emotional and behavioural problems. Receiving education, of course, means attending school. For many young people being looked after, this can be a major challenge for their carers. Getting children to school, however, not only helps with education. The above study showed that children who were good school attenders were less likely to have long term psychological difficulties.

The importance of 'listening'

Very few children who have emotional and behavioural difficulties receive any formal treatment. Only children with the most severe problems are likely to receive specialist help. For most children with such difficulties, the best that parents, carers or teachers can do, is likely to be the only treatment option. For most children, however, this is also likely *to be the best option*. I learnt, in my many years working as a child psychiatric social worker, that labelling a child as a psychiatric case, unless they are truly ill, was sometimes more damaging than the problems they already had. Even if a young person will attend a clinic, this is no guarantee that they will conform with any treatment programme. Parents, carers or teachers will also have a much deeper knowledge of the children they are involved with, than professionals can obtain in the allotted consultation time.

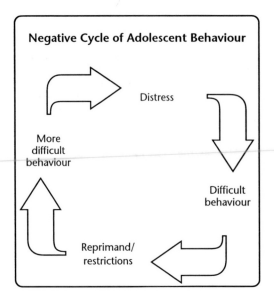

Negative Cycle of Adolescent Behaviour

Distress

More difficult behaviour

Difficult behaviour

Reprimand/ restrictions

Being available

The first difficulty for the parent or carer is finding out what is the problem. Difficult behaviour is often a communication from the young person. The challenge for the parent or carer is to find the time to listen. In a recent survey (Katz and Buchanan 1998) of 4,000 boys' and girls' views about their families, parenting 'style' crucially divided the high and low self-esteem young people; as well as the depressed and the non-depressed and those who were alienated from school and those who were not.

High self-esteem children had parents who 'listened', who 'respected' their young, who gave the 'right guidance', who treated everybody in the family 'equally' and who laid down the 'right rules'. Being loved was not enough. The young people wanted loving, encouragement and careful guidance and rules. The vast majority of high and low self-esteem children felt they were 'loved'. Children with low self-esteem felt they had parents who were critical, authoritarian and inflexible. Most parents or carers want the best for their child but if they get into a cycle of criticism that undermines the young person's confidence, they will fail. Without positive encouragement the young person feels they cannot succeed.

Breaking the cycles or 'setting children up to succeed'

When difficult adolescent behaviour is entrenched, it can be extremely difficult to 'turn a child around'. The first step is to create opportunities to hear what the young person is communicating by their behaviour. In the survey of young people mentioned earlier, young people with high self-esteem were those with families who did things together. A number of studies now note the importance of 'family togetherness'. It is possible that by doing things together, opportunities arise not only for the young person to have positive experiences but also opportunities arise to communicate between family members.

The next stage is to find a way of setting the young person up 'to succeed'. The earlier research on 'recovery', however, gives scientific validity to what parents, carers or teachers have always done to help their troubled young people. For example, when a teenage girl is showing signs of being 'withdrawn', those around her set up a range of activities to 'bring her out of herself'. When an adolescent boy is mixing with a group of young people on the edge of delinquency, those around set up a range of activities, or 'compensatory experiences' to divert him from trouble. 'Compensatory experiences' can be found in the four systems described earlier; the person, the family, school and the community.

A simple analysis of a young person's strengths and difficulties can help in planning compensatory or diversionary experiences. In the following analysis, for example, it may be profitable to involve the uncle who shares an interest in football with his nephew.

Apart from pharmaceutical treatments, some of the most successful treatments for young people with more problematic emotional and behavioural disorders are based on behavioural or cognitive behavioural approaches. Behavioural approaches are based on the simple presumption that most behaviour is learnt. Problematic behaviour may be the result of failing to learn the necessary skills to deal with a situation, or having learnt the wrong skills. The two year old living with a depressed mother will learn

Person	Family	School	Community/ wider world
Strengths	*Strengths*	*Strengths*	*Strengths*
Strong/athletic	Likes uncle	Could have a bigger role in school sports	Good local resources to encourage sport
Likes football	Uncle plays for local football team		
	Supportive wider family		
Difficulties	*Difficulties*	*Difficulties*	
Finds school hard	Father chronic alcoholic Mother mental health problems	Behaviour problems in school	
Concentration poor	Difficult relationships in family		

Antecedent	Behaviour	Consequence
What happened before	*Behaviour*	*What happened as a result of the behaviour*
Mother depressed	To obtain any response	Mother responds

that the only way to obtain mother's attention is to have a temper tantrum. This behaviour becomes a problem when the girl goes into school at the age of five. Teachers are inclined to react badly to children who have tantrums whenever they want the teacher's attention!

Much can be learnt about the causes of a child's behaviour by an ABC analysis.

In this example, in order to help the child learn how to get teacher's response, the child will need to be noticed when she is **not** having a tantrum.

Foster carers may think 'why does David go to school happily everyday but on Friday there is always a problem?' an ABC analysis may suggest that there is something at school on Fridays that is a problem for David. Alternatively, a foster carer may be surprised that David never wants to go to school but is happy to go on Mondays. In both these cases missing school avoids the problem at school so is likely to encourage the child to stay away. On the other hand, it may be that meeting up with other truants is more fun than school.

Once the foster carer has found out what the problem is, they may then negotiate with the school and the young person to see if going to school can be made more rewarding and staying away less satisfying.

In another example, it was found through an ABC analysis that a girl who was involved in glue-sniffing always came home through a particular park that was a well-known glue-sniffing haunt when she was not met from school by her mother. The local police were told about the park and this dispersed the group. In the meantime, the girl was encouraged to get involved in an after-school dance-group on the days her mother could not meet her.

Cognitive behavioural techniques are based on the assumption that young peoples thoughts, or perceptions of the world, influence how they act or behave. These 'therapies' focus on helping the young person to challenge the perceptions that lead on to the problematic behaviour.

The aim of the approach is to help the person 'rationalise' their responses. A range of

Antecedent	Immediate reaction	Possible alternative explanation	Possible alternative action
Teacher tells me I got it wrong in front of the whole class. I felt angry that she showed me up.	Teacher does not like me. No one likes me. School is a waste of time. There is no point coming to school. I can do better out of school. I can look after myself. Storms out of school	I could have got it wrong. Most people get things wrong sometimes. Teachers have to let you know when you get things wrong. Maybe the teacher was a bit unfair.	Slow down, stop and think. I could try catching up with the teacher after the lesson to see if I can talk it through with her. I could tell my tutor that I was upset by the way I was told off. I could talk to my foster carer to see if she has any ideas.

techniques has been used with younger children. For example, with younger children who are aggressive and impulsive, a helpful technique can be to give the child a card. On the card is drawn traffic lights: **red** for stop; **amber** for think; **green** for go. At a quiet time, the foster carer can use the traffic light card to teach the child the strategy of stopping and thinking before reacting.

The Best That Can be Done — Limiting the Harm

Young people in turmoil are exhausting, stressful and demanding. By the very nature of their work, foster carers are dealing with children and young people in turmoil. Children's turmoil is like a fever. Some fevers can be alleviated before they become too serious, by the strategies suggested here. Other fevers have to run their course. As the child passes through the turmoil, the challenge for the carer is to limit the damage the child inflicts on themselves, and to survive intact themselves. Carers never know how successful they have been. The results of their labours will not show up until long after their foster child has moved on. There are many examples of turbulent adolescents grown into quieter adults who look back and remember the dedicated care they received from their special people. These dedicated people have the qualities so well described by Kipling:

*If you can keep your head when all about you
Are losing theirs and blaming it on you,
If you can trust yourself when children doubt you,
But make allowance for their doubting too;*

*Or being lied about, don't deal in lies,
Or being hated, don't give way to hating,
And yet don't look too good, nor talk too wise;
If you can dream…
If you can meet with triumph and disaster…
…Yours is the earth and everything that's in it.*

(Adapted from Kipling *If-*)

References

Buchanan, A. and Ten Brinke, J. (1997) *What Happened When They Were Grown up? Outcomes from Parenting Experiences.* York, Joseph Rowntree Foundation

Buchanan, A. and Ten Brinke, J. (1998) *Recovery from Emotional and Behavioural problems.* NHS Executive, Anglia & Oxford. University of Oxford

Buchanan, A. and Ten Brinke, J. (in press) Children at Risk of Emotional and Behavioural Disorders in A. Buchanan and B.L. Hudson: *Parenting, Schooling and Children's Behaviour.* Aldershot, Ashgate

Buchanan, A., Wheal, A., Walder, D., Macdonald, S., Coker, R. (1993). *Answering Back, the Views of Young People Being Looked-after on the Children Act 1989.* CEDR, University of Southampton

Cheung, S.I. and Buchanan, A. (1997). High Malaise Scores Amongst Children and Young People who Have Been in Care. *Journal of Child Psychology and Psychiatry*

Katz, A. and Buchanan, A. (1998) *Factors Associated with High and Low Self-esteem in Boys and Girls. - The Views of Young People.* Report to Mental Health Foundation.

Rutter, M. and Smith, D. (1995). *Psychosocial Problems in Young People,* Chichester, John Wiley & Sons Ltd.

Sweeting, H., and West, P. (1995) in *The West of Scotland Study*

Webster-Stratton, C. in Buchanan, A., and Hudson, B.L. (1998) *Parenting, Schooling and Children's Behaviour.* Aldershot, Ashgate

2.5 Teenage Fostering

Jan Hawkins

Working with others - on the same board (or on another maybe). I'm playing chess, why the hell are you playing draughts. What do you mean, the chairperson thinks we're playing backgammon?

The above was my first thoughts when deciding what to write in this chapter which I have written in my own way, in my own style. I hope it will not only help foster carers to enjoy fostering adolescents, but also that social workers and other child care workers, as well as academics, will better understand this complex task.

We have been fostering for 15 years now. Our initial registration was for young persons of 2 - 10 - our first placements being two boys of 8 and 10. Our own two children were two and four. We, (like so many others,) **did not want teenagers!** Our family was not, we claimed, experienced or equipped to cope. Our fostering training consisted of eight Wednesday night sessions of two hours duration which focused heavily on the importance of the department, the role of social workers, and how difficult it was for social workers to manage to do everything they had to do each day. (The underlying message being you would be best probably not to expect a reply.) Strangely, we pursued the registration process.

Our introduction to adolescent fostering was by default, we were offered an 11 year old girl on an emergency basis. It transpired that she was 13 years old. Therein starts our tale…

I really believe that one of the biggest factors in our continuing to foster, lies in the make-up of our family - our two were only young. We have always attempted to treat the young people in our care with the same amount of honesty and respect that we have afforded to our own two. We have not always succeeded, 'attempted' is the operative word.

The other factor is probably a miriad of individual strategies which we apply whilst living with adolescents, our own included, essentially attempting to second-guess and defuse potential problems. Life is very much akin to games of chess, which, when played multiplicitly, is really exciting and rewarding since, much as no two chess games are the same, neither are young people. Equally it would be foolish to apply the same strategies more than once, the game would never be won - stalemate is no solution - no one should lose.

The following are a few of our strategies, there are surely many more, these are not listed in order of effectiveness:

Listen, hear, and respond. Many young people are used to being ignored or disregarded. They are constantly asked, especially the 'looked after' young person, for their thoughts and feelings, which are subsequently filed, recorded and noted but very rarely actually actioned in such a way that the young person feels of any value. Just try to imagine how alien it is to explain the reality of situations, to acknowledge that adults do not always fully understand the emotion and feeling of rejection experienced, to a young person who believes that if he shouts long enough that someone will give in. This is learnt behaviour, it has always worked before, after all they want to be treated like adults, but their development often leads to childish behaviour.

All carers should have mandatory training in child development, not charts extolling the various virtues of a group of learned people delivered on an old OHP in a church hall. Most carers appreciate good quality training delivered in a professional manner. They need practical advice. I once attended a course which put it all into focus for me. The trainer, Margaret Burton, explained the various targets, which each child should be able to reasonably expect to achieve, and that which needed to be offered by the parent or carer in order to achieve that target. Interestingly she then went on to chart the various responses which may be expected if the child was deficient in any area. Behaviours were noted and ages allocated to the behavioural responses. It became apparent that a fifteen year old girl who lived with us was probably not being deliberately obtuse when asked to go and sort out her room

- and an hour later it was to be found in the same mess. Margaret asked whether we would expect a younger child of four to undertake such a task? She suggested that if we were to approach the problems, which we were experiencing in a different manner, perhaps at the level of response of a young child, that it may be more effective. I started to go to her room with her, to encourage her to group her belongings, and to offer praise for each task. It worked.

Stealing - often the issue that many children raise as a problem, is a behaviour, which many carers find extremely offensive. It is. However, it may not always be what it seems, could the items have been moved? Could someone else be using them? How can you be sure which person is the offender? Always ask questions of yourself, try not to offer a knee-jerk reaction! If you have identified stealing as your achilles heel to any young person, then prepare yourself for a challenge. If you are sure of the offender's identity, and only if you are positive, then quietly talk to that person. Often young people expect a reaction, such as fury, of lost emotion, they immediately have gained 'control of the board'. Try to present differently from their expectation, discuss the issue as a family. Perhaps money is missing, identify the money as a budgeting issue, do the young people manage their money properly? Would it be more helpful to break down the allowance they receive weekly into smaller daily sums, then bi-weekly? Notice allowance, not pocket money.

Somehow we seem to have differing ideas as adults about the terminology since one infers a more realistic management of finance as opposed to an attempt at the world record for 'disposal of cash at speed for totally useless items'. How many young people spend seven days waiting for the cash, and seven minutes disposing of it? Another stealing highlight is precious essential items (photos, keys, toys, tickets etc.). Do not make them accessible, in the case of keys and tickets for example, provide the young persons with their own special toy, you can also put photos which the young people bring with them into decent frames, as you do your own.

Finally stealing to feed habits, be they ciggies, booze, sweets, drugs or fruit machines, all major issues for which all carers need to be prepared. Try to be honest yourself and set achievable goals. If the young people need money for these addictive behaviours, the usual education, health or social responsibility chats do not work. Try to involve yourself in some small way, acknowledge their habit, talk with the young people about the 'buzz' of the activity, try in some way to offer another activity, for example have treats around the time of their usual exit from the home, show the latest video, invite an old friend, go trainer shopping! Just try to curtail the 'fix'. Do not attempt to stop it immediately. Vera Falberg a well respected American writer about young people and their behaviour, gave a lecture in London several years ago. In her address she reminded us to always offer a substitute for anything which we, as adults, remove from a young person's life, not food for cigarettes or computer consoles for amusement arcades, but perhaps a physical activity involving a group or the whole family. Try camping - good toilets and showers being a priority, where the site has no club house or arcades. Young people are able to lose the pressure (often self inflicted) of habitual activities

Lying is very difficult to prove to the offender. Sometimes fantasy has a hand to play, especially in the blatant "I've been to Florida" person who later goes on to say " I've never flown before". These lies are usually light-hearted and the young person often smiles along with you when you point out, maybe several days later, that you had 'wondered'. Ask yourself, many times a day, whether there is any damage in the fantasy? If there is, and there can be, you need to find out why the fantasy is so important to that young person, what can you realistically replace it with without destroying a part of the adolescent that you are trying to nurture? The face-to-face liar is an interesting one, often the best tactic being to 'agree to disagree' with a proviso that the discussion may resume, at a later stage, when evidence has been compiled. Do not fall into the trap, however, of obsessively pursuing your argument, it is often just a way of gaining your attention on a one-to-one basis. Sometimes a good quality laugh, repairs the sensitive issues and, as the adult, we opt to leave well alone. There is often a good case for prioritising which issues to deal with and which to 'file' in your overloaded mind. Lies are, after all, often very negative to most relationships.

Many young people have developed a survival technique around them. They need to re-learn the value of reality and of their place within the real world. This has to be one of the biggest gifts that we, as carers can provide to those in our care, they need to discover who they really are, not who everyone has told them that they are. All adolescents have to achieve this goal, the hardest part of all is to like who they discover they are. One of our leavers wrote on one of the many forms which these children are asked to complete, that the thing that she had enjoyed most about living with us was finding out that she liked herself. People ask us why we foster.

Swearing - I do not like it. Thus far young people have been very respectful - although the odd mistake does occur - more reality for me! Generally peer pressure dictates that our children listen to bad language and schools are rife with it, it can often be amusing listening to young people explaining to their friends that 'she' will not have bad language in the house - and then noticing how difficult it is for them to formulate a sentence without using swear words. Some young people even go as far as to check what is, and is not, swearing, since in their own families swearing is a normal everyday form of communication. This can be a big problem, especially for the visiting parent perhaps if their child becomes embarrassed by them.

Strategies need to be in place to reassure the young person that as an adult you can appreciate the pressure that their parent may be under, and that you do not want a big issue to be made out of it. A very good tactic, especially if you have younger children of your own, is to explain to the adolescents that you do not want to be in a position where the younger children get into trouble at school for using bad language, which they learnt at home. We explain to our teenagers that the little ones would find it very easy to learn, but possibly difficult to unlearn just as the adolescents had.

Drink, drugs, sex - ' been there, seen it, bought the tee-shirt' is my best advice to carers, which may not be the detailed personal information that many adolescents yearn for. To be fair to the young people most of their unique experiential activity is just a re-mix of those activities in previous generations, it is important to remember this and try to always recall how ultra sensitive you were, as well as try to recall the massive highs, and lows which we all experienced during that awful time between middle school and college, university and work.

Advice, education, open honest discussion and acceptance of the reality of life all help. If the young people start to talk about issues such as drugs and use terminology which you do not understand then ask. Often they are amazed to learn that you understand the pressures of their lives. However, you will need to manage to balance the care and concern angle. It is not wise to enter into the secrets game where your involvement infers permission or the forbidden fruits ideology which strengthens the resolve of even the most passive teenager. There is a lot of literature available to young people about the risks of drugs, read it yourself, arm yourself with information. You will be in a better position to help the young person should you discover that they are 'stoned out of their minds' if you have read the information. You will realise that there is little value at that time in ranting and raving. Indeed it will do little to help any one. The best tactic is to provide a quiet, calm. warm environment, with reassurance that the often frightened young person is not alone. The following day is the time to express your concern, health, risks of harm and vulnerability are your tools with an understanding that the young person often does not take the 'stuff' knowingly.

There is a lot of drink 'spiking' nowadays, terrified clubbers identifying themselves as potential victims by not knowing the rules - never accept drinks from anyone you do not know and buy bottled drinks, as they are harder to slip anything into. Do not leave drinks unattended The liquid drugs are very powerful, they cannot be detected. Warn the young people. One of ours willingly took a cocktail of drugs, her life is now full of sadness. She is still the same lovely person that we once knew, but a big part of her has changed. She is psychotic with no prospects of work and a mental health label that will stay with her forever.

Sex is not an issue provided that communication is established from the outset.

Legal perameters have to be adhered to by carers. However, alongside this, we need to respect the individuality of each relationship. Teenagers experience the same highs and lows of emotion that we ourselves once endured. It is wrong to say that as a teenager, that they don't understand real love, indeed acknowledged intensity of each emotion means that, by virtue of their hormonal balance they feel deeply. We can, as adults, attempt to guide them, but only the individual can experience their own innermost feelings, both good and bad. Little is to be gained from a young person actually confessing to having started a sexual relationship, just to be confronted by the arguments that they themselves anticipated. Take deep breaths, try to be proud that this young person has shared something with you of immense personal importance, make sure that they took precautions, as you have constantly reminded them in the past. Discuss the implications of unwanted pregnancy, but do not panic, you have 72 hours in which to apply for the necessary medication to administer.

The young women need to be aware of some of the side effects of various medications, alongside the implications of long term contraception. Remember there is always someone the young person can talk to. It may not be you. Make their chosen person accessible to you too, not to break confidences but for reassurance! There is a good chance that if you have been excluded from the discussion then the lines of communication did not exist initially. Remember that young men also may have a need to feel able to share information with you. Pregnancy is an issue which they too, need to be able to discuss. Never assume that our education system has prepared these young people for all of the issues. One confident young woman who we cared for from 15 years old, announced that she could not possibly be pregnant, after all she had not 'slept' with him. It was so sad, and yet when we sat down and ploughed our way through the basics she told me that it all started to make sense now. She felt that her lack of understanding was probably due to constantly changing school, but also may have much to do with the way in which the information was presented in large groups. She certainly had managed to disrupt most large groups in her school career, never mind

the potential with a group of hyped-up adolescents.

Rock and roll does not count now, it is raves. A whole new concept in fear and anxiety for the average parent or carer of adolescents. All of the above apply, and yet another 'rite of passage' for our young person to pass. Nothing can really prepare you. I guess that I manage by talking to other parents or carers who had survived the ordeal. It helped a little and mine survived. Try to remember that often once is enough, and that we too had our festivals, clubs, discos or whatever. We survived.

Our own children are often the unspoken heroes. They manage to share their families, their lives, their physical space, their everyday living with perfect strangers. Mine claim that, unlike their genetic link and consequential relationship, they have managed to bestow the title of 'sibling' onto many. Some they have (and still do) loved. Several have only had moments of reason, one or two have been openly snubbed. We have to be realistic and understand that our chosen path can be rocky. We need, where possible to include our whole family in decisions.

Confidentiality can be an issue. Ours have never needed to know the finer details of young people's lives. Often however the young person gives versions which social workers would dispute. Is that important? The only information ours ever wanted to know when they were young was whether or not their possessions might get damaged and as they grew older they needed to know where our boundaries lay in respect of times, language and behaviour.

As a family we seem to have developed a fairly laid back approach to most issues, our own children object to social workers excluding them from the obligatory visit to MacDonalds and the trips to bowling alleys and other intermediate group venues. They dislike the way in which they are prevented from entering our lounge when these people decide to make a visit. They also object to the fact that their opinion is very rarely sought. They also claim that when they are asked for their opinions, these are then dismissed. To be fair to ours though, since they have had an opportunity through the private fostering agency to express their thoughts, they have learnt the power of speech. They seem to feel supported by the caseworker designated to our family and are always included in all activities. Discrimination is not an issue. Our two are absolutely amazing really. To everyone who says "aren't you worried about the effects on your own?" Yes, is the short answer, but we have always tried to include them in everything. I might even be tempted to say that the experiences that we have had practising on other families' teenagers may have improved our strategies with our own.

Try to remember to give yourselves time too, easier said than done. Remember that after fostering there needs to be another life, just in the same way that any parents need a life of their own. Try to steer clear of guilt. Do not think about what you did wrong, instead concentrate on the good aspects of a placement. Even if the experience was bad on the whole we need to remember that for many young people it is not possible to cope with the complexities of an ordinary family - their previous life experience has done little to prepare them, indeed often all they have learnt is that becoming close to anyone is a painful

and dangerous experience. Forgive them for not responding to your family and wish them all the best in their lives. A smile costs nothing.

Please do not set out to change these teenagers in the image of you. It is an impossible task to produce your own children into images of yourselves despite their genetic materials. Imagine how difficult it would be to mould an unknown quantity. Remember that the diversity of lives strengthens us all. Often the young people have practical ideas and suggestions which we have incorporated into our families' norm. Respect their past. It helps them to respect themselves.

If we consider the concept of playing chess once more it would be good to remember that only one set of rules apply. It would be true to say though that many people try to bend the rules. I have often sat in a room of fellow professionals and realised that they are playing a completely different game to me. The social workers, parents, even the chairperson all seem to have their own agendas. They all claim to want to know what it is that the young person wants. How often do they listen and hear?

2.6 Fostering Siblings Together

Shelagh Beckett

This chapter will consider the sibling dimension of children who enter public care. The significance of relationships between brothers and sisters will briefly be considered and the ways in which separation from parents and much that is familiar, may impact on siblings.

Many foster carers have children of their own and some will also have one or more children already in placement. Child-to-child relationships are important not only to the children involved but also to their parents and carers. Children's relationships with each other will have some impact on the quality of their experience and the outcome. For example, whether or not the new child entering a foster family is accompanied by their own siblings will affect the individual child, separated siblings and the dynamics within the fostering household. In addition sibling groups bring with them, diverse and sometimes distorted ways of behaving in relation to each other. Some children will have experienced sexual and other forms of abuse, one child in the sibling group may have been the main butt of parental violence whilst another was the 'good child'. Older siblings may have assumed the role of care-giver to younger siblings when parental illness, absence or other problems have limited or affected parenting by adults. Patterns of behaviour and roles which were largely regarded as functional within the birth family are less likely to be perceived in the same way when children are accommodated or looked after. The experience of entering care is also likely to have a significant impact on siblings because large numbers of children will experience separation from some or all of their siblings.

Looked After Siblings

There is remarkably little material available about siblings who enter the looked after system. This is perhaps surprising given that 80 per cent of the general population have one or more siblings. Various estimates have been made about the numbers of children in public care who are part of a sibling group. Berridge and Cleaver (1987) in their study of foster home breakdowns, estimated that three fifths of children aged under eleven when they entered care were accompanied by one or more siblings. For siblings in short term fostering, more than half were separated from at least some of their brothers and sisters.

The Department of Health document, *Patterns and Outcomes in Child Placement* (1991) stated that between one third and one half of all admissions to care involved sibling groups and that the majority of these were concentrated in the pre-adolescent age range. Clearly, estimates vary. It is also important to recognise that there is a difference between the numbers entering care and those who remain in care over the longer term. Reliable data on sibling groups and how they fare, is sadly lacking, not least because it would seem that many local authorities, do not collect and monitor information relating to siblings. This suggests that the needs of sibling groups may not be recognised as requiring any special attention or resources. In particular any unmet need may fail to be recognised and consequently will not receive attention at a strategic level. In the absence of adequate information it is hard to plan services.

Looked after children are amongst the most disadvantaged in our society (Bebbington and Miles, 1989) and increased professional attention has focused on the importance of reducing any secondary damage that might be caused by the experience of being 'in care'. Whilst not always easy to achieve, it is acknowledged that children in care should ideally experience as much continuity as possible such as placing them in their own neighbourhood, to match placements to identified needs including those of race, culture, religion and language, to avoid changes in placement and for children to remain at their current nursery or school.

Legal and Policy Context

The Department of Health (1991) recognised that sibling relationships merited closer attention and found that there were *'few references to siblings in local authority policy documents or practice guides'* (p. 27).

The Children Act 1989, was the first piece of British child care legislation to specifically refer to siblings and their placement needs. The Act required local authorities to place a child with their sibling(s) *'...so far as is reasonably practicable and consistent with his welfare...'* (section 23.7 b).

The number of children who may be placed in a foster home is set out in paragraphs 2 and 3 of Schedule 7 to the Children Act. This prescribes a usual fostering limit of three children, however, this limit does not apply if the children are siblings. In practice however, there are often other limitations which may affect whether or not siblings can be placed as a group. For example, the lack of departmental policy and guidance, insufficient resources focused on the particular needs of siblings, some children entering public care whilst some or all of their siblings remain at home; and later the situation breakdown which may lead to others subsequently entering public care. The implications of these differing arrangements for children has attracted little attention. These children will experience a range of emotions and much skilled and sensitive work is necessary to both assess and meet the children's needs.

The extent to which local authorities have responded positively to the wider needs of sibling groups, is difficult to determine. However, my own survey (Beckett, 1993) of 16 local authorities revealed that the majority (over two thirds) had no policy framework for siblings, did not monitor information relating to numbers and placements such as whether children were placed with some or all of their siblings. Similarly just over half of the local authorities had no overview of the number of foster carers able to take sibling groups. Such gaps in information, make it difficult to identify need and to match service provision accordingly.

Guidance on family placements issued in respect of the Act 1989 state that:

> *Procedures for taking overall stock at regular intervals of the available pool of foster carers who form the major resource of the service will make plans for recruitment and training more responsive to likely future needs; in respect of the numbers and range of foster placements and ensure that resources are more effectively used.*

Training for foster carers has developed considerably in recent years, encompassing a wider range of issues and needs. However, the additional demands and skills which might be required in caring for a large sibling group with diverse needs, roles and rivalries is something on which few, if any, carers are likely to receive preparation or training. This is not surprising since they receive little attention at departmental level and social workers may feel poorly-trained and ill-equipped to address the needs of sibling groups.

Sibling Relationships

Although sibling relationships and children's attachments to each other have attracted less research attention than parent-child relationships, it is clear that attachments develop between siblings from an early age (Schaffer and Emerson, 1964). Children spend a great deal of time interacting with siblings and significantly more than with their parents. Research has shown that by the age of one, infants spent as much time with their elder sibling as with their parent (Lawson and Ingleby, 1974) whilst children in the four to six year age range spent twice as much time with each other compared with in the company of parents (Banks and Kahn, 1975). This research was carried out in respect of predominantly white, western cultures and levels of interaction may be even higher for other ethnic groups.

Apart from high levels of interaction, it is also evident that siblings can be a familiar and reassuring presence. Stewart (1983) reported that approximately half of his sample of three and four year old children acted to provide comfort to a distressed younger sibling when left alone in a strange situation.

When two or more siblings are separated from their principal attachment figure and cared for in the same setting, their distress can be minimised by interaction between them. This is the case even when siblings are too young to take on a care-taking role. It seems likely that being with siblings may serve to reduce children's anxiety in stressful and unfamiliar situations, such as, admission to a residential nursery (Heinicke and Westheimer, 1965). Whitaker et al. (1984) found similarly that children in residential care benefited from the presence of their siblings.

Whilst relationships between siblings can provide familiarity and serve to reduce stress, it must also be recognised that sibling relationships typically include much rivalry and relatively high levels of aggression. Woolfson (1995), based on a survey of several thousand families, found that in over 75 per cent of the families children used violence against each other. The term 'violence' encompassed acts such as throwing something at another person, grabbing them hard, aggressive shoving, slapping, kicking, biting or punching. The child's own temperament has also been highlighted as a factor in sibling conflict, with children who are hostile, active, intense, or unadaptable in temperament more frequently having conflicting relationships with siblings (Boer, 1990, Munn and Dunn, 1988). Siblings play a significant role in shaping one another's development by influencing self-esteem for example. Not surprisingly sibling relationships themselves will, in part at least, be influenced by parenting behaviour. Dunn and McGuire (1992) found that differential treatment by a parent was linked to greater sibling conflict:

> *Maternal differential treatment is linked to the quality of sibling relationships: the more differential maternal treatment is shown, the more conflict and negative behaviour the siblings show to each other.*
> (Dunn and McGuire (1992) p. 72).

Parental favouritism is related to increased hostility from both less favoured and more favoured siblings (Boer, 1990). Dunn and McGuire draw attention to differences in the way conflicts are managed between siblings as compared with peers. They note important differences in how conflicts are initiated, played out and resolved with peers and siblings. They refer to research by Rafaelli (1991) which showed that sibling relationships were more tolerant of conflict than those with friends, and

could provide a context in which differences between individuals were clarified. In respect of the looked after population, a proportion of children will not be full siblings, sharing one but not both parents. The extent to which this may impact upon children's relationships with each other is likely to depend upon a range of factors but has not - to the best of my knowledge - been the subject of any study.

Whilst we need to understand a great deal more about sibling relationships, particularly when these may be influenced by factors such as neglect and abuse, it is clear that siblings have a significant impact on each other and one which must be considered in service planning. Although siblings may not always appear close to one another their relationship has the potential to be both supportive and enduring over the longer term. As Ainsworth stated:

> *...despite current differences in activities and interests, and despite rivalries or other causes of ambivalence, siblings have a background of shared experience over a relatively long period of time, which not only promotes similarities in their perception of situations and in value systems that influence their decisions, but also promotes mutual understanding, without necessarily requiring explicit communication.*
> (Ainsworth (1991) p. 47).

Placement Patterns and Resources

There is a dearth of research in respect of local authority placement patterns and provision for siblings. However one local authority study of looked after siblings (MacLean, 1991) found that 37 per cent of children were placed with all their siblings, 22 per cent placed with some of their siblings and 41 per cent separated from all siblings. The reasons given for these placement patterns included serial admissions, sexual abuse within the sibling group and placement unavailability.

Evidently whether or not siblings will be placed together is likely to be determined by a range of factors, some of which, are resource-based. Examples of this include:

- Lack of availability of a foster placement to accommodate a sibling group at the time the children enter public care.
- Some foster homes that in principle could accommodate a sibling group may have been filled by the placement of two or three unrelated children.

- Some foster carers who may be interested in caring for siblings lack the necessary space within their own home.

My own study found that only seven out of sixteen local authorities had information about the total number of foster carers and how many of these were able to accommodate one child, two, three or more. In the absence of such information it is difficult to target the use of resources and to recruit accordingly. The extent to which strategic planning takes account of siblings is likely to impact on the availability of resources. For example:

- The additional issues involved in meeting the needs of sibling groups may not be recognised or receive scant attention.
- The local authority may have little or no information about placement patterns relating to sibling groups and is relatively unaware of the extent to which siblings are placed together or separately.
- Recruitment drives may fail to stress the need to keep siblings together.
- Staff may lack training, skills and experience in working with and assessing siblings.
- Foster carers may be provided with insufficient support to enable them to cope with both the practical issues and other demands presented when fostering a sibling group particularly when the group comprises three or more children.

It is also evident that separate placements will have a considerable impact upon parents and the wider family. The extent to which placement patterns may influence the frequency of parental visiting and the likelihood of restoration home is, as yet, not understood. However, it seems reasonable to suggest that the separation of siblings will at best complicate matters and at worst may have a significant adverse impact.

Although initially separated through placement unavailability the chances of this changing are likely to diminish unless strenuous efforts are made from the outset. That is, it is much harder to re-establish a sibling group once children have been separated for a significant period of time. There are many factors which can contribute to this in addition to resource issues and the amount of social work effort required to bring about a change in the status quo. In some cases attachments will develop between children and their carers who may express a long term commitment to keep the child or children placed with them. In other cases, lack of contact and the children's own feelings will play a part, for example a child may feel angry and abandoned by siblings with whom they no longer live.

Contact Between Siblings

Significant numbers of children in foster care are separated from one or more of their siblings because only part of the group has entered public care, or for those siblings who need to be accommodated together, a suitable resource is not available. Research suggests that more than half of children with siblings are separated from at least some of their brothers and sisters as a consequence of care (Berridge and Cleaver 1987, MacLean 1991). Given that the majority of sibling groups in foster care are concentrated in the under 11 year age group, it is clear that considerable efforts are required to promote contact.

Foster carers of children in separate placements have a crucial role in facilitating contact but one which may not be sufficiently recognised and incorporated in planning. It is important that foster carers, the children's' social workers and link workers meet, with members of the birth family as appropriate, to draw up plans for contact between the children as well as the wider family contact.

There may be a tendency to underestimate the strength of attachment between children particularly when they fight, argue and compete for adult attention. Developmental delay or the impact of neglect and abuse can also contribute to an understandable focus by the professionals, on the needs of each child as an individual. Unless contact is planned in a way which is meaningful for children, their relationship with one another is likely to suffer and this in turn may lead to the significance of the relationship being minimised in the future. As Le Pere et al. (1986) have stated:

> *An important first step in maintaining sibling bonds is their placement together in foster care...In the event that siblings are separated in foster care, their*

contacts must be seen to be as important as contact with biological parents. In fact, as the literature indicates, these contacts may be more important. Sibling visits may prevent major readjustments when siblings are reunited with biological or adoptive parents.

(p. 41-42)

Sibling contact should be planned in such a way as to maximise opportunities for children to spend 'real' time together.

Checklist

- Have those involved in caring for and working with the sibling group met to draw up a written plan for contact between the children? The plan should ensure clarity about the level of contact which can be managed between the foster carers and what will be arranged by the social workers involved.

- Do the children regularly have time to be together, to play, to share meals and help one another?

- Do they go to bed and wake up in the same house on at least some occasions? For example consideration should be given to foster carers taking it in turns to have the whole sibling group for a week-end perhaps once every two or three weeks.

- What practical and financial support do the foster carers need in order to promote contact?

- Have foster carers met to discuss the children's behaviour, routines and any special requirements?

- Do they broadly agree on how they will manage the sibling group - for example, recognising that siblings' roles may be distorted, that safe care practices will need to be in place?

- Is any specialist advice needed with regard to behavioural issues in the sibling group and how best to manage these?

- If some contact sessions are being assessed, what framework is being used and who is involved in this process?

- How and when will contact arrangements be reviewed?

Assessment Frameworks

There are a range of frameworks available to social workers involved in the assessment of parents, parenting skills and parent-child attachments. Similarly there are comprehensive guides to assessing family functioning in the context of child protection and risk assessments. Whilst it can be argued that further work is still needed to refine and validate assessment frameworks in respect of parent-child relationships, it is clearly the case that the assessment of child-child relationships and those between siblings in particular, has received far less attention. A Department of Health publication (1991) included checklists as a basic tool for studying the way siblings behaved towards each other. It noted the importance of recording behaviour and understanding the context in which this had developed, suggesting that the following aspects were significant:

- the children's position in the family

- gender

- cultural and family expectations for each child

- the emotional age at which each is functioning

- the extent to which children have a shared history and family experience

- the role each child is perceived to have played (if any), in the sibling group's admission to care or accommodation.

I have been unable to locate any other sibling assessment frameworks available for general use. Individual practitioners and authorities may have developed material for local use. Wider dissemination and discussion of such frameworks is urgently needed. It is also crucial that any assessment of siblings is not done in isolation but includes direct work with each child. This work should promote opportunities for the child to share information, feelings and any distorted perceptions about their siblings. For example, a child may blame their sibling for the family being split up, for dad going to prison, for mum being ill, or similar events. Jewett (1984) has written about the 'good-bad split' which occurs in some sibling relationships:

It is not infrequent for two children in the same family to respond in quite different ways to their loss of or separation from a parent. One may seem to lock herself into the provocative 'bad' child role, while the other, fearful of rocking the boat and driving the caretaker away, becomes 'too good to be true'.

(p. 116)

She points out that there is a danger that work is focused solely on the 'bad' child and that the unresolved feelings of guilt, pain, sadness and anger of the 'good' child may not be recognised, only to surface later. This needs to be considered in cases where the placement of one sibling is at risk of breakdown or has already disrupted. There is no simple response to such situations. In some instances it may be right for all the children to move from the placement and in others not. There is a desperate need for agencies to monitor, learn from and to share such practice dilemmas and also for independent research.

Local authority systems for reviewing and managing child care plans and decision making, including adoption panels, have a key role to play in ensuring that detailed assessments are conducted in respect of siblings. In the absence of informed and reasoned decision-making, it seems very wrong that a child is permanently separated from siblings.

Foster-siblings

Until very recently the relationship between a child or children entering the foster family and the family's own children, has attracted little research and professional attention. This is perhaps surprising given, as Part (1993) has asserted, that practice wisdom 'has it that the attitude of foster carers' birth children can make or break placements'. Her own research was based on a postal questionnaire with responses from 75 children. The vast majority (80 per cent) stated that they liked fostering even though difficulties were acknowledged. Doorbar, in her report on the results of her research meeting foster siblings (chapter 3.4) are confirmed in the findings of Reed (1996) and Kavanagh (1987).

Safe Care

There is now a greater awareness of the impact of sexual abuse upon children and an increased understanding that carers are entitled both to preparation and to full information prior to placement. However, the specific implications for child-to-child relationships have received less attention, such as, the potential impact on other children in the foster home and the consequences of sexual abuse upon sibling relationships.

It is clear that children can and do involve other children in sexually inappropriate and abusive behaviour. A study of 66 families who had experience of fostering or adopting children with a history of sexual abuse found that 86 per cent of placements were made with families who already had other children (Macaskill,1991). The incidence of sexual activity directed by the abused child to another child in the family was high - occurring in 51 per cent of placements.

In the study there were fourteen 'birth' sibling placements, in eight of which, some sexual activity had occurred between siblings. This included siblings masturbating together or trying to engage in sexual intercourse. Some of this group seemed particularly unaware of the normal boundaries to such behaviour, acting in a sexually explicit way in front of others (including other children in the family). Macaskill noted, as others have, that such patterns of behaviour:

…were often difficult to break, because they had been learned over prolonged periods. Practical steps had to be devised to monitor sibling relationships. Attempts were made to educate and re-educate them about relationships.

(p. 87)

In other sibling groups different patterns of behaviour were evident. Rather than behaving in a sexual way towards a sibling, children were sometimes highly protective in situations where they perceived, accurately or not, their sibling to be at risk of a sexual approach. Pierce and Pierce (1990) reviewed 43 cases of adolescent intra-familial offenders, they found the sibling relationship was the most significant in terms of who was abused:

20%   were natural, step- or adoptive sisters

9%   were foster sisters

16%   were foster brothers

5%   were natural brothers.

Available research clearly suggests that birth and foster sibling relationships are significant in planning safe care, particularly in respect of children who have previously experienced abuse and appropriate training for carers is extremely important.

Outcomes

Siblings and restoration home studies suggest that one of the best predictors of restoration home is the maintenance of contact (Millham et al., 1986). As stated earlier, the separate placement of siblings may have important implications for achieving restoration with family.

Farmer and Parker (1991) found that children's prospects of successful restoration home were higher for those children who returned with their siblings. Although the reasons for this are not clear, it seems likely that children can offer valuable support to each other in re-establishing roles and relationships within the family and in the overall process of adjusting to change. Research on children's adjustment to other significant life events supports this. Research which has considered children's adjustment after divorce has found that siblings can provide an important source of support (Wallerstein, 1985).

Farmer and Parker found that children returned to families where there were changes amongst the children in the household (for example, a new partner who had introduced additional children into the home) fared less well. This group had the poorest outcome. Rivalry and competition for parental time and attention would seem to account for at least some of these failures. Social work efforts may also have played a part by tending to focus on the adult relationships and adult-to-child relationships rather than paying sufficient attention to those between the children themselves.

Fostering and permanent placements: placement patterns and outcomes

Early research on disruption associated sibling group placement with an increased risk of disruption (Kadushin and Seidl, 1971, Boneh, 1979) but more recent research findings suggest the contrary may be the case (Barth and Berry,

1986, Berridge and Cleaver 1987, Borland et al., 1991). Berridge and Cleaver found a considerably higher rate of disruption (50 per cent) for children in long term fostering who were completely separated from siblings compared with those who were accompanied by some or all of their siblings (26 per cent and 33 per cent respectively). Their finding was similar for short term and intermediate fostering where children fared better when placed with siblings.

A recent review of more than 1,000 adoption placements made by 48 local authorities and 21 voluntary adoption agencies found that 43 per cent of the adopted children had been placed with at least one sibling (Dance, 1997). In relation to looked after children she notes that:

> even allowing for the fact that there may be a number of cases where there are no other siblings in care, the proportion of children placed with a sibling seems somewhat low.
>
> (Dance (1997) p. 33)

In Children's Interests?

The reasons why sibling groups are or are not being maintained is as yet, little understood. Whilst assessment of the children's needs may lead to a planned separation, there is a marked absence of discussion about practice in this area and whether or not any assessment frameworks which are being used are appropriate. Is it a valid part of assessment to ask children about whether or not they might wish to live together or separately? To what extent decisions to separate siblings are 'resource- driven' or 'needs-led' remains questionable. My own small scale research and practice experience, combined with an awareness of the national shortage of foster carers generally, leads me to conclude that large numbers of children are separated from siblings primarily because of resource shortcomings.

The Way Forward

The difficulties inherent in corporate parenting are considerable and whilst efforts are being made to improve the care experience for children in general, more attention needs to be focused on siblings. Whilst resource constraints play a significant role, it is also suggested that currently the particular needs of siblings may go largely unrecognised in many social services departments.

In order to improve the fostering service for siblings, a range of issues need to be considered. These include:

- A fundamental review of the way foster carers are recruited, trained and remunerated.

- Local authorities should ensure that information systems in respect of looked after children include sibling status.

- The current pool of foster carers available to take sibling groups should be reviewed together with existing placement patterns and any resource shortcomings identified.

- Targeted efforts to recruit carers for sibling groups where additional placements are required.

- Recognition of additional support to carers who are looking after sibling groups. For example some carers may need heavy duty washing machines or financial help to purchase a larger car.

- The more effective management of contact when siblings are in separate foster placements.

- Greater attention focused on the review process, such as, ensuring an appropriate balance between individual and sibling needs and incorporating the sibling dimension in plans from the outset.

- The development and evaluation of assessment frameworks for use in work with sibling groups.

- The development of more sophisticated training and research in respect of sibling relationships and outcomes.

In short, if the best interests of the child are to be considered when placing a child in a foster home then the whole question of siblings and sibling contact must be considered.

References

Barth, R.P. and Berry, M. (1988) *Adoption and Disruption* Aldine de Gruyter, New York

Boneh, C. (1979) *Disruptions in Adoptive Placements*, Massachusetts Dept. of Social Welfare

Borland, M., O'Hara, G. and Triseliotis, J. (1991) Placement Outcomes for Children with Special Needs, *Adoption and Fostering vol 15*, 2, pp18-28

Dance, C. (1997) *Focus on Adoption: A Snapshot of Adoption Patterns in England - 1995* BAAF

Farmer, E. and Parker, R. (1991) *Trials and Tribulations: Returning Children From Local Authority Care to their Families* HMSO

Jewett, C. (1984) *Helping Children Cope With Separation and Loss*, Batsford

Kadushin, A. and Seidle, F. (1971) *Adoption Failure*, Social Work, 6 July pp32-37

Kavanagh, S. (1987) Younger foster siblings as therapeutic tools, in *Adoption and Fostering vol 11*

Macaskill, C. (1991) *Adopting or Fostering a Sexually Abused Child* Batsford BAAF

Milham, S. Bullock, R. Hoise, K. and Haak, M. (1986) *Lost in Care* Gower, Aldershot

Part, D. (1993) Fostering as Seen by the Carer's Children, *Adoption and Fostering vol 17*

Pierce, L.H. and Pierce, R.L. (1990) *Adolescent/Sibling Incest Perpetrators* in Horton, I., Johnson, B., Roundy, L. and Williams, D. (Eds.) *The Incest Perpetrator: a Family Member No One Wants to Treat* Beverly Hills, CA: Sage

Rhodes, P. (1993) Like Any Other Job: Paying Foster Carers, *Foster Care vol 75* pp6-7

Reed, J. (1996) *Fostering Children and Young People with Learning Difficulties: The Perspectives of Birth Children and Carers. Adoption and Fostering vol 20*

Rosenthal, J.A., Motz, J.K., Edmonson, D.A. and Groze, V. (1991) A Descriptive Study of Abuse and Neglect in Out of Home Placement, *Child Abuse and Neglect* 13:249-60

Wallerstein, J.S. (1985) Preliminary Report of a Ten Year Follow-up of Older Children and Adolescents. 24 pp545-553

Wedge, P. and Mantle, G. (1991) *Sibling Groups and Social Work - a Study of Children Referred for Permanent Substitute Family Placement* Avebury Academic Publishing Group, Aldershot

Whitaker, D.S., Cook, J., Dunn, C. and Rocliffe, S. *The Experience of Residential Care, from The Perspectives of Children, Parents and Care-Givers, Final Report to the SSRC* Department of Social Policy and Social Work., University of York 1984

2.7 Family Link Care

Julia Waldman

In this chapter I want to describe a particular type of programmed respite care for families with children with disabilities, commonly called in the United Kingdom 'Family Link Schemes'. By looking in a critical way at the features of family link schemes I hope to be able to provide connections to some of the broader contemporary debates about foster care, the special needs of children with disabilities and their families and moves towards 'professionalisation' of foster care.

My interest in writing about family link care comes primarily from my role as family link carer and my perception that family link schemes often seem to be somewhat invisible within the wider activities of family placement work. I have been a carer for seven years and in that time have maintained a caring link with the same family and the same child. This singular experience is very personalised and thus it is inappropriate in this chapter to draw significantly upon this as representative of family link care. It does, however, mean that I do bring an experiential perspective to the wider practice debates about this arguably niche form of family-based programmed care.

Promotional material aimed at the general public helpfully summarises the purpose of a particular family link scheme as follows:

> ...links a child with a disability to a carer in the community for short periods of respite care. Caring full time for a child with a disability can be extremely hard work and short periods of respite care may be just what the parents want, safe in the knowledge that the child is well cared for.
>
> The scheme offers parents the chance to spend a few hours shopping, meeting friends or spending time with their other children.
>
> The 'Link' provides the child with a new positive experience and an opportunity to make friends and widen their social circle.
>
> (Portsmouth City Council, 1997)

Conveyed within these statements are a number of features that appear to be common to family link schemes. These are explored below.

The ethos of family link, it can be argued, is largely strength-based. The family of the child with a disability is generally seen to be coping and the link recognises that part of a coping strategy is being able to have 'time out'. So, unlike many foster care situations, the intervention is not always problem-based and attempts to work within a social model of disability. The possibilities for having 'time-out' that many families with non-disabled children take for granted, are not there when caring full-time for a child with a disability, as the following quote exemplifies:

> I need a rest. You know, I just need to put my feet up and go to sleep. That's what I'd like to do most of all. I'd just like to sleep for a weekend, the whole weekend would be just marvellous.
>
> (BBC, 1998)

Another quote sums up the pressures of care:

> 24 hours a day, 7 days a week, 365 days a year care required
>
> (Nash, Waldman and Wheal, 1996)

The social exclusion of disability means that the world of after-school activities, sleep-overs or trips to the local park are limited for many disabled children. Parental care often involves an intensive dependency.

For this reason family link schemes usually emphasise that they are intended to provide an opportunity for the linked child to broaden their social networks and opportunities.

Another feature is that, whilst the link carers are caring for the child, it is actually the parental or family needs that are seen as equally if not more important than the child's. Russell (1989) highlights earlier work by Oswin that identified:

> an inherent tension in the fact that respite care is frequently directed to parent relief and not seen as part of a coherent local authority child care policy for all handicapped (sic) children.

The dual issues of meeting two sets of potentially competing needs and family link as part of a wider network of services for children with disabilities remain critical in contemporary child care policy and practice and will be explored in more detail later on in the chapter.

Another distinctive feature of family link care is that carers are recruited and supported to work with one family and usually one child in a family. The relationship, although framed by statutory and agency requirements, is essentially a personal one. One ex family link co-ordinator interviewed for this chapter commented that when a caring link ceased nearly all the carers did not request a new link with another family. Unlike other forms of foster care, for many link carers it is not a recurring role. This raises interesting questions about the motivations and interests of link carers, as well as resourcing and planning issues for the agency. This is another area to which I will return later.

Family link schemes offer a respite service. This can mean different things but commonly it means *planned and regular* breaks for the family with a child with a disability. Rather than being a crisis-driven intervention, family link care operates by family and link carer negotiating a mutually acceptable arrangement for periods of care that become part of both family's normal routine. This might mean an afternoon a week, one day per fortnight, one weekend a month and less commonly periods such as a week during holidays. Thus the link arrangements should be exemplifying short-term programmed care and the notion of shared care. Again this feature is highly pertinent to the recruitment strategy for link carers. They will often be people who would not consider other forms of foster care but who feel they can make a specific commitment to moderate amounts of planned time. Such carers will often be working full time or have a range of other commitments. They would or could not accommodate children on an emergency basis about whom they would have very little information.

Whilst working in partnership with parents of all looked after children is becoming more of a practice reality since the Children Act 1989, family link arrangement cannot exist without both family and link carers working together to meet an identified respite care need of an individual child. It requires an open and

respectful relationship if the notion of a home from home for individual children is to be realised. Implicit is a need to balance a fine line between a relationship that has elements of both formality as well as more 'old fashioned' good neighbourliness. It is in some ways anomalous to the growing emphasis on foster care as a semi-professional activity. This ambiguity is both a strength and potential weakness of the scheme. One of the arguable strengths is that parents of children with disabilities are also a part of the wider population in which there is frequently suspicion of social services and an association of social work intervention as stigmatising and a sign of failure. (Powell, Waldman and Lovelock, 1994; Waldman and Wheal, 1996).

Currently family link schemes are run and managed within a variety of settings including the voluntary and statutory sector. A scheme may be part of the disabled children's team, family placement team or provided within family centres. They may be part of a general fostering service or situated within a setting co-ordinating a variety of services for children with disabilities. Given the previous issue there may be sound arguments for placing the scheme at a distance from the mainstream social work functions and where it is visible within a network of provision for children with disabilities.

There is a sensitive negotiating task to be carried out in supporting parents in a way that they experience as helpful and empowering, whatever the setting. To share the care of their child with another family will generate a range of feelings for parents. If link carers are motivated by a sense of community this may be less threatening for the parents, yet this can place the child second in the hierarchy of those to be helped. If families are familiar with health or social services based provision they may also have certain expectations about standards of care.

Thus whilst family link schemes will target recruitment at the broad population, the approval procedures must be as rigorous as other forms of foster care.

The two extracts from promotional materials demonstrate the way carers are targeted:

> *because only short periods of care are needed, the scheme is a way that people can help children while carrying on their normal lives in terms of work, leisure commitments and holidays.*
> (Warwickshire Local Authorities, 1998)

Link families are ordinary families in the community: they may be couples or single... They will have a real interest in children and a genuine desire to help a child with a disability and their family.

(Portsmouth City Council, 1998)

Training and approval processes will vary across local authorities and agencies. Carers need not only to engage with the information and awareness raising covered in the training, they will also need to think about the issues that arise when caring for children with a range of specific and special needs. The practical and emotional dimensions of the caring role will also need to be addressed. For the agency recruiting carers, there is a need to think carefully about how to distribute energy and resources to the different stages of the approval process with an expectation that only a small number of potential carers will see the process all the way through. Such questions may include the appropriateness of mixed-training with other foster carers whose needs and knowledge of 'the system' may be different to link carers.

Family link carers are paid for their time, though this is usually played down as expenses. This presents a picture that it is essentially a good will activity but parents of children do not feel carers are out of pocket and the money sends a message that the caring task is not an imposition or charity. Choosing to claim for the time is the carers decision and some do not. However it can, in my view, provide a useful reminder of the formal element of the relationship and not lull carers in to thinking the arrangement is a friendship. Carers, as with other foster care, have to adhere to agency policy in caring for children and the formal element of the role is an important protection for all parties involved, but crucially the child.

The final feature of family link care is the placement process. Again, unlike many forms of foster care it is recognised in family link schemes that a carefully managed staging process is needed to work towards the link family looking after a child successfully. There is an expectation that relationship-building will need to happen before the child stays with the link family at their home, the common care environment. Not only does the child need to feel comfortable with their potential carers but also the other family

members need to have built up sufficient trust for the child's parents to feel confident about leaving their child with a new family. This indicates the need for the matching process that should be part of careful pairing of parents needing a link with a caring family. This may include attending to racial, cultural and religious dimensions. Consequently each link arrangement will be unique and individual and so will the formal and informal boundaries that frame each relationship that is partly a working and partly a personal one.

Having identified some of the common features of family link schemes I now want to move on to explore some of the issues and questions that help to understand how and why family link schemes can be regarded as a niche service in the context of foster care.

In some ways the family link scheme has some resonance with recent developments in adult disability services and direct payment schemes. Once a family link scheme co-ordinator has negotiated an arrangement with a family they generally play a low key role in the arrangement, with trouble-shooting being the most common reason for contact. Although annual reviews of care plans are now required by law, the frequency and nature of these reviews are very variable. This places a great deal of responsibility on the linked families to sustain and manage the link. If both sides of the link feel that 'things are going well' then this model can be maintained, albeit in a passive way, with energy focused upon sustaining the status quo. However, one merely has to scratch the surface of this to reveal a number of problematic issues that are centred on the contemporary social context of disability.

Children's needs do not stay the same. A year in the life of a child is a long time and they may undergo many physical, emotional and cognitive changes. A child with a disability is a child first and foremost and their care needs cannot simply be measured by their impairment. Family link care is intended to be a long-term intervention. As my own experience demonstrates the period of care may encompass key transitions in a child's life; starting school, moving to secondary school, the onset of puberty as examples. This suggests that all parties need to be aware of, and consider the implications of, a child's development to the caring relationship. The link carers may begin by caring for a vulnerable child and find themselves caring for a young person who is looking for ways to increase their independence and/or who have different kinds of personal care needs. Simply, for example, older children are heavier and, depending upon their development and progress, may have fewer or more complex care needs. Yet it may be difficult to raise and address very sensitive situations without the aid of a third person. Perhaps values and views on adolescence are very different between the families and tensions may arise about when and how to recognise a child's emergent maturity. Parents of teenagers with disabilities may find themselves in need of a more specialist respite care for their child and both link parties in this scenario need to explore the viability of the family link without either side feeling that they have failed in some way.

As the carer recruitment strategy described earlier shows, link carers may well be people who have little contact with social services or related health services. Yet studies of children with their disabilities and their families have frequently shown that a number of false assumptions often exist about knowledge of, and take up, of support resources. *Making Connections* (1998) identifies some of the problems:

> *'Disability' itself is a contentious term which is often limiting and unhelpful.*

There may be cultural, racial and linguistic barriers which make parents reluctant to assign to their child certain 'disability' labels and relative marginalisation of certain groups in society may inhibit access to information about services.

Parents of disabled children may face similar barriers to those of disabled people in accessing information by being house-bound or having limited free time. Professionals can make false assumptions about the abilities of middle class parents to access information. Parents already 'in the system' may be falsely assumed to know more about the full range of available services and benefits than they actually do.

A situation may present where a linked family is lacking appropriate information and support and linked to a carer who also has very little information about needs and

services for children with disabilities. Their 'ordinariness' can also be re-framed in this context as non-specialist. Successful family links need to be bound by a set of clear expectations which are regularly reviewed to take in to account changes involving any of the three parties involved. Family link should not be seen as a cheap substitute for specialist residential respite care. It may be quite reasonable to request a modest aid for adapting a link carer's home to accommodate an individual child's needs, for example a handrail in a toilet. If, however, a carer feels in need of a lot of additional equipment it raises the question about whether that home setting is appropriate for the particular needs of that child. These needs may not have been apparent when the placement began.

When a care relationship has a personal element, and this of course applies to all foster care, the ending of a care relationship becomes critical in how it is managed. Without accessible support, link carers and linked families may struggle to maintain the link and be unable to face up to the reality that the link care is no longer able to meet the needs of the child and/or parents. The Children Act 1989 states that local authorities have

> *a duty to provide services to minimise the effect of their disability and to give them the opportunity to live a life which is 'as normal as possible'.*
> (Open University, 1997)

The Children Act, Section 17 also applies.

Unfortunately normality may mean provision of more specialist support or conversely release from a maternalistic care situation that gives a young person little autonomy and freedom to make their own choices. Many young people may choose not to go and be looked after by grandparents or other family member for example. So a child in a link situation should be given all possible opportunity to express their own views about the family link situation. For the parents desperate for a break they may feel pressured to maintain a link, even when it seems past its 'sell by date'.

For the link carers they also may feel pressured to keep the caring going, the role may become bound by a sense of duty. Carers and families need access to independent support to address such issues. Yet unlike other fostering situations the family link co-ordinator has to be working in the interests of the child, parents and carers. This can put them in a position of managing competing interests.

In looking at the place of the family link scheme in the contemporary mixed economy of health and social care if the 'person first' and community-based ethos of the scheme can be maintained this suggests it has continuing relevance to children with disabilities and their families by emphasising access to ordinary experiences that all children in society should be entitled to, including being 'just another citizen'. It also implies, however, that family link care is specialist in the sense that it is serving a particular need for both child and family and that the care is necessarily limited.

Parents, children and carers need to have a clear sense of purpose and an awareness of their place in a wider network of support services to appreciate the particular function of family link care. This means that the changing needs of children and families are not problematised but viewed as inevitable and expected. Growing in and out of relationships is part of all human relationships, a care plan cannot determine the personal dimensions of those relationships, but the support that should be attached to such a plan can go a long way to limiting the damage 'messy endings' can cause and to make the relationship as fulfilling as it can be for all parties whilst it is working.

References

BBC Radio 2 (1998), *Getting a Break*, extracts from Radio 2 programme *Why Do We Care?* June 10, http://www.bbc.net.uk/education/carers/gettin.htm

Kahan, B. (Ed.), (1989) *Child Care Research, Policy and Practice*, London:Hodder & Stoughton

Making Connections (1998) *Enabling Information: A Report on Improving Access and Raising Standards in Information Service for Disabled People and Their Carers in Scotland*, http://cil.gcal.ac.uk/Connections/saif/EnablRp/Background/Background2.html

Nash, S., Waldman, J. and Wheal, A. (1996) *Information Needs of Families in Wiltshire*, Southampton: Nash & Waldman

Portsmouth City Council (1997) *The Family Link Scheme Issue 1*, Portsmouth: Social Services Department, Portsmouth City Council

Open University, (1997) *Law Cards England and Wales, Course K201*, Milton Keynes: Open University

Powell, J., Waldman J. and Lovelock, R. (1994) *Future Services for Royal Naval and Royal Marine Children and Families*, Southampton: CEDR

Russell, P. (1989) Handicapped children in Kahan, B. (Ed.), *Child Care Research, Policy and Practice*, London: Hodder & Stoughton

Waldman, J. and Wheal, A. (1996) *Children in Need Research Project*, Southampton:University of Southampton

Warwickshire Local Authorities, (1998) *Give us a Break 25 August 1998*, http://www.warwickshire.gov.uk/press/augbreak.htm

2.8 Family and Friends who are Carers

Ann Wheal

Introduction

This chapter is based around a small piece of research carried out by Julia Waldman and me at the University Southampton on behalf of the NFCA for the Department of Health; a session at the International Association of Schools of Social Work in Israel 1998; a literature review and my own personal experience of caring for my grandson whilst my daughter-in-law was in hospital following a car crash.

The first part of the chapter looks at what I believe should be the way forward for friends and family who are carers; the current situation; other research and other people's work is also covered. The difficulties and dilemmas when friends and family become carers are then highlighted and examples given of how different agencies, different regions and different individuals all respond to these carers differently.

The second part of the chapter looks at what is needed to enable this type of care not being seen as second best. It suggests the policies and practices which should be in place to ensure the best interests of the child are met and that these carers must be adequately and appropriately trained and supported.

Terminology

At this point it may be useful to note that the use of the separate terms 'friends' and 'family' is deliberate. 'Kinship care' is part of professional usage in the international arena but not used commonly in the UK. Other terms in use in the UK are 'de facto care', 'district vetted', 'child specific' and 'self-presenting foster carers'. There may be more. These terms often give misleading and impersonal interpretations to a specific type of care. The term 'stranger carer' when referring to the remaining group of carers is also an emotive term for some people.

Network care is a term which is more inclusive and will be used in this chapter. It encompasses the range of social networks in which children may be supported and nurtured. In this chapter the common feature is that the substitute carer has an existing personal relationship with the child and/or the child's primary carer. The term child may also mean children.

A Suggested Way Forward

Whenever a child or young person cannot live at home, in many cases, the best place for them to live is either with family or with friends. For this type of care to be successful new ways of thinking need to be explored. It seems to me, both from my professional and personal experience, that consideration should be given to the idea that in reality there are two types of network care and that each will require different decisions and different levels of support.

The first is where social services are involved from the start where it is decided that what is best for the child is to stay within the friends and family network rather than with a stranger carer. This type of care can be monitored and supported and the best interests of the child established as the basis for the placement. What is needed here then is a base line for approval as foster carers similar to that for stranger carers. Are lesser standards required simply because the carer is known to the child?

The second type of network care arises in a time of personal family crisis — a death in the family, mother has accident, father has a heart attack. Should the other agencies such as health or the police refer the situation to social services? Some would say that this smacks of too much of the 'big brother' syndrome which would not be acceptable. It seems that what is needed is publicity, similar to that for carers of the elderly or disabled, where the family could learn what support is available and how to access it, or where other agencies guide the network carer to the most appropriate form of support. But then, how does that conflict with the rights of the child? Are their wishes and feelings being considered? How will their well-being be monitored?

A suggested way of establishing the different care situations is to use a grid system, similar to that used by Wiltshire Social Services, for example, where the level of service initially offered to the client is based on answers to a set of predetermined and graded questions. In the case of network carers, the questions might cover such things as support required/necessary, likely length of care, information requested, training needed, details of the carer(s) as well as details and age of the child, their health, education and any other special needs or cultural requirements plus appropriate specific information such as, 'is a court order in place?'

Family solutions to family problems seems to me to be the way forward for many children but, in order to ensure the best interests of the child are considered, there is an urgent need for a change of attitude, a new way of working and better and different training for the carers, social workers and managers.

The Current Situation

There has been a marked increase in the number of network carers both in the UK and elsewhere and the following table shows the estimated usage internationally as a percentage of the known total of carers in each country:

New Zealand	75%
Sweden	25%
Poland	90%
USA	33%
Belgium	33%

Fostering Kinship: An International Perspective on Foster Care by Relatives, Ed. Roger Greef (1999).

Exact numbers for the UK and Ireland are not available at present. In Ireland, in the future, care agencies will be required to compile separate registers for network placements, which will assist in the identification of trends. It is anticipated that at least a quarter of all placements in Ireland in the future will be network care. Difficulties arise in the UK because of the variety of terms for these placements and the possible alternative legal frameworks used. Statisticians providing data will only know the term used in their particular area so the collection of data about network care has so far proved to be inaccurate in many cases.

The following three quotations highlight a universal change in attitudes to network care:

> *In the recent past kinship care (in the family and the social network) has developed very quickly, from being a kind of 'second choice' foster care it is becoming more and more a 'first choice'. It is increasingly becoming the policy of foster care organisations that social workers should look first into the family and the social network.*
>
> Riet Portengen and Bart van der Neut, Netherlands
> Ch.4 Greeff, (1999).

> *It's a growth industry*
>
> Care manager, UK

> *In Sweden there has been little research on kinship care. But the debate concerning kinship care shows that it is a controversial issue and that attitudes and values are polarised. Many social workers do not show a commitment to the principle of kinship placement though others do. Different localities adopt noticeably different perspectives on kinship care.*
>
> Eva Berherhed, in *Foster Children in a Changing World*, European IFCO Conference, Berlin 1994. Votum Verlag (1995).

Rapid growth of network care has not been accompanied by the development of policies to ensure that:

- the rights and needs of the child are met in the best possible way
- these carers are appropriately trained and supported
- social workers are trained to enable them to carry out the specialised role in this type of care in a professional and supporting manner

There are many theories about the reasons for this rapid growth such as the shortage of stranger carers, greater involvement of families in the decision making process, government initiatives on promoting the family. There may also have been a shift in attitudes on the importance of family life and values.

The Research

The aim of the research was to identify the training needs of this group of carers, their social workers and the managers (*Friends and Family as Carers, Identifying the Training Needs of Carers and Social Workers*, Ann Wheal and Julia Waldman, (1997)). Training is discussed later in the chapter. However, carers and social workers were eager to discuss many other issues which were not part of the remit of the research project.

The research reflected demographic and geographic diversity. The authorities were also chosen for their apparent different levels of use of relative and friend carers. The researchers met, and spoke to on the telephone, carers, child care and family placement social workers, adoption and fostering managers and policy makers. The additional source of information was national and international material, both published and unpublished.

The challenge to this work was presented by the disparity of the care situations encountered which were embraced by the term relative or friend care. The relationships which existed between child and carer before they took on their new role varied greatly and included uncles and aunts, parents of the friend of a child, neighbour who befriended a young child, friend of the carer, male friend of the family, teacher of a child, friend of mother, step-father, older sister and grandmothers, many of whom were lone parents.

Grandparents were also the largest group. The reasons for caring for their grandchildren were varied but included parental death, long term mental illness and drug addiction.

Circumstances and contexts were infinitely variable, along with the attitudes and expectations of carers. In the majority of situations, the children were in situ, often staying with a relative or friend as a result of a crisis. Assessment procedures usually happened after the child was placed which is very different to the normal pattern of recruitment and assessment for 'stranger' carers.

I just thought, I don't want to see her in a home, that was the initial thing. It wasn't until about two weeks later when we got a visit from social services and we had to read all this stuff, all these forms and then we had to sign it and then had a meeting and so I had to take a lot of time off work

Carer

The range of carers' motives also present special challenges. For many carers the need for formal involvement with a local authority was often only driven by the need to access financial support. For these families the focus of local authority involvement should be on using the strengths and values of the extended family, and how allowances support the continuation of family stability.

Other People's Work

Howard Dubowitz, *Kinship Care: Suggestions for Future Research*, Child Welfare League of America (1994) noted that despite its widespread use, little research has been done on kinship care, instead there are deeply felt ideological beliefs, illustrated by the comment:

I'd rather my child be placed with my worst relative than with a stranger

Dubowitz recommends that research should be undertaken to look at whether the children are adequately protected and receive appropriate care. He also suggests another important area of research should concern the families of origin and the emotional health of these families, their reasons for, and satisfaction with, caring for the children. He would like professionals to be interviewed to ascertain their views including their ability to monitor kinship placements whilst avoiding being overly intrusive.

In the NFCA research children were not interviewed and I would recommend that their views should be canvassed. My own experience of talking to young people suggests that in some cases the young people feel that the grandparents side with their own child (the parent) instead of being independent like other carers — *Answering Back*, Buchanan A, Wheal A, Walder D, McDonald S, Coker R, University of Southampton (1992).

The next two comments highlight the need for sound and consistent policies:

In Poland, shifts in political regimes and social policy has affected kinship care but the commitment of extended families is remarkably resilient, continuing strongly whether supported, ignored or opposed by the state. There is now pressure on the state to recognise kinship care as kinship fostering particularly with the growing awareness of children's rights and human and individual rights in general and the development of active citizenship.

(Abstract IASSW Conference, Israel 1998,
Zofia Waleria Stelmaszuk, Poland)

Valerie O'Brien in Ireland (O'Brien, 1996, 1997 in R Greeff (1999 Ch. 8) carried out research in the Eastern Health Board area in 1995. The study both qualitative and quantitative, examined the evolution of relative care networks following an emergency placement of a child in a relative's home. The study traced the process through decision-making, assessment and post-assessment stages. It also provided base-line data on a population of ninety-two children.

O'Brien suggests in *Evolving Networks in Relative Care — Alliance and Exclusion* that there should be :

● recognition that there may be conflict over access and support
● network meetings
● multi-disciplinary services working together

My experience as a network carer was that it was almost impossible to persuade different agencies to work together in the best interests of the child. In fact, one hospital consultant refused to allow me to be present when a planning meeting was being held for my daughter-in-law's return home from hospital, still suffering from head injury difficulties. I had asked that any planning should include a plan for the care of her one year old son at that stage being cared for by me.

Another piece of research by Kosenen M, (1993) *Descriptive Study of Foster and Adoptive Care Services in a Scottish Agency*, Community Alternative Vol.5, no. 2 Fall shows that network care seems to be more successful, in that the young people maintain better and more frequent contact with their parent(s) and stay within their own community. This means they also usually stay at the same schools and keep the same friends. Children fostered with family or friends are usually placed with siblings and are more likely to return home when there is no longer a need for outside care.

Dilemmas

Many network carers who might like support do not get it because:

● they are unaware of what is available
● they are emotionally involved in the situation
● they (mistakenly?) believe that they should be able to cope because they are family
● they feel there is a stigma in becoming involved with social services.

The following shows how difficult network care is to regulate, yet these same dilemmas show how important is the need for clear guidelines to ensure that these carers and the children are treated fairly and receive the best possible service.

As mentioned earlier, many grandparents may have failed their own children and also many of the families have a history of mental health or addiction problems. If this is the perception of this type of care, it is not surprising that attitudes of professionals vary so much. It is important that an unfair stigma does not become attached to all network carers that creates prejudices which are difficult to eradicate.

There is concern amongst some grandparent carers of seeing a repeat of the parenting problems they had experienced with their own children, which had in turn, caused them to have to care for their grandchildren. For social workers, does that automatically make these people unsuitable carers? Is it possible for a poor parent to become a good grandparent? Many would say 'yes'.

If a carer is caring for a child voluntarily should they be treated in the same way as someone caring for a child who is subject to a court order? Should they have the choice of keeping the arrangement purely private or should they be required to register the situation with social services in order to protect the rights and well-being of the child? Should this decision be age-related to the child and/or the carer? Is it necessary for network carers to meet the stringent requirements of stranger care or are there times when these standards may be relaxed, especially if the child is in situ and seems happy and well?

The transitional period during which carers and their families make the adjustments to living with a new family member is clearly a difficult one for many. As a carer explained who was looking after a teenage friend of her daughters:

...it was very disruptive for the other children and it upset them...because they knew the family they were knowing what was happening and I had to explain an awful lot more than I would have done normally, stuff that you don't really want an 8 or 9 year old knowing about.

There seems to be no hard and fast rules and social workers will need to learn new ways of working to ensure each carer receives a service appropriate to their circumstances and that of the child.

Cultural issues play a major part in some families' decision to care. As one black adoption and fostering manager said:-

There are particular challenges with culture and social circumstances, particularly with the black community — the community I'm part of. My experience of growing up is that if your mother or father whoever, can't look after you for whatever reasons, its an automatic thing that your aunt, your uncle whoever takes over. It's nothing to do with the state.

My personal experience again supports this. A colleague, when discussing with me some of the difficulties we had experienced said '...*is very lucky that you could look after him. He could have gone into care.*' This is something no-one in the family would have considered. If my husband and I had been unable to care for our grandson, another family member would have done so.

There are also difficulties regarding placement of mixed race children or where the friend or relative carer is from a different race:

...if it wasn't of the same origin exactly (network carer), where do we stand on trying to make a same race placement, versus placement with a relative and where does that fit in with the Children Act philosophy

Social worker

Carers on the other hand seemed to eschew the 'blood is thicker than water' ethos.

Often network care has been seen as the cheap option and cynics would say that it is the reason for the increase in the use of this type of care. There are also cultural differences which may cause conflict even within the same social services department:

Families should not be paid

Manager

This sort of view may give social workers further dilemmas in knowing when, or even if, to offer financial support.

Since 1989 in New Zealand there has been a significant shift from stranger carers for children unable to live with their parents to children living within the family if at all possible. The Maori people:

see a child not as the child of its biological parents but as a child of the whanau — a communal responsibility and much of the policy and practice in New Zealand is based around this ethos

Jill Worrall (Greeff, 1999, Ch. 12)

If a similar statement was devised in the UK some of the present dilemmas might be avoided.

Another possible difficulty was noted by a social worker during our research:

The obvious split loyalties that might occur given the number of scenarios such as the child disclosing to the friend concerning incidents perhaps or her developing concerns independently about the child as to where loyalties would lie... There could well be difficulties in the relationship between mum and this person caused through her taking independent action, or the right action of a foster carer if she brought her concerns to the local authority.

When I was caring for my grandchild whilst my daughter-in-law was in hospital, I sought the support of an excellent health visitor who was a great help. Should she, for example, have reported our family circumstances to social services? I would hope not, certainly not without telling us. It might have been helpful to us though, and indeed many others in difficult circumstances, to have known about other support services that might have been available. We would have liked help with:

- coping and letting go when the child returned home

- preparing for and helping the child to again live with the mother and/or father

- helping the parents to cope with the natural jealousy they feel when they observe the bond that the child has developed with their carers.

All of this was extremely painful. It also surprised us, and put stress on otherwise good family relationships. If we had not been so emotionally involved in the situation, we might have expected it.

Another dilemma relates not just to the child who is being fostered, but also to the siblings of the carers. Much has been written recently about foster carer's siblings in a traditional fostering context, but support is also required for network siblings too. After all, they suddenly, often without warning, have one or more children in the house with whom they have to share with their parents.

> The caregivers reported that feelings of jealousy and resentment were expressed by their own children, even if they had left home before the children came. One young man was heard to say, when he heard his cousin calling his mother 'mum', 'You can't call her that! She's not your Mum! You've taken everything of mine, you are not taking my Mum'.
>
> (Greeff , 1999, Ch. 12).

In our research, the differences in attitudes and expectations amongst carers, especially towards social services, was particularly notable. Social workers interviewed were very aware of the effects of these differences and the dilemmas this caused them. For example one felt:

> ...as far as doing any work or any sort of assessment, I didn't do very well there at all. The children were always well cared for and happy when I saw them, but there was this big barrier 'why are you here' why are you asking questions like this?

Training and Personal Development

The type and content of training suggested during the research complements the suggested new way of thinking on network care.

Carers and social workers who participated in the research were each asked what they considered to be the developmental needs of themselves and of the other party. Both groups had strong views of the others needs. Some of these ideas would not come into traditional thinking on training; others should already be an integral part of good practice. Additional details are contained in the research report to the NFCA (Wheal and Waldman, 1997). A summary of the responses are highlighted below under generic headings.

Communication

Both groups identified that many carers need help in dealing with the statutory procedures; form filling, speaking out at meetings, attending court and understanding choices that might be available including being given clear information about the implications of different types of care orders affecting children and carer's roles. Carers also felt that social workers should ensure carers are given sufficient information about such things as children's and carer's rights; what is going on, being up-front, open and honest. Both groups acknowledged the need for help in handling complaints.

Child and family matters

Carers wanted help in dealing with family relationships; handling contact with other family members; dealing with their own and the child's trauma; explaining situations as they arise; coping with grief; managing changing relationships with their own children and managing differences in values and priorities between carers, parents and children, e.g. religion, culture, sexual identity. Additionally social workers felt carers needed help in maintaining the identity of the child, dealing with the long term effects on the child, siblings, carers and extended families as well as generally coping with the emotional side of caring.

Social workers felt they needed help, knowledge and understanding to support carers including when to offer additional support if appropriate e.g. respite care. They also wanted help in how to explain about and support families in managing contact arrangements and helping families cope with emotional ties and family conflicts. Carers felt social workers should learn to know when to offer advice or help and when to recognise the family can cope alone. Carers highlighted the importance that families should not be penalised because they are related to the child. They also felt there was a need for better understanding of the fact that family and friends know the child, know the history, know and are in contact with other relatives and may be the best option for children, especially if the extended family is able to offer support.

Information needs

Carers felt they needed guidance on what they are allowed to do in such areas as giving advice on contraception, parental responsibility, holidays, attendance at father's funeral, smacking and discipline, baby-sitting. They also wanted guidelines on looking after children generally, and specifically information on allowances. They particularly felt they should be given more information about what is going on, what to expect, what might happen, short and long term planning and the roles of the different professionals. Social workers also mentioned that carers should be given information on what sort of behaviour they might expect from a child who has had a disrupted life or who has been abused and also general information on the broader issues of bringing up children.

Social workers wanted to know what options they can offer carers and children in relation to care planning and financial support and requested clarity on relevant policies. They also felt they needed advice on how to present necessary information in a non-threatening way, for example local authority policy on corporal punishment.

Managing the situation

Carers identified that they needed help to understand the child protection system. Additionally social workers felt carers needed help to cope with knowing, understanding, and the reasons why a child had been abused. They also felt carers needed help to implement prevention of contact or how to adhere to supervised contact. Family loyalties, allegiances, and relationships obviously playing a very strong part in the conflict.

Carers wanted help when dealing with schools; in knowing what extra help is possible from the school; how to avoid the stigma of the child being 'in care' and getting others to recognise them as 'parents'. They also wanted help to manage the prejudice of the local community who may make assumptions that the child has been abused and see the carer as part of an abusive family.

Social workers felt they needed help to plan these specific placements in partnership with all other groups as well as when to use the different court orders. They also felt joint work with children's social workers and family placement workers should take place, particularly in carer/care setting assessments.

Interestingly social workers felt they needed help to cope with their own emotions. Although not mentioned specifically, it may be that carers and the child also need similar help.

General

Carers felt that social workers should be aware of the importance of keeping promises and that they should be trained in giving pastoral support; communication skills, listening; time management. It was also felt that social workers needed to understand the importance of working with, and being sensitive to, the needs of the child and carer. Carers also wished for the development of a family-centred approach to caring by, for example, organising meetings to suit the family - time and place, and returning calls as promised.

Social workers on the other hand felt they needed guidance on when to use family and friends as carers; weighing up and making the decision, including value judgements - family background not quite meeting approval criteria; weighing up quality of care against attitude which may not, in other foster carers, be acceptable. They also wanted help in making the assessment and balancing speed to give a child stability with quality and depth in assessments; on treating every situation on its individual merits, recognising diversity with this type of care and helping families to decide without placing undue pressure on them.

Social workers also felt they needed to learn coping strategies for dealing with situations such as being aware that some families will need to, and others will **not** want to, work with social services. They need to know when to stand back and allow carers to cope as appropriate and what they should do and what their position is in such circumstances. As one carer said

I'm a parent myself - I've got nothing to learn

Specific advanced training topics suggested by, and for social workers, were separation and loss; the place of culture in human behaviour; goal setting linked to family strengths; negotiation and conflict resolution; building problem solving skills in families; building community networking skills in families; assessment skills, using culturally competent assessment instruments.

In the light of our findings Ronny Flynn has produced two training packs for the NFCA - a survival guide for foster carers and a training manual for social workers.

The book for foster carers is a self study workbook. It aims to help carers who are approved as foster carers, or in the process of being assessed for approval, so they are able to provide the best quality of care for the child or young person they are looking after. It differs from other material for foster carers by exploring the implications for carers already being connected with the child in some way. It is in three sections covering such topics as 'official' relationships with the local authority, the legal position, divided loyalties, family relationships etc.

Policy Issues

This final section looks at what I believe is needed to develop network care into an integral and essential part of the foster care system. Evidence suggests that network care has been subject to patchy and limited policy attention. There is a picture of growth rate which has not been paralleled by policy development which would assist in promoting best practice in the use of relative and friend carers.

Several social workers summed up the apparent lack of awareness of policies on network care, or of their use, by saying:

> *I don't know of any policy decisions in this area, that's not to say we haven't got any, its just that I've never unearthed it or worked with it*

> *Many of these placements are made on the 'hoof' for expediency and cheapness*

> *Contact with parents varies from case to case it's very difficult to manage. It's a very sensitive issue that certainly requires a lot of careful monitoring. There are no guidelines on this*

A senior manger adequately described the whole question of policy and practice:

> *They have tended to evolve these placements, rather than being thought through and it is time now to sit and think about it and how we're going to deal with them in the future, because as I say, I think there is going to be far more of them*

Clear information linked to choices and responsibilities should be given to potential carers early on in the care planning process.

An early decision needs to be reached on which term is to be used to cover this group of carers. During the research different terms were being used even within the three participating regions. The disparity of terms not only makes the collection of accurate data difficult and monitoring almost impossible, it also means that the level, quality of service and financial support network carers receive varies termendously.

There is also a need for a fundamental debate about the status of network carers and how far policy should seek to define the nature of the relationship between the child, the carer and the 'State' as represented by the local authority. There is a need to continue to debate in what way can an essentially private relationship between the child, their family and the carers, work effectively and be properly resourced, without compromising the qualities of intimacy which in best practice underpin this type of care. **To judge effectiveness in terms of the welfare of a child inevitably means some form of intrusion.** Should this intrusion be of the same order as for 'stranger' foster care is a question that emerges from the resentment some carers, participating in the research, felt towards the private nature of many questions asked in the assessment process.

From March 1999 there will be a new set of Standards for Foster Care (Ch. 2.1). These standards will apply to network carers where the carers have been approved. Policy decisions are also needed as to whether they should also apply to the second group of carers mentioned on the first page of this chapter.

Other policy issues that need to be addressed are:

- Should the notion of network care be better promoted, to enable children to stay within their own families or social networks?

- Should the special value of the intimate and private nature of network care be promoted to ensure it does not become to be seen as second best as foster care becomes more 'professionalised'?

- If the suggstion for two groups of carers is considered, should one be called foster carers and the other carers with say the first group being paid full allowances/salary and the second not? What will happen if someone from the second group asks for financial assistance in order to be able to maintain the status quo? Will the carers be able to move from one group to the other if circumstances change?

    Alternatively, we could look at the system of payment suggested by John Hudson in the Conclusion - those who care for expenses ony, those who care in return for pay below the economic rate and those who care for pay at the same rate as anyone else caring for a child with a similar level of difficulty. Clearly the debate on payment for network care needs to be openly discussed and directives issued to enable network carers to be adequately and appropriately financed.

- Is training to be compulsory for all network carers? When care is crisis-driven it makes it difficult for social workers to raise the topic of training early on and when a care situation is already established requests to attend training carry litle weight. Decisions on training should also include when it should take place and in what form.

- Is the development of an advocacy system for network carers needed?

- Consideration of the promotion of shared care for network carers, particularly older care-givers.

- Is there a need for standard foster care information to be adapted so that material speaks more directly to the experience of relative or friend carers?

Clearly network care has expanded in recent years. Policy decisions need to be made as a priority to ensure the child is given the best and most appropriate type of care possible and that those caring for the child are given consistency of support and adequate advice and training.

The political climate and research debate all now lean towards the importance of the family. If in times of crisis a child can stay within the family network, in most cases, this will be in the child's best interest. Policies and resources must be available to ensure that this can successfully happen whenever possible.

References

Buchanan, A. Wheal, A., Walder, D., Macdonald, S., Coker, R. (1993) *Answering Back, Report by Young People Being Looked After on the Children Act 1989*, University of Southampton

Bergerhed, E. (1995) *Foster Children in a Changing World*, Documentation of the European IFCO Conference, Berlin 1994, Votum Varlag

Dubowitz, H. (1994) *Kinship Care: Suggestions for Future Research*, Child Welfare League of America

Duerr Berrick, J., Barth, R.P. (1994) *Research on Kinship Foster Care: What Do We Know: Where Do We Go From Here?*, Child Welfare League of America

Greeff, R. (Ed.) (1999) *Fostering Kinship: an International Perspective on Foster Care by Relatives*, Avebury

Kosenen, M. (1993) Descriptive Study of Foster and Adoptive Care Services in a Scottish Agency. *Community Alternative*, Vol 5, No 2, Fall

Wheal, A., Waldman, J. (1997) *Friends and Family as Carers - Identifying the Training Needs of Carers and Social Workers. A Research Project and Report*, National Foster Care Association

Waterhouse, S. (1997) *The Organization of Fostering Services: A Study of the Arrangements for Delivery of Fostering Services in England*, NFCA

2.9 Private Fostering

Carol Woollard and Beverley Clarke

Private fostering raises a kaleidoscope of issues of both a theoretical and practical nature. These must be openly and honestly debated for progress to be made and public and community awareness raised. This chapter examines the most prominent of these issues and discusses the possible ways forward.

The term 'private' in private fostering is unfortunate. It suggests something conducted outside public scrutiny, entirely the affair of the purchaser and provider, without reference to the citizenship context in which it takes place. It connotes a concept of parent/child relationship in which the child is viewed as a commodity or possession of the parent who has parental 'rights' rather than parental 'responsibilities', and in which the rights of the child are subsumed.

In the first part of the chapter, a health visitor who has had to deal with the practice and consequences of private fostering in her daily work, and who has subsequently established a special interest group within the Community Practitioners' Health Visitors' Association (CPHVA), gives a feel of private fostering. There will then be an attempt to analyse the issues raised and relate them to the wider issues of child care and the socio-political framework in which it takes place.

Case Study

Buki, a two year old West African, first came onto my case load via a child protection case conference. Her mother lived on an estate on my patch, and she was privately fostered with a white family in a neighbouring borough. Some of Buki's foster carer's own children had been taken into local authority care. Buki suffered a broken arm whilst being thrown by the carer's 16 year old son and his friend. Following a period of hospitalisation she was taken into local authority care and placed in a children's home. Her parents were encouraged to visit her and take her home, but somehow seemed reluctant to do so, as this to them was a better form of child care with social services supporting their child care needs.

Buki's father was a student, and her mother worked long hours as a cleaner to finance the family. Mother was currently pregnant with her second child and found it difficult to cope with Buki's constant crying and wanting to be picked up.

My role as the family's health visitor was to encourage them to have their daughter home, and support them with their parenting skills. It was also to raise their awareness of the implications of private fostering, and the profound effects of their action on their daughter. The act of commissioning this kind of care, and perceptions of British child care need to be addressed, in the African community and by all other users. This was demonstrated at the time of my visit by a family friend of Buki's mother who requested the name of the children's home for her own two children.

With lots of encouragement and support around issues of child rearing, Buki's parents removed her from care. Mother gave up her cleaning job to spend more time with Buki. By the time the baby arrived Buki was more settled with her family and was able to accept her new sister.

Although I no longer have responsibility for the family, I often see Buki's mum with both girls when I visit on the estate. She confesses the guilt that she suffers through lack of awareness of the care she commissioned for her daughter. Buki is now over 10 years old, confident and doing well at school. Her early experiences have, however, left her with one handicap. She has a fear of staying overnight outside her own home, especially with a 'white' family.

Definition

Private fostering has a legal definition as set out in the 1989 Children Act.

'A privately fostered child' means a child who is under the age of 16 (or 18 in the case of a child who is disabled) and who is cared for, and provided with accommodation by, someone other than a parent of his, a person who is not a parent of his but who has parental responsibility for him, or a relative of his.' (Section 66) *A child is not a privately fostered child if the person caring for and accommodating him has not done so for a period of less than 28 days, and does not intend to do so for any longer period.* (Section 67)

The numbers of children privately fostered within England and Wales are unknown. The Department of Health, since the implementation of the Children Act in 1991, has ceased to require local authorities to give annual returns, because the previous statistics were clearly inaccurate and misleading. It is perhaps more relevant to consider the various categories of children in placements which fall within the legal definition of private fostering.

Save the Children Fund's, African Family Advisory Service (a project which worked inter alia on the needs of West African privately fostered children and the issues raised) estimated that at any one time during the late 1980s there were between 6,000 and 9,000 children of West African origin in the UK. In the 1950s and 1960s the children were mostly the offspring of students. Often in inadequate housing and similarly to Buki's parents, needing to make practical arrangements for their children. The placements were essentially for the duration of their studies, and their plans were usually to return to West Africa. By the 1980s, many arrangements were being made by parents who were working full time, with no time scale for their children's placements, or by people who were primarily domiciled in West Africa, but who wished their children to be brought up in the UK. There is also a significant number of Chinese children, most of whose parents work unsociable hours in catering, who find it practicable for their children to be cared for by others.

There are children from other ethnic groups who are brought over to this country in response to crises elsewhere: for example Russian children who came over after the Chernobyl disaster, and Bosnian children who were rescued from the conflict. There are also overseas children who are brought over for adoption, and who, because of irregularities, have not come within the scope of being 'protected children' so are technically, privately fostered.

Another category of non-British children is that of children attending language schools or on cultural exchanges who are boarded out with families for periods exceeding 28 days. Children at residential schools for whom arrangements are made during the school holidays with non related families, may also be privately fostered. There are a number of British children, mainly teenagers, whose parents have moved house, but who wish them to remain at their original school to complete their studies. They have made an arrangement with friends. Finally there are the young people who, because of family problems, have voted with their feet and have gone to live elsewhere.

It was with this disparate range of children in mind that Part IX and Schedule 2 of the Children Act were formulated, together with the guidance and regulations in Volume 8. Until the legislation is superseded it is to these that the practitioner and student should refer.

Literature

Private fostering has been represented as the 'cinderella' of child care services, but attempts have been made to raise its profile. The most significant piece of research remains that of Robert Holman in the late 1960s whose book *Trading in Children: A Study of Private Fostering* was published in 1973. Holman's description and analysis of placements of West African children in the Midlands is relevant to placements today, despite the fact that legislation and regulation have changed. An essentially descriptive study of private fostering was published in *West African Families in Britain. A meeting of two cultures* edited by June Ellis in 1978. Laurie Joshua of SCF's *African Family Advisory Service* unpublished studies and lobbying were largely responsible for the inclusion of private fostering within the remit of the Children Act, and his subsequent pressure on SSI resulted in a Department of Health funded project published by SCF on *Private Fostering: Development of Policy and Practice in Three English Local Authorities*, as well as encouraging SSI to carry out an inspection in three further local authorities.

The SSI inspection report was accompanied by *Signposts: Findings From a National Inspection of Private Fostering* which is a practical DIY manual for local authorities. Section 3 contains a series of pro forma documents to be used by social workers and others involved in hands-on practice. An earlier publication produced by the Race Equality Unit of the National Institute of Social Work *Black Children and Private Fostering* had a similar hands-on focus, with a good introduction on the issues for African children, and some pro forma tools for practitioners. The British Agencies for Adoption and Fostering, in collaboration with the CPHVA Special Interest Group, have produced two manuals in easily comprehensible language for parents considering, or who have made, private fostering placements for their children, and for private foster carers. Social workers and health visitors should encourage the dissemination and use of these manuals as an essential means of improving and maintaining the standards of care for children.

Political Philosophy and the Role of the State

The 1989 Children Act guidance on private fostering states early on that 'a proper balance needs to be maintained between parental private responsibilities and statutory duties towards private foster children.' This balance was a matter of considerable debate during the Act's parliamentary passage (see Hansard 27 April 1989), and is always open to interpretation.

The interpretation of 'private' in part IX of the Children Act was a nicety of balance and conflict avoidance: local authorities were asked to 'satisfy themselves that the arrangements are satisfactory and that the foster parents are suitable. They do not approve or register private foster parents.' They are left to decide how they can signify that they are satisfied, without actually giving 'approval'; and private carers are left knowing that they have been scrutinised, but wondering about the conclusions. Unless it is challenged by case law or altered by statute it will continue to affect what happens in reality.

Race, Culture and Child Rearing Assumptions

The 1989 Act for the first time in child care legislation included issues of race; and the

need for these to be addressed in private fostering arrangements was enshrined in Regulation 2.(2)(c) 1991: 'whether the child's needs arising from his religious persuasion, racial origin and cultural and linguistic background are being met'. The accompanying guidance recognised that the practice of some ethnic minority families in placing their children trans-racially and trans-culturally could in some instances pose a contradiction for local authorities.

Case studies undertaken by SCF concluded :

> *Most foster carers professed themselves to be free from prejudice by the very nature of the act in taking children from another ethnic group into their homes. By their comments, however, some displayed attitudes that many would regard as insensitive and others as frankly offensive: for example one told a Nigerian child that he was 'white underneath' when he cut himself. One social worker witnessed the teenage son of a foster carer making racially offensive comments to the foster children, unchecked or unheeded by the foster parent. Others, who declared themselves 'colour blind', saw no reason to keep foster children in touch with their culture and language, or to seek opportunities for them to meet up with others from their ethnic group.*

The practical aspects of caring trans-racially (such as hair and skin care, health needs, and searching out multi-cultural toys and literature) are succinctly covered by *Caring for Other Peoples' Children*. A number of studies have been undertaken during the 1980s and 1990s on attitudes to race and the emotional effects of trans-racial placements, of which Lynda Ince's *Making it Alone* is a continuation of the discussion. She demonstrates how feelings of isolation and alienation, and identity stripping can occur. For some, these feelings and processes are irreversible, preventing later identity unfolding, leaving young people confused or struggling.

The views of parents, private foster carers and children, have sometimes been found to be mutually reinforcing. There is evidence that some West African parents have considered that 'white' per se is 'good', or that their children will readily reassimilate into their racial group on return, despite minimal contact and lengthy placements; while private carers have been blinkered by the prevailing social attitudes around them.

SCF research into social workers' attitudes on private placements noted that the concept of problem frequently arose when social workers spoke about the West African parents, while the parents who commissioned the placements appeared to be satisfied with the basic care. Laurie Joshua has suggested that comparative reviews of the literature of childhood socialisation in Nigeria and Britain demonstrate contrasting and conflicting values. The British construct of abuse is primarily one of individual and familial pathology; the African one of problems of social infrastructure. Whilst British professionals inevitably operate within a British value system, they should question their assumptions and be open to understanding the values of others.

Inter-departmental Issues - Home Office Affairs

The inter-cultural international aspects of private fostering are further complicated in a small but significant number of cases of issues of immigration and criminal justice. Liaison and coordination with the Home Office (immigration and prisons sections), International Social Services, and overseas embassies and high commissions should be regarded as a matter of policy as well as of practice.

The economic and socio-political forces which bring people to Britain see individual families caught in a web of immigration law or dealings that fall outside legal parameters, and children's welfare can suffer as a result. Local authorities need to be aware, and have policies in place, to deal with the children of these families. A number of West African children are being brought into Britain on their parents' passports, but then parents return home leaving no-one with legal parental responsibility in the UK. There is no regularisation of entry and exit immigration data on this, so that it is possible for some children to become stranded with no means of tracing the whereabouts of their parents.

Parents may also be in the UK without valid visas, and who therefore prefer to keep a low profile from official bodies. Professionals may be left with the dilemma of knowing that a privately fostered child is not legally resident in the UK, and knowing that even if they do not wish to inform the Home Office, the child's

access to education and health care may possibly be restricted.

Some children in private foster care have parents in prison, often on drugs related charges. When they are foreign nationals, they may be deported or sent to serve their sentence in their country of origin. If the child's private foster placement has not been notified to the local authority, and/or the parent has not mentioned the child to the criminal justice authorities, the familial ties may unwittingly be cut. Liaison is essential between the different groups such as probation, prison staff, social services, working with the private foster carer and child, as well as The International Social Services and The Home Office to ensure the best interests of the child are met both in the UK and elsewhere.

Private Fostering and Other Aspects of Child Care in Britain

Standards and comparability with local authority care and childminding

It has already been noted that differing value systems about state intervention, race, child rearing and child protection may be subsumed within private fostering. Social workers interviewed in the SCF study spoke graphically of the differing standards in physical and emotional care and child care planning, and the tensions that this created for everyone involved.

The guidance on private fostering under the 1989 Act made some bold statements of principle and practice: 'The attention of local authority social services is drawn to the publication: *The Care of Children: Principles and Practice in Regulations and Guidance*... This will assist practitioners and supervisors to relate law to practice' i.e. the *same* principles and practice that applied to other aspects of child care; and ' The major similarity between local authority family placements and private fostering is *the nature of the experience for the child*. Specifically, the *minimum visiting frequency* by the local authority *is the same*.' (my italics). And in addition: 'Private fostering and childminding of children under eight for reward *are similar*. Both are private arrangements to care for a child and money is paid directly by the parent. The role of the local authority is supervisory, regulatory, advisory'.

However, the fact that double standards have remained, despite legislative efforts, is influenced by assumptions about parental authority. The SCF study points to the continuing dilemma:

If private fostering is essentially a private arrangement between two parties, it is predicated on an assumption that the parent(s) are actively exercising their parental responsibility and have a continuing overview of the welfare of their children. Whilst this is a correct assumption about the situation for many private foster children, it may not happen for children from abroad and/or whose parents are not resident in this country or whose parents live and work far from where the children are placed.

Child protection

The inclusion of private fostering within mainstream legislation does enable practitioners more readily to consider other aspects of the Act as applicable to private fostering, notably Part V (Protection of Children) and Part III (Children in Need). The guidance in relation to unsatisfactory care spells out the various options of the social worker vis a vis their own regulatory functions - e.g. issuing requirements, the return of the child to a parent or relative, accommodating the child under Section 20, or offering support under Section 17 of the Act. Failing these, if the child is suffering or likely to suffer significant harm, 'the procedures under Part V of the Act should be invoked immediately. This is the only way that the local authority can seek to remove the child against the private foster parent's wishes'.

In a study in one area in 1989 eleven private foster homes were **known** within a particular local authority. Amongst these homes, two care givers were over 70 years of age; several of the foster carers had experienced significant difficulties in raising their own children; two of the foster families were described by the social workers as 'multi-problem'; one foster father had a conviction for violence and another for indecent assault; two foster families had prior applications to foster for the local authority refused; one family's own child had been received into the care of the local authority. The vulnerability of privately fostered children continues to cause concern in many areas. Utting in his report *People Like Us* (1997) notes that:

Private fostering is clearly an area where children are not being safeguarded properly, indeed an unknown number are likely to be seriously at risk.

Children in need

The SSI inspection report *Signposts* specifically included a section on the relevance of the concept of 'children in need' to private fostering. It reiterated Section 17 (10) with its deliberately wide definition of 'need' to reinforce the emphasis on preventative support services. It emphasised that services to the privately fostered child should not be confined to children at risk of significant harm. Each local authority had the flexibility to determine its own level of services, but the definition in Part III could not be substituted. The local authority has the option to consider providing the person with parental responsibility with services under Section 17 to safeguard the welfare of the child, and to enable the parent to continue to look after him.

How far in fact Part III is being used in relation to privately fostered children is not clear. A telephone survey of local authorities in which it was known that there were a significant number of private foster placements was undertaken by SCF in 1992. Virtually none had included private foster children in their policy statements categorising children in need. One of the three local authorities in the SCF study amply demonstrated that Part III could be used to develop wider community resources, such as attempting a partnership approach with the private carers; encouraging them to attend support groups and providing resources to develop their understanding of the racial and cultural background of the children for whom they were caring. It is hoped that a community development approach, with family support services, will be echoed in London and other metropolitan areas from which many of the children emanate so that the need for private fostering will be circumvented.

The Future for Private Fostering

Since 1980 when SCF inaugurated its Overseas Childrens' project various groups have been formed and meetings held to encourage the relevant agencies to work together on policy and practice. Since 1993 BAAF has held twice yearly 'Practice Issues Groups' on private fostering topics. The groups have taken the form of one day low cost seminars, enabling a wide range of social workers and interested parties to get together and share notes over a raft of concerns. SSI and the Department of Health have been kept in touch with these discussions. In addition the CPHVA Special Interest Group on Private Fostering has met about four times per year. Membership of this group is not confined to health visitors, and the regular attendance of involved social workers and those undertaking occasional research has enhanced its proceedings. Fringe meetings and concurrent sessions on private fostering have been run at recent CPHVA annual conferences, raising the profile for many who were unaware of the concerns and difficulties.

The establishment in law of a registration system for private foster carers has been debated since the research of Holman who came out strongly in favour of a system similar to that for childminders. The passage of the 1989 Children Act was a prime opportunity in which private fostering registration could have been enacted. However legislators at the time were still enamoured of the **private** responsibilities of parents, and were convinced that it was they who should have full responsibility for finding placements and ensuring that their children's needs were met. As Utting has commented:

> Public policy is founded on the conviction that family relationships and family values are essentially private. So private indeed that public policy hesitated to pronounce on what they are or should be

In addition the legislators considered that a system which scrutinised placements child by child ensured that the particular needs of each individual would be met. In effect they implied that registration would be less child-centred.

The disadvantages of registration would be the financial cost, both to the nation in this major change, and to the parents, as the cost of placements would inevitably have to be raised. If registered placements were too costly there is the fear that underground placements would be made, rendering a group of children even more vulnerable. The system might not be easily workable on a local basis as users of

private foster care and the carers themselves tend to come from disparate geographic areas. Some would find a registration system overly bureaucratic for instance for British teenagers who stayed behind with family or friends in order to take their GCSE examinations when their own family moved.

Despite these objections, the advantages of registration are apparent. Parents wanting to make placements would know whom to approach, confident that there would be an honest broker. Standards could be set; there would be quality control; and training and support to carers could be offered. The system would be open to public scrutiny, and the movements of the children who disappear could be traced. Child protection issues would more readily be addressed and resolved. There would be improved liaison with other agencies, such as general practitioners and education.

It is ironic that childminding in which children are usually cared for only for a number of hours per day and in which daily parental contact is the norm is more heavily regulated than private fostering in which children are often absent from their parents for months and even years. The debate on registration will not die down. Utting has been unequivocal in his recommendations. He has enumerated the options as, firstly, to leave things as they are. This he thinks is the 'worst of all worlds' as it gives the **appearance** of safeguards which are ineffective in practice. Secondly, there could be deregulation. This would not only 'abandon children to their fate', but also be a potential 'honeypot for abusers' because of safeguards elsewhere in the child care system. Thirdly regulation could be enforced, but this would 'burden social service departments with commitments they cannot realistically fulfil'. He therefore strongly advocates registration as the only viable option. Privately fostered children:

> should have the full protection of statutory regulation...It is proposed that private foster carers should be required to seek approval and registration from a local authority before taking on any children, as is currently required in the case of childminders and providers of day care services. To do so without registration would be a criminal offence. It should also be an offence for parents to place a child with unregistered foster carers.

There needs to be a National Commissioner for Children, who, as in many other European countries, can both investigate complaints, and also, if supported by a properly staffed unit, coordinate the needs of children interdepartmentally in policy, legislation and practice. Until such is established it is highly likely that the needs of some privately fostered children will continue to fall between stools. If the Government took seriously its commitment to the International Convention on the Rights of the Child it would be wishing to make progress in this direction.

References

African Family Advisory Service. (1997) *Private Fostering Development of Policy and Practice in Three English Local Authorities*. Save the Children

African Family Advisory Service. (1993). *A Research Study into the Development of Policy and Practice in Relation to Private Fostering Arrangements In Kent*. Unpublished Study

African Family Advisory Service. (1993). *A Research Study into the Development of Policy and Practice in Relation to Private Fostering Arrangements in Hampshire*. Unpublished study

African Family Advisory Service. (1993). *A Research Study into the Development of Policy and Practice in Relation to Private Fostering Arrangements in Shropshire*. Unpublished study

Batty, D. (1995) *Caring for Other People's Children. A Guide for Private Foster Carers*. British Agencies for Adoption and Fostering.

Batty, D. and Wrighton, P. (1996). *Your Child and Foster Care*. British Agencies for Adoption and Fostering.

Ellis, J. (1978). *West African Families in Britain. A Meeting of Two Cultures*. Routledge and Kegan Paul.

Federal Ministry of Culture and Social Welfare. (1990). *Report of the International Workshop on Child Abuse and Neglect. Implications for National and International Social Work*. FMCSW,Victoria Island, Lagos

Fox Harding, L. (1991). *Perspectives in Child Care Policy*. Longman

Health, Department of (1991). *The Children Act 1989 Guidance and Regulations. Volume 8. Private Fostering and Miscellaneous*. HMSO

Health, Department of (1994). *Inspection of Facilities for Mothers and Babies in Prison. A Second Multi-Disciplinary Inspection and a Study of the Social Work Arrangements for the Children of Imprisoned Foreign National Mothers*. Department of Health

Health, Department of (1989). *The Care of Children. Principles and Practice in Regulations and Guidance*. HMSO

Holman, R. (1973). *Trading in Children. A Study of Private Fostering*. Routledge and Kegan Paul

Ince, L. (1998). *Making It Alone*. British Agencies for Adoption and Fostering

Joshua, L. (1991). Private Fostering. *The Need to Safeguard, Protect and Promote*. Talk given at the ADSS Conference, 1991

Joshua, L. (1992). *Review of the African Family Advisory Service. Consolidating for Change*. Unpublished. Save The Children

Race Equality Unit (1993). *Black Children and Private Fostering*. National Institute for Social Work

Rae Price, J. (1998). Voices of the Future. Article in *The Guardian*, 29.7.98.

Social Services Inspectorate. (1994). *Signposts. Findings from a National Inspection of Private Fostering*. Department of Health

UK Joint Working Party on Foster Care. (1998). *Consultation Document on National Standards in Foster Care*. NFCA

Utting, Sir W. (1997). *People Like Us. The Report of the Review of the Safeguards for Children Living Away from Home*. Department of Health. The Welsh Office

2.10 Safe Caring

Kate Rose and Anne Savage

Introduction

The Kaleidoscope Project was formed in 1995 as a joint Salford ACPC/Social Services and National Society for the Prevention of Cruelty to Children (NSPCC) initiative. The aim of the project was to identify needs and develop services for young people and their families where sexual abuse is an issue. As workers seconded from these two agencies, we have been privileged to have the opportunity to consider ways that a variety of needs could be met through direct and co-working, groupwork, training and consultation.

The views expressed in this article are the views of the authors and are not necessarily the views of the NSPCC or Salford Community and Social Services.

A common theme throughout the Project's life has been referrals by a variety of professionals (teachers, nursery and family centre workers and foster carers) who have been concerned about aspects of young people's behaviour. In many cases, for these children it is known, or concerns exists, that they have been sexually abused. This chapter is a result of our experiences of working with a variety of professionals in a range of settings; we seek to suggest and build a model for helping foster carers to unpack for themselves and the children they look after safe ways of caring. We suggest ways for adults to articulate and clarify why activities are done in certain ways (i.e. from mealtime and bedtime routines to more subtle activities such as hair cutting or family photos). Once activities are clarified for the adults, we propose to explore how adults can assess activities that are always OK, never OK or open to misinterpretation. Finally we consider how routines and activities can be explained to young people and how these can be checked out as having been understood. This then becomes our understanding of the concept of safe caring.

A Theoretical Basis

In order to consider the practical aspects of safe caring it is necessary to develop some theoretical basis. If we considered experiences in our own childhood, it would be easy to remember situations in which we have felt vulnerable, whether this be because of our size, our lack of language or emotional maturity to describe what we really wanted to say or feel. Indeed, many of our experiences in childhood are moulded by messages and truisms held by society generally. How many of the assumptions passed down through generations are still around today, e.g. children should be seen and not heard? Whilst we no longer say this directly to children, we need to ask ourselves how we promote children and young people having a say. How these messages are tackled within families may differ, but there are still these views within the popular press and those who have the power to influence many of the policies and decisions about children's lives. Young people in our society have less power, less of a voice and less status than adults.

For children who are looked after by the local authority there are additional hurdles that serve to increase a young person's vulnerability. Entering the care system is a significant life change experienced by young people who have most commonly experienced some form of abuse or traumatic experience. The consequence for us of abuse on healthy development is that there becomes an increased range of feelings, questions and muddles a young person must cope with and make sense of in order for healthy development to continue. However, in our experience it is these young people who often have less life skills and positive coping strategies to draw from. It is these young people who are removed from a familiar, even if abusive environment, into a world of new ways of living that need to be understood by them very quickly.

It would follow that for young people who have been sexually abused their inherent vulnerabilities are compounded even further. Suzanne Sgroi (1989) outlines that for a young person who has been sexually abused all of the following effects will be significant:

- 'damaged goods' syndrome
- guilt
- fear
- depression
- low self-esteem and poor social skills
- repressed anger and hostility
- inability to trust
- blurred role boundaries and role confusion
- pseudomaturity and failure to complete developmental tasks.

Our experience confirms Sgroi's belief that the first five effects are relevant in some way for all children who have been sexually abused. Secondly that the latter effects are additional for children and young people who have experienced intrafamilial abuse. The advantage of this framework for us has been that it allows the behaviour and personality of the child to be understood in terms of the root cause of what they are coping with. In determining what 'treatment' would most benefit the child we can make assumptions that all these issues are relevant. This framework is important in helping carers understand a child's day to day functioning. The task becomes defining within this framework which issues are most relevant for the child at any particular time.

Any child or young person who has been sexually abused will have experienced a distorted relationship.

In our experience the effects of this distortion on the young person is crucial to understand, e.g., how they understand love and affection. Further there are consequences for the carers when these children enter the care system. For the child, adapting to a new environment will be another hurdle for them to overcome.

The challenge therefore is for these systems of support to enter the young person's distorted world in a way that will take all the above into account and provide experiences and role models for positive change.

Safe Care - Setting the Scene

Given the knowledge of children's vulnerabilities it is important to consider how 'professional' carers understand these needs. When the local authority assumes a shared responsibility for children and young people, many are placed within existing family units (foster homes) or within residential placements. The 'corporate' parent is an adult-centred body. The context that the organisation creates to fulfil its duties and responsibilities are also characterised by adult thinking. For example, the making of plans for children and young people looked after often occur through formal meetings with reports, and minutes and 'chairs'. Likewise reviewing progress, and recording their successes, uses systems, language and style most easily accessed and understood by adults. The result of this is that the 'systems' we have can act to create substitute parenting that is not easily accessible and understandable to any child.

As previously suggested, given that the children and young people local authorities become responsible for are often the most vulnerable, the capacity for them to become further excluded just through the functioning of the organisation is enormous. The key as to how the corporate parent enters the world of the child lies, we believe, in a model for 'safe caring'. The facets of such a model can become the mechanism though which:

- The adults develop an understanding of the inherent vulnerabilities of the children they look after.
- The adults unpack and make sense of how their thoughts, feelings and actions impact on children.
- The adults are able to make decisions about parenting that are based on these understandings; and most importantly.
- The process that the adults use to explain their decisions to the children they are responsible for, and monitor and review the appropriateness of these decisions.

As parents we know that if we are unable to make ourselves understood to our children and they have no control or power of negotiation the outcome for parent and child is negative. This is a demanding task as parents to our own children. For the 'corporate' parent and looked after child, where the child has with them the knowledge and experience of abusive parenting, the potential for alienation is much higher.

A Model for Safe Care

Any model for safe care is based upon the adults taking responsibility for the care they provide and the experiences they offer the children and young people they look after. The process for achieving this could be described as follows:

1. *What can I assume about any child coming into my care?*

This initial stage demands that the carer has an overview of the theory around child development, attachment, grief and loss, as well as the specific effects of abuse and the general vulnerabilities of children and young people. The carer then has a range of knowledge from which they can draw in order to begin to make sense of the child's perspective, for example, there will be an impact for every child leaving their birth family. A carer's understanding of separation theory will allow them to make provision for this in their care. This is relevant not only on the first night when the child arrives, but also on a longer-term basis. For the pro-active carer, having knowledge of the theories can build their confidence to adapt their practice to meet the individual needs of the child. For example the carer might ask specifically what the child's routine at bedtime was, when the child would be seeing parents again, or what reassures the child when they are sad. Whilst it is inappropriate to expect a foster carer to be seen as a 'therapist', we should not underestimate the capacity of the foster home to be an environment to allow the child to change, and develop their potential.

2. *How I parent, and how this affects any child*

All carers have their own routines, styles, tolerances and strengths in caring for any child. In the first instance it is important that any carer understands what these are for them, and why they exist within the household. For example "We have our tea at 5.30 pm every night so that we can eat together as a family, and have the meal cleared away in time for Coronation Street". For a couple it is necessary that they also acknowledge how they parent together. This process should clarify for carers why they do what they do. This exploration then needs to extend to the support systems for the family. For example, grandparents' roles and interactions within the family. The process of doing this will inevitably lead carers to be able to acknowledge the impact for any child they look after. For example, for families where tea is eaten together at 5.30 pm there is an impact for a child who is not used to this.

3. *How does my parenting specifically impact on a child who may have been abused?*

The emphasis in the process is to bring together the carers theoretical knowledge from 1 (above) together with the personal insight gained in 2.

At this point the purpose is to evaluate a number of things:

- In any decision or task, whose needs are being primarily met.
- The impact of this on the child who has been abused.
- Identifying from this what, if anything, needs to be changed for that child. Thus creating a clear rationale for what happens in the home.

A practical framework for carers to work through has been outlined by Ray Wyre. He suggests the use of concentric circles (fig. 1.) as a way of breaking down and evaluating the families norms. The core circle represents those tasks, rules and outcomes that are always safe. For example dressing gowns are always worn over nightwear when downstairs. The second circle represents those tasks, rules and outcomes, which are open to misinterpretation, according to individual outcomes. For example, photographing children on their own. The third circle represents those tasks, rules and experiences that are never safe. For example, a looked after child sitting in the lap

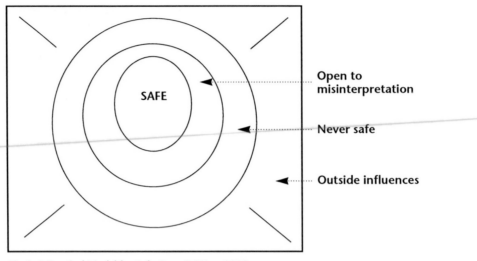

Fig.1. A Practical Model for Safe Care, R. Wyre 1998.

of a male carer for a story. Surrounding this framework are those outside influences within which we live and work, including local authorities' policies and procedures, health and safety guidelines. For example, the number of children carers are approved to look after. It is important that foster carers have a working knowledge of these.

Mapping the day to day care of children looked after, in this way, will develop a rationale for safe care. The advantage of doing this is that there is clarity about what a carer can offer a child. It must be acknowledged that professional carers cannot 'parent' a looked after child in the same way as their own children. Therefore there will inevitably be gaps for the child in how the professional carer meets their needs. The carer can be clear about what they can and cannot be responsible for in relation to the child. A wider task then becomes how those needs might be met elsewhere. For example, a child may lack a sense of physical closeness within the household. Therefore part of contact arrangements may focus on encouraging a non-abusing parent to cuddle their child.

4. How do I explain safe caring to all the children in the household, and check out that it is understood and still relevant?

The fourth stage in the process is the mechanism by which the adults become accountable to the children for everything about the household. This accountability is based on the knowledge that if children understand decisions, they are more likely to be successful and sustained. The process of developing this model also raises opportunities for children who are looked after to become empowered. For carers' own children it provides an opportunity to 'have a say' in the household. The benefit of this level of accountability is that it also fulfils the need to be accountable to the local authority. In our experience children actively seek information about their placement as this often provides them with a greater sense of security.

It is possible to break down the needs of the child for information into the immediate, short and long term. For example, prior to placement it may be assumed that a child has fairly fundamental needs. (See Appendix A). The suggestion for using this tool would be that it is completed by the carers during the process of approval and kept updated. The minimum expectation is that a social worker provides this information for the child prior to arrival at placement. (Even if it is done in the car on the way.) Secondly (using Appendix B) the worker might facilitate the child in deciding what they want their new carers to know about them. The purpose of this would be to reassure and involve the child, in the transition from home to foster care. Specific information in relation to racial and cultural heritage, language, religion and disability is included on the adult centred admission forms and in a more obscure way in this form.

Following the arrival of the child at the placement, we are aware that the settling in process over the first few hours involves a lot of information giving and receiving. This often occurs between the adults. Appendix C outlines a tool for allowing the child to enter into this discussion. In our experience a common question for young people at this time will be, when they will see their birth family again. In order to facilitate the worker acknowledging the importance of this question for the child, (see Appendix D) this form can be completed before the worker leaves. This is a mechanism by which the question can be answered in a way a child can refer back to, without needing to remember. If the worker is not the young person's longer term allocated worker, this form is still relevant as it will acknowledge the issue and identify where the responsibility for resolving this lies.

In the longer-term, where the plan is that a child is expected to stay in placement for longer than a couple of months, safe caring remains relevant and should evolve to serve the following functions:

- To check out that the child has understood the initial information.

- To continue to identify any distorted messages a young person may bring to the placement and establish ways of correcting these.

- To provide an opportunity for 'rules' and boundaries to be discussed and agreed, particularly as new situations may be presented.

- To review the understanding of the child's needs that develop over the course of the placement, in conjunction with the looked after children's documentation.

A straightforward way of doing this might be for the carer to provide for each child in the household a folder. This could include within it a number of sections:

- The information that is relevant to all members of the household (Appendix E).

- Work that comes from specific issues for that child (Appendix F).

- A record of achievements, for example pieces of work, certificates, hand and foot prints.

- Photographs, importantly those photographs that link the child's past and present experience.

- Information generated by the statutory process.

For all of these sections it is important that the child is involved in creating their own material. In our experience the discussion is as important as the end product. The aim of this is that the child has a record of their placement that they own and they can take with them, whatever the circumstances of their move. Through this process, the corporate memory can also belong to the child who is looked after.

Safe Care - Why Not?

In the process of thinking through issues around safe care for ourselves we have discussed the principles outlined with a range of professionals, including foster carers. There have been a number of responses, which have caused us further thought which we would wish to consider.

In our experience, foster carers are anxious about the possibility that children in their care may make an allegation against them, or a member of their family. The National Foster Care Association have produced a book, *Safe Caring* in response to this fear. This document is essential for foster carers in beginning to question the care they can provide. We need to acknowledge that children are abused within the care system. It is only when the perspective of the child is considered that a context for any allegation can be fully understood. We have already established that for a child coming into local authority care, they bring with them their previous parenting experiences, both healthy and unhealthy. These experiences are the framework that guides the child in trying to understand their new environment. Carers can never fully know the child's framework or how they apply it. Therefore there may be examples of safe care from the adult's perspective, which don't feel safe for the child. For example taking a photograph of a child who has been photographed for the purposes of child pornography. Given that we don't know all the child's experiences, it becomes necessary to work from the assumption that placements can never be entirely safe for the child. Maybe allegations are therefore inevitable.

For us, the Safe Care Model (Fig. 1.), provides the opportunity for any allegation to be unpacked within the context of the care provided. It also expects that carers review their practice and that the child becomes an integral part of changing and reshaping it where necessary. For a local authority investigating an allegation of abuse, the first question might be, 'did this happen' and if so, 'why and what does it mean'. Carers should be able to demonstrate what happens in a placement and why, if they have developed safe caring.

A consequence may also be, that adults who seek a vulnerable child to abuse may be dissuaded in a climate with this level of accountability. An environment in which the child has a strong voice is to be welcomed and encouraged, even where that voice is one of complaint.

Where there is a high level of accountability, there will be a corresponding level of transparency of care within the household. It would be usual for a positive care environment to be described as being underpinned by honesty, respect for each other and openness. This would be true from the adult's perspective. The question from a standpoint of the safe caring model would of course be, 'how does the child or young person know and understand that this is the case?'. Looking at this in detail will involve unpacking the norms adults may take for granted. This may feel a lengthy process, however, our view is that any extra time spent in planning and developing these issues as part of a safe care policy for a household would ultimately enhance the positive experiences of a looked after child in any placement.

There are a number of jargon terms used widely within the world of social work that we suggest carers would benefit from defining for themselves. Firstly, is the area of

'confidentiality'. How does the child know what will happen to things they reveal during their stay. Secondly, involves clarifying the issue of secrets. Whilst this word and the distortions around it are most commonly associated with children who have been sexually abused, it will impact on all children in some way. Clearly, it is impossible to have no secrets in the household. Therefore some attention to definition and explanation for everyone is useful.

Finally, concerns the issue of privacy. Again, all households have norms around personal boundaries and space. A safe caring policy will allow the child to define the boundaries for themselves around this e.g. when the bathroom door is closed, no one else is allowed to go in. An advantage of defining such terms also allows for discussion around the sanctions available should aspects of safe caring be overstepped. This allows for the reinforcing of agreed norms and messages and some checking-out that they are still relevant. This is then the spirit of openness that can be offered to children looked after.

We are aware that professional carers perceive themselves and are perceived as low status in terms of the work they do. This may be due to a societal view as well as opportunities for training and qualifications these tasks hold. As a consequence, the needed 'therapy' for a young person in the household is often obtained outside the home. We would suggest that the process of caring for a young person within the home is a vital part of the therapeutic process. Typical opportunities for carers might include: managing challenging behaviours; responding to questions and sorting out muddles; planning, preparing and responding to a child at difficult times, i.e., contact with birth parents. This is the process whereby the distorted messages, low self-esteem and confidence, worries and muddles are all dealt with on a day to day basis as a part of daily living. It may be that carers do not even recognise the significance of these tasks as part of their work, or the subtle changes they nurture in the young people they care for. Whilst we are not advocating that one form of 'treatment' is more beneficial than the other, we are aware that vital information gained both by the foster carers or outside worker may not always be shared. In our view, the best outcome for the child involves the regular sharing of information between all professionals. All work, whether formal or informal, with the young person needs to provide consistent messages to them.

A child who has been sexually abused can present particular challenges to carers in relation to their behaviour. Carers cannot take away any inappropriate sexual knowledge that a child may have. In our experience carers worry about managing behaviours in a way that is appropriate to the child, safe for others and avoids the child becoming socially isolated. For example how to manage a child who seeks to touch the genitals of adults and children. There are no quick fixes or easy solutions but breaking the process down may make it more manageable (Appendix G provides a practical way for carers to do this). If the model for safe care, explained previously is followed, carers can at least ensure that they can reduce their own fears. Carers would need to develop an understanding of healthy development, including sexual development. They also need to understand the impact of sexual abuse on that development and its relationship with the child's emotional, moral and mental functioning. In the light of this, a carer needs to review how their own norms may impact on a child. For most families, openness about the issues of sexual behaviours, sexuality and sex education feel difficult. For a carer of a sexually abused child there is the added facet of needing to correct distorted messages. It is important therefore that carers are not only clear what their own 'norms' are and how they are explained but where the gaps lie. For example, carers may not feel comfortable with providing information about anal sex to a young child. For the child who has been abused in this way, the distorted knowledge is there and they may have real worries and fears.

Challenging behaviours are often the process children use to both regain a sense of control of their confusions and work out the meaning of the experiences they don't have the maturity or context to understand. Carers will be able to provide reassurance on some fundamental messages, for example, it is wrong for adults to touch children, bodies are private, in this house no-one touches others with their genitals. The carer may also be able to provide some choices for the child in coping with their feelings, depending upon what need the behaviour was meeting. For example, 'in this house to show we like each other we…'. They can also then inform the caseworker

of the gaps for the child, they feel remain unmet and may need to be met outside the placement.

Another area of concern highlighted to us in the course of our work has been in relation to disciplining a child. We feel that if carers develop their practice along the same four-step process, the mechanisms of discipline and boundary-setting used in the household will not only be clear and understood by all members, but can also reflect the individual differences that may also exist. For example, a child whose experience of neglect was to be shut away in their room for long periods of time may not be appropriately disciplined by being sent to their room, and an alternative for that child considered and planned for.

On reflecting on the philosophy and tasks associated with safe caring it may feel like a tall order. Certainly we are suggesting a lot of thinking, discussing and planning is involved. At the end of the day we expect that few practical changes may occur within the running of any household. However, we are aware that the discussing and planning tasks may feel onerous for individual households to undertake on their own. For this reason we are suggesting that the initial process is undertaken and supported through the recruitment and training procedures of the agency. Further that an ongoing review of safe caring and accountability of practice occurs through regular review and supervision of carers, including identifying ongoing training needs. We are aware there is a current trend towards employing carers as professionals and view this positively. This is a way of both validating the role of caring for young people who are being looked after and ensuring consistency and the ongoing quality of care experienced by the young people.

Conclusion

The aims of this chapter have been to provide some practical solutions to the process of clarifying, assessing and checking out activities within the home. This then forms a discrete safe caring policy for each household.

In our experience, the time and energy involved in developing safe caring practices within the foster home is an essential component of care for children looked after.

We understand the principles of safe caring to be relevant in all settings where children live, learn and play. We have introduced this safe caring model and considered its practical application not only with foster carers, but also in nursery and residential settings. We would hope the potential is even wider still. Some of our ideas have come directly from our involvement with young people and foster carers themselves and has been shaped by their views. If the priority, as central government has suggested, is to safeguard against future abuse within the care system and to ensure that children who are looked after have positive experiences, we would advocate that safe care policies and practice must become the norm.

References

National Foster Care Association (1994) *Safe Caring*, NFCA 7067

Sgroi, S. (1989) *Handbook and Clinical Intervention in Child Sexual Abuse*, Lexington Books, USA,

Wyre, R. (1998) Model used with permission from lecture given to a Conference on Professional Abuse on 11 March

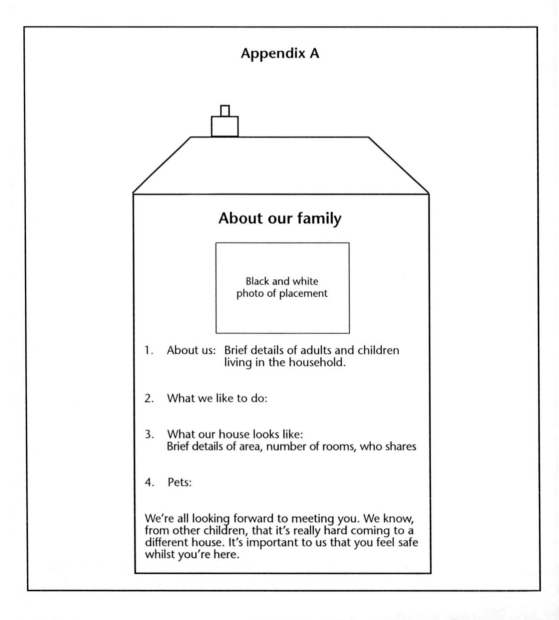

Appendix A

About our family

Black and white
photo of placement

1.   About us: Brief details of adults and children
living in the household.

2.   What we like to do:

3.   What our house looks like:
Brief details of area, number of rooms, who shares

4.   Pets:

We're all looking forward to meeting you. We know, from other children, that it's really hard coming to a different house. It's important to us that you feel safe whilst you're here.

Appendix B

Stuff ABout Me

What I want to be known as (called) ....

The important people in my life are ....
(Family, friends, other adults)

My family links are ....

The language I most like to talk in is ....

What food I like ....

(Tea/breakfast/supper)

....

Dislike ....

I have strong beliefs about ....

My favourite TV programme ....

My best game ....

To look after me properly you need to know that I have to :

Go to bed at ....

E.g., wear glasses when ....

Take medicine at ....

(Anything else)

....

The most important thing I've brought with me is ....

What I've not got now that I need is ....
(i.e. Roller blades, Mickey Mouse sweatshirt)

What I need to happen if I'm:

Scared ....

Sick ....

Sad ....

Silly ....

(Anything else)

....

What can be done to make it OK tonight ....
(i.e. foster parent, social worker, parents etc.)

At bath time I

....
(i.e. wash myself, need help, don't wash hair)

At bed time I

....
(Need light on, don't like 2 pillows)

If I wake up at night

....

Questions I have are ....

....

Appendix C

What Does a Child Need to Know

Where will the young person sleep?

Where will the young person keep their things?

Who lives here?
- What does the young person call us?
- Who lives long term and who is passing through?
- Who do I go to for different worries?

Basic needs and routines - eating/bathing/bedtimes etc.

What would the young person like to know about me and the family?

Acknowledge with young person they may feel different, but not have a way of talking about this yet.

How do I explain to others why they live here?

Acknowledge that there may be some things that might need to change over time to suit the young person.

Boundaries, rewards and punishments. (What they need to know today).

Reinforcing there are no secrets in this house.

Practical stuff:
- School
- Friends
- Contact (Ref. Appendix B 'Stuff About Me').

Appendix D

My name is   ....   (Worker placing child)

Your social worker's name is   ....   (If different)

Phone number   ....

You can phone me   ....   (time, when)

You can see me/social worker will contact you next on   ....
(Explain time age-appropriately, i.e. when it's daylight next)
You will speak to/see again (mum/dad/siblings/gran etc.)   ....

On   ....

You are living with   ....

At   ....

Because   ....
.
For   ....   (time)

On the next school day, i.e.   ....   you won't be going to school.

Or, you will be going to school and   ....   will take you and collect you.

Appendix E

This section needs to reflect the current practice of safe care within the house. Some examples may be:

- Routines: including bathing, transporting, meals, bedtimes etc.
- Physical contact: between adults and children; how we comfort children; boundaries during play.
- Privacy: general boundaries and guidelines, e.g. toileting.
- Sexualised behaviour: boundaries that exist in the house.
- Discipline: the range of sanctions that are used within the household.
- Health and safety: for activities about the home, coping with emergencies, i.e. fire drill.
- Visitors to the house: understanding and commitment to the households safe care practice.
- The fundamental messages that underpin everything that happens in the house (mission statement).

This might also include broad issues of respect, judgements, morality, language, culture, religion. There also needs to be more specific messages for children who are looked after; i.e. being in care is not their fault; not the only one; not replacing/in competition with birth parents; it is right that plans are made with them about their future.

Appendix F

This should reflect the individual needs and solutions for the child/young person raised during the course of the placement. For example:

- For a child who bedwets - the immediate management together with reassurances of actions for the causes, i.e., we will talk together to Jean, our health visitor.

- Identify what the child needs to happen to cope with the feelings they may have after contact.

- Healthy expression of individual feelings as alternatives for the child.

Appendix G

Managing Behaviour

We frequently receive referrals from colleagues with regard to challenging behaviour of a young person. For example, a foster carer reporting that a young person is smearing 'all the time'. What is often useful is to have an accurate description of what actually is being talked about. A framework for breaking the process down is offered through answering the following questions:

1. What is the behaviour that is of concern?

2. What is the **frequency** this behaviour is exhibited, - daily, weekly, time of day, any patterns or routines?

3. **How long** does this behaviour last?

4. What is the **intensity** of the behaviour - is there any distress, is the young person in control, what need does it meet?

5. Who else is involved and what is their reaction?

6. What happened directly **before**?

7. What were the **consequences** - what happened after, what did you do, what did the young person do?

8. What are all the possibilities for **why** a young person might behave in that way?

9. Why does it bother you?

10. What are the long term consequences if this behaviour does not change?

11. How can this behaviour be managed in the short term?

Analysis/Understanding of Behaviour

List all the reasons you can think of why a child might behave in this way:

Why does it bother me?

What will happen if this behaviour does not stop?

What can I do now to make a difference?

What help/support do I have?

Behaviour:

Frequency: Day   Time   Duration

Intensity:

Others involved:

Triggers:

Consequences:

2.11 The Role and Work of the GAL

Cathy Caine

Introduction

The term 'guardian ad litem' (GAL) is a legal term for a person appointed by the court to represent the child's interests in court proceedings.

The guardian has a special position in relation to the child, because it is the GAL's responsibility to safeguard and promote the welfare of the child, and to ensure that the court is informed of the child's wishes and feelings. The GAL is professionally independent from other parties and works impartially with parents, carers and professionals at all stages of the court process.

In Scotland when an application for adoption is made a 'curator ad litem' may be appointed. Adoption cases may be heard in the Court of Session or more usually in the local Sheriff Court. At other times where a child's case comes before a children's hearing, a 'safeguarder' may be appointed.

Much of the work of these two groups are similar to the role of the GAL. Further information may be found in *BAAF Practice Guide (Scotland)*; Lexy Plumtree, *Child Care Law in Scotland*; *The Children (Scotland) Act 1995, Regulations and Guidance, Volume 2, Children Looked After by Local authorities*; *Greens Annotated Acts, Children (Scotland) Act 1995*, Norrie. K. McK.

Appointment of GAL

Foster carers most often meet with GALs who are involved in proceedings issued by the local authority social services department for a Care or Supervision Order, or an application for an order in respect of a child who is already the subject of a care order, e.g. contact order or freeing order.

Whatever the application, the GAL will be appointed by the court from a panel of GALs. The panel of GALs will be largely made up of experienced social workers who are not employed as social workers by the local authority making the application. This is set out in regulation, in order to obtain an independent professional opinion of the child's interests, and how these can best be met. In making an appointment, the court will take into account as far as possible the child's ethnicity, culture, first language, and gender, if sexual abuse is an issue. Sign language and other communication skills may also be relevant for the child or family members, and some GALs may have these skills. Occasionally, the child may be represented by a GAL from a different culture, or one who is unable to communicate directly with the child, e.g. due to lack of sign language. In such cases the GAL will probably request assistance from another professional familiar with the child's culture and language.

If the child has had a GAL in previous proceedings, efforts will be made to appoint the same GAL to offer some continuity to the child, unless there are specific reasons against this.

The same GAL is usually appointed to represent all the children in the family who are subject of proceedings. The GAL has a duty to look at the interests of each child separately, in addition to the children's shared interests due to their family relationships. Because children's needs and experiences within the same family may differ, plans for each child may be in conflict, in which case the court may consider appointing a separate GAL for a particular child.

The GAL is appointed for the duration of the proceedings and the role finishes when the final order is made. The GAL has a duty to advise the court about the need to avoid delay in the proceedings, unless it can be shown to be advantageous to the child.

The Child's Solicitor

The child has a legal representative in the same way as other parties to the proceedings are legally represented. The GAL will appoint a solicitor from the Children Panel (solicitors with experience of children's work), to represent the child's interests in court. The solicitor will take instructions from the GAL about what is the best plan for the child, taking into consideration the child's wishes and feelings. With an older child who has good understanding of the proceedings, if the GAL and/or the child's solicitor find significant conflict between what the child wants, and the GAL's view of what is best for the child, the solicitor will represent the child's views and the GAL will continue to present an independent view to the court about the child's interests. The GAL may bring the solicitor to meet the child at the fosterhome, or arrange for the child to visit the solicitor's office.

Safety Issues

The GAL should show their identification card on the first visit, along with the letter of appointment from the court. As with any professional visiting a child, it is important that the child feels comfortable talking to the GAL, but is not cut off from support during meetings. The age of the child and the rapport built between the child and the GAL will influence how all concerned will consider how best the child can feel safe, and make arrangements for the foster carer to be easily accessible should the child feel uncertain.

For many children who have been abused, the bedroom may not feel a safe place to meet with the GAL. The child may wish to show the GAL around the house, but meetings will usually take place in a 'public' room with the door open, or perhaps walking in a local park.

The Child's Agreement to Assessments and Examinations

During the course of proceedings, the child may be asked to take part in medical or psychiatric examinations, or other assessments. The person, usually the social worker, arranging the examination will explain to the child the purpose of the examination and what it will involve. The GAL is responsible for advising the court on the key issue of whether or not the child has sufficient understanding to refuse to take part in any examination or

assessment. This is not solely related to age, but depends on the child's ability to grasp the issues and the potential long term consequences for themselves, of agreement or refusal. The GAL's assesment of the child, and discussions between the child and the GAL about the issues involved, will influence the GAL on what to advise the court. Painful issues, such as tests for genetic disorders and AIDS, justify lengthy consideration and heart searching for all concerned.

Some assessments are done 'on paper', which means that the nominated expert evaluates the information recorded by other professionals, and draws their own conclusions, without any face to face contact with the child.

The GAL and the Child

To prepare an independent report to the court about what is best for the child, the GAL has to:

- gather information about the child
- evaluate whether the child has suffered significant harm (if appropriate to the application)
- assess what the child needs
- assess whether the person or people with parental responsibility are able to meet the child's needs in the long term
- evaluate the care plan prepared by the social services department, and the alternative plans put forward by the parents or any other parties

The GAL also has a specific duty to advise the court on the child's wishes and feelings.

The process of gathering and analysing information about the child and family usually involves interviews with the people who have played a significant part in the child's life.

- Interviews and meetings with the child.
- Interviews with the parents and other significant relatives and friends.
- Examination of records about the child and family, held by the social services departments and other agencies.
- Interviews of professionals who have been involved with the child and family; and may include people who have cared for the child in the past.

- Obtaining expert opinion on factors relating to the child, the parents, or the proposed plans (sometimes).
- Observation of contact between the child and the parents or proposed carers (sometimes).
- Research into particular factors eg genetic disorders (sometimes).

Each GAL is different. There are no procedural guidelines about how the GAL carries out their work in preparing their report, beyond court requirements and professional ethics. GALs may manage their workloads in varying ways, and do the GAL work alongside other employment.

The issue of being independent, and being seen to be independent, may also have an impact on GALs behaviour. As part of their efforts to act impartially, a GAL may not give very much feedback in response to information or news. Lack of reaction does not indicate that a GAL does not value and consider what has been said by the child or the foster carer. Equally, a GAL may be unwilling to put forward an opinion until late in the proceedings, when information from all the significant people concerned has been considered.

Meeting the Child and the Foster Carer

Most GALs want to meet with the child early in the proceedings, and so start to learn about the child in every respect. The GAL will usually write or telephone foster carers within a few days of their appointment to introduce themselves to the child and the foster carers, explain their role, and arrange an initial meeting with the child and the foster carers.

GALs should offer written information about their responsibilities to the child, which should include how to contact them, and the address of the panel manager, in case there are any concerns about the GAL's behaviour.

This early stage of the proceedings is of special importance if the child and family have been recently separated. Research indicates that the chances of successful reunification of a child and parents reduce significantly after a separation of six weeks. The GAL will want to find out from the child and the foster carer,

how the child was feeling and behaving on arrival, what changes occurred over time, and the experiences they had relating to contact with family members. If the child seems to be finding the changes hard to cope with, this observation should be reported to the GAL (as well as the social worker), and the plans and visits may be adjusted to assist the child.

With a young child or baby, the GAL will be making direct observations and asking questions, to learn from the foster carer and the child. If a child is able to speak or communicate through play, most GALs will also plan to work directly with the child, to seek to understand the impact of their experiences, their needs, and their wishes and feelings about the important people in their life. Some children are unable or unwilling, e.g. through fear or divided loyalties, to express their feelings directly, and it may not be possible for the GAL to build a relationship of sufficient trust for this work to take place.

It is helpful to everyone if working boundaries are negotiated, for contact between the GAL, the child and the foster carers, bearing in mind the task the GAL has to do. If the child and foster family have a routine for contact visits, leisure activities, meals, bath times, bedtimes, the GAL should be told so that as far as possible the child, the GAL and the foster carer may make mutually satisfactory arrangements for meetings. For example, a surprise visit by the GAL in the middle of the child's birthday party is usually most unwelcome.

It is helpful to clarify who the GAL wants to meet, so that appropriate arrangements can be made, e.g. a quiet room for direct work with the child or a private conversation with the foster carer about the child's behaviour when the child is at their playgroup.

Continuing Work Between GAL and the Child

Although the GAL will explain their role to the child at the outset, it is helpful if the foster carer is able to reinforce the explanation, should the child become confused. Because the GAL needs to find out what the child wants for the future, and the GAL can be seen as a very powerful person, the child can feel let down when their wishes appear to be unheard, or court proceedings are extended for many months.

It is likely that direct work with the child will be concentrated in the early weeks of the proceedings, so that the GAL can make the necessary assessments.

When this work is largely completed, other factors in the proceedings may have an impact on the GAL's activity, and the GAL may not need to visit the child so often. For example, if one of the parents enters an alcohol rehabilitation unit for a three month programme, the GAL may not be involved in lengthy meetings with the child, but may want to keep in touch on a monthly basis.

At turning points in the proceedings, e.g. when there are changes in the parents ability to care for the child, or fresh information indicates a need to change the care plan, the child and the foster carer may hear the same information in two versions, from the social worker and from the GAL. If this causes confusion, it is advisable to clarify the facts with the social worker, and the GAL, and explain what may happen as a result. This may have an impact on what the child wishes, and so the GAL will want to listen to the child's views, and the foster carer's observations.

The GAL may accompany the child for a meeting with an 'expert' appointed by the court, to give an opinion on some aspect of the proceedings.

The child may have anxieties about contact visits and other meetings, and worry before and after meetings which involve the GAL. It is important that the child knows that the GAL wants to understand about the child, and that the child does not have to 'please' the GAL or other professionals. The child should understand from the GAL what their situation is, and what the GAL is doing for the child.

The Final Court Hearing

In the last few weeks before the final court hearing, the social worker has to prepare the care plan, and the GAL must write the final report. The GAL will discuss their recommendations with the child, and record the child's wishes and feelings. These reports will be distributed to the parties, by the court.

Before the final hearing, the GAL will talk to the child about whether or not they wish to go to court. Some children may wish to see the court room and learn what happens in the

court. They may wish to listen to the whole process, and learn what is being said. Although children may want this experience, it is not generally thought by GALs and other professionals, to be in their best interests, and some judges will refuse to allow the child to stay during the hearing.

There may be a conflict between the child's rights, the parents' rights, and the court's desire to carry out its business efficiently. In addition, most professionals would want to prevent the child from reliving painful past experiences.

At the final hearing, the court (i.e. the judge or magistrates) will decide on what court order is appropriate, if any. This may determine where a child lives and with whom, and may make future contact arrangements.

The orders are unlikely to contain any surprises, but the child or the foster carer may not understand the court's decisions or reasons. This can be a difficult time for a child who was hoping to go home, or to have some certainty about the future, and it may be hard for the foster carer to reconcile their own views. The GAL will usually make a final visit after the hearing to explain what happened and the reasons why, and to wish the child well for the future.

It is the social worker's role to continue working with the child, and the family placement social worker may be able to offer support to the foster carers if the outcome of the proceedings causes distress.

Concerns About a GAL

If the child or the foster carer has any concerns about the GAL (e.g. lack of contact, unreliability, behaviour), they should usually speak to the GAL directly and seek an explanation and a remedy. If this feels too difficult, or the concern is more serious, the child or the foster carer may contact:

- the child's solicitor
- the social worker
- the panel manager for the GAL

The priority will usually be to resolve the problem so that the GAL can complete their work to a good standard. However, on rare occasions, if the GAL's integrity is in question, and/or the GAL is discredited in the court, the court may make an alternative appointment of a GAL for the child.

Arrangements for Panels of GALS

Panels of GALs are in place around the country under a variety of arrangements. Some are managed by the local authority 'at arm's length', others are grouped under a single management on behalf of several local authorities, and some are managed by voluntary organisations. Whatever the arrangements, the regulations which set out to achieve independence from social services departments apply. GALs may be salaried, or work on a self employed basis. In either case, they are required to submit returns detailing how their time is spent on each case. Panel managers are required to monitor the work of GALs against national standards, and use a variety of mechanisms to carry out this task, including feedback from courts, complaints, reviewing court reports, and case returns giving details of their work.

Panel managers make training available for GALs on a range of issues, including communicating with children.

If foster carers want more information about the work of GALs, a GAL or panel manager can be invited to speak at a foster care association meeting.

Recent Developments

In July 1998 the Department of Health, the Home Office, the Lord Chancellor's Department and the Welsh Office, published a consultation paper entitled *Support Services in Family Proceedings - Future Organisation of Court Welfare Services*. This paper proposes combining the three current services which represent children's interests in family proceedings under one unified service. This would include as one service:

- probation officers who act as court welfare officers in private proceedings
- the part of the Official Solicitors Department which represents children's interest in proceedings with unusual circumstances (such as those with a substantial foreign element)
- guardians ad litem

It is suggested that this national organisation would offer greater flexibility to represent children's interest, according to the needs in family proceedings and more national access to legal representation.

At the time of writing, the deadline for consultation on this paper has not been reached. It is anticipated that there would be a considerable lead-in period because of the necessity to change the law to enable these proposals to be realised.

References

Health, Dept. of (1991). Patterns and Outcomes in Child Placement, HMSO

Health, Dept. of (1996). Reporting to Court under the Children Act, HMSO

Health, Dept. of (1996). Implementing National Standards, DH

Health, Dept. of (1991). The Children Act 1989 Guidance and Regulations, volume 7 Guardians Ad Litem and other Court Related Issues, HMSO

Health, Dept. of SSI (1995). What does it mean for us? The Findings and Key Issues Arising From an Inspection of Four GALRO Panels October 1994 - January 1995 , DH

Health, Dept. of (1995). A Guide for Guardians ad Litem in Public Law Proceedings under the Children Act 1989, HMSO

Liddle, C. (1992) *Acting for Children* The Law Society

Lindley, B. (1994) *On the Receiving End* Family Rights Group

2.12 Child Protection

Sue Cart

Introduction

Child Protection is a highly contentious area of interface between public, professional and political tensions. This has been most recently informed by the publication of *Child Protection, Messages from Research* (1995), produced by the Department of Health.

The emphasis that children in need of protection are on a continuum of children in need, and that there should be a change of emphasis which embeds investigation within family support. It has greatly influenced current thinking and future policy.

Background

The aim of statutory agencies is always to try to support the child within their family. In most cases this can be done by the provision of support services. The child protection route is one way of providing the support if the parenting has fallen to an unacceptable level below that which can be tolerated.

Agencies work with many more families and provide help without the risk of the child ever reaching a dangerous level.

Child abuse is an emotive subject; one about which almost everyone has a view. Society and individuals are quick to judge. Expectations of statutory agencies change over time and on occasions intervention is criticised for being extreme, with the apparent inappropriate early removal of children; or too lax as in cases when children were not removed from home and died at the hands of their parents or carers.

The reality is that it is impossible to totally predict human behaviour; some parents neglect their children out of ignorance but would never intentionally harm them. Some threaten to hurt their children but do not do so; other people hurt their children without any predicting factors.

There is no crystal ball which distinguishes between those that hurt their children and those that do not, therefore children can never be totally protected and sadly children will continue to be harmed and some even die at the hands of their parents.

There is a responsibility on everyone to report concerns about the safety of any child to a statutory agency quickly. In order to do that people need to be able to recognise abuse, to accept and understand it is harmful and to have some idea of what is likely to happen as a result of the reporting.

You may as a member of the public recognise that someone is harming a child in some way. Alternatively a foster carer looking after a child who has been abused previously may have to deal with the aftermath of that abuse, or when a child makes a new allegation that they have been abused, child abuse will come to the forefront of the carers mind. The impact of this information will depend on one's own personality and life experiences

Most people grow into adulthood without any knowledge or experience in their personal life about child abuse; others will have been victims themselves and it is a sad fact that some will go on to become abusers. People who abuse children are from every social strata, culture and religion, they may be male, female, within the family, a friend or stranger. There are some common themes in the backgrounds of abusers but no predictors and it does have to be acknowledged that the majority of children who have been abused grow up to become extremely caring, and protective of children as a result of their previous experiences.

The aim of this chapter is to look at the different types of abuse, at the child protection procedures and the role of the foster carer, in caring for an abused child. An abused child is a hurt child, usually caused by the actions of adults. Child abuse is not a new phenomenon but the recognition of it and how we respond to it has changed over a period of time. Society as a whole has gone through a process of recognising the plight of the abused child and we as individuals go though a similar process. In the 1800s children were the possessions of their parents and were not recognised as valuable individuals in their own right. Children went up chimneys to clean them or worked in factories; their care and safety was not at the forefront of people's minds as it is now, but gradually the florid symptoms of physical abuse were identified.

Types of Abuse

Physical abuse

Physical abuse was first identified in 1868 when the 'battered child' syndrome was described in Paris. Doctors recognised and reported that children were being battered and injured deliberately rather than accidentally. It was difficult initially for society to believe that physical injuries were being caused by deliberate acts or non-intervention on the part of parents or carers and it was felt that they must be caused by some deviant outside the family or that the parent and carer had inflicted them when drunk or drugged. Gradually it became clear that parents **were** hurting their children and physical abuse was recognised and acknowledged; children were removed from the parents in extreme cases and the parents were prosecuted.

Failure to thrive

The next stage was a recognition that some young children were not growing and developing as they should, either because they were not being fed or because they were being neglected in other ways with their physical and care needs not being met. This phenomenon brought about the recognition of a state categorised as 'failure to thrive'.

Emotional abuse

Another reason that children were not developing properly was because they were being emotionally abused or rejected. They did not receive stimulation such as positive talking to which would be reciprocal and encourage them to be animated, did not receive praise and encouragement but instead denigration and sarcasm. Some parents had a distorted view of what their child was capable of and had expectations far higher than a child can achieve, putting unfair pressures on them.

All of this maltreatment can severely adversely affect a child's emotional and behavioural development and can seriously distort their personality and their growth. This type of abuse is more difficult to identify because the wounds and scars do not show externally. It is necessary to carefully observe behaviour to elicit evidence of whether this type of abuse is occurring, or has taken place.

Neglect

Some children are neglected. They have not been held, rocked or cuddled to give physical comfort or groomed for physiological comfort and to feel proud about themselves. Children who are being neglected may become listless, apathetic and careless about their own safety, they may not grow properly, be clad properly, or receive any necessary medication or treatment. As with children who are being emotionally abused, they may become withdrawn or alternately aggressive, or seek attention by inappropriate methods. They may crave attention and respond positively to anyone, even strangers, without being circumspect and having a healthy wariness of strangers.

Sexual abuse

A further type of abuse which is as damaging as any of the others is the sexual abuse of children and over the past few years society has begun to recognise that children are being exposed to pornographic material or being engaged in, or exposed, to inappropriate sexual activity. It can be identified by:

- direct reporting - the child told someone
- indirectly observing behaviour that the child demonstrated
- their drawings
- through something they say
- medical symptoms
- pregnancy
- changes in demeanor or presentation.

Children can suffer a number of different abuses at the same time.

As mentioned previously, we as individuals go through a process of recognition of abuse. A range of feelings and sympathies can be elicited ranging from disgust, revulsion, anger and not wanting anything to do with the abuser to indifference, incredulity, shame, sanctimonious righteousness and judgement. We can positively reframe these feelings, become resigned, accept that it has happened and try to achieve some understanding and tolerance towards the abuser as an individual whilst being horrified by their actions. This is the double bind that children as victims often have to endure; loving the person but hating and not understanding what they are doing. As people working with children we go through this cycle of feelings every time we have to care for children who have been subjected to abuse; however we should also acknowledge that these feelings are normal and they should not stop us positively helping children. One never, ever, becomes 'used to' child abuse or inured to its effects; it is a fact of life that we have to accept. If it does begin to distort our ability to protect and care for children then it is important to share this with someone.

Recognition of Abuse

The identification of child abuse is the key factor in our ability to protect children from its re-occurrence. The categories of abuse detailed in the previous paragraphs may happen either separately or together, some children are physically abused; others may be sexually abused as well and will suffer some emotional trauma as a result. The children may become more vulnerable because of the grooming processes involved in past abuse; therefore carers need to be alert to indicators of abuse and seek immediate advice if this is noticed. Foster carers should be given information and training to help them to identify signs of abuse. They also need to understand the increased vulnerability of the children they foster, and know how and when to gain advice and support. Physical abuse often leaves marks and is therefore more easily identified; but children also sustain bruises accidentally. If they have bruising in areas which are unusual, or multiple bruises or bruises caused by an

implement then these may need to be brought to the attention of the social worker. The bruising may have been caused accidentally or by other children; or there may be a medical explanation; it will need to be checked and no one will be criticized for pointing it out. In fact quite to the contrary, as the child's carer, allegations may be made against the carer and by taking a proactive stance carers are reducing the possibility of that happening.

Bite marks, burns, scalds and fractures should always be drawn to the attention of the agency when they happen. The carer and whoever has parental responsibility need to know what is happening to the child; these are all significant events that need to be recorded and the cause may bear further exploration. A child who is regularly bruised may be un-coordinated in some way; their eyesight may need testing but it does need to be explained. It is particularly important to note marks or signs when a child has been away from the carer and to let the agency know; it may be that the child is being bullied at school and marked as a result. If they are being re-abused during contact with their previous abuser, the carer is likely to be the first and only person to note the signs either by marking or in their behaviour. Time is of the essence as some marks, for example bruises, can disappear within 12 to 24 hours.

Some indicators for sexual abuse have been mentioned earlier and they and the other types of abuse can cause children to display signs of post-traumatic stress disorder. These may be flashbacks (sometimes triggered by a sensory image or smell) when they re-experience the feelings when they were being abused or they may have nightmares, gaps in memory, sleeplessness, depression, anxiety or guilt.

It is really important when caring for abused children that during initial contact, a carer asks permission before touching them, that their privacy is respected, that they are treated with respect and dignity as people with rights of their own; the carer is then beginning to reconstruct them as whole individuals. Carers should listen to their views and wishes, explain things wherever possible, use appropriate praise and boost their self-esteem. Children may have lived in families where domestic violence has occurred and family rows may assume inappropriate significance. One important aspect of fostering abused children is to remember they have learned mal-adaptive behaviours and need to re-learn what is appropriate. In order to help them and to protect carers from allegations, there needs to be very clear 'house rules', not just for abused children but for all children in care. For example, no-one should ever walk around undressed, everyone should wear dressing gowns as a minimum and this should be normalised by the explanation of warmth, privacy and the wearing of slippers as well.

Sometimes when carers hear a catalogue of abusive incidents that have occured to a child they will wonder why the child never told anyone in order to stop it. Maybe they tried and no-one believed them or listened to them; maybe there was no one person that they could trust to tell. They may have been living in fear of harm to themselves, their brothers and sisters or their pets. Children are very suggestible and easy to convince that some imagined threat will come true. Very young children have vivid imaginations.

The abuser may have used other emotional pressures saying that they would go to prison and the whole family would suffer as a result, which may have happened; alternatively they may twist what actually happened in order to make the child believe that they instigated the abuse or caused it in some way. The child may receive some gift or apparent benefit from being abused and feel it is their fault, and if they tell it is they who will get into trouble. Abusers often have a natural way of inveigling themselves into the lives of children and seducing them into being abused. In some families the abuse may have started at a very young age and become the norm in their early life; because they do not have the knowledge that abuse is illegal and unacceptable they are unable to recognise that what is happening is wrong and to report it to anyone. What carers must always reiterate to the child is that it is never, ever the child's fault. They could never possibly have been responsible for what happened even if they were given a reward; children are used to being told what to do by adults and that the abuser knew that and used it to their own advantage.

Disabled children are particularly vulnerable to abuse due to their dependency; because they may need to be cared for in a variety of settings by a variety of carers (which in itself can be abusive). For those with communication difficulties their inability to convey what is happening to them increases their vulnerability. They can be abused without intent by carers if they have, for example, ill-fitting callipers, if they receive too little or too much medication, if they are forcibly fed or restrained, if their personal care is carried out without privacy or if they are over protected or under stimulated.

Procedures and Practice

There is a solid legal framework intended to protect children which is kept under regular review and amended from time to time. The most recent piece of legislation which is in force now is the Children Act 1989, which places a statutory duty on local authorities and organisations such as the NSPCC to investigate when they have any suspicion or receive an allegation or disclosure that a child is suffering or is likely to suffer significant harm. This is not an optional power, they have to investigate, it is a legal duty and the focus is on the safety of the child.

There are also good practice guides and procedures based on the Department of Health guidance. All agencies such as police, health, social services and education, are required to co-operate in child abuse matters.

Allied to this is a responsibility on each and every one of us to make sure children are kept safe and to act immediately if there is any information that all is not well with a child, even if the information is passed on anonymously. The earlier the statutory agencies are alerted the quicker action can be taken to protect the child; abuse rarely stops without some form of intervention and it usually gets worse. Intervention at an early stage can often prevent its re-occurrence and certainly should prevent it worsening.

In 1972 *The Memorandum of Good Practice on Video Recorded Interviews* was published which gives guidance to be followed when interviewing child victims for criminal purposes. This describes rules of evidence and social workers and police officers are specifically trained in order to ensure they are complied with. Many areas now have specially equipped video suites with video cameras, two-way mirrors and medical examination rooms on site in order to minimise the investigation process by reducing the time and distress to the child.

Recent legislation has also been enacted to ensure the whereabouts of convicted paedophiles are known to the police, following their release from prison.

It is tempting to think that child abuse is rare but sadly it is not. Local authorities collect statistics about the prevalence of child abuse and in March 1998 there were 2.8 children in every 1,000 who were on a child protection register. About 100 children a year die as a result of an identified deliberate act; many others suffer lasting incapacity.

Statistics indicate that most abuse happens within the family group, and in the majority of cases where children are killed the perpetrators are parents, but a number of abusers are foster carers. However good the checking and screening process, it is a sad fact that some children go on to be abused in their foster home.

When information is passed to a social services department there are set procedures drawn from Department of Health that must be followed; these guide the process and are intended to ensure that the investigative and assessment process is thorough without being insensitive or damaging.

The procedures are formulated by a multi-agency working party, the Area Child Protection Committee (ACPC) which is comprised of senior members of all the key agencies involved in protecting children. These may be social services, education departments, the police, health authorities, probation, and NSPCC; district councils are represented, and sometimes the armed forces. The ACPCs parameters encompass the local area: they not only maintain current child protection procedures but also develop local policy and inter-agency training. Their purpose, in addition to the above, is to prevent abuse and to develop treatment strategies. They also convene in-depth reviews when children are severely injured or die as a result of child abuse occurring in their area, or if there is an element of public interest, to ensure that learning from the incident can be promulgated.

It may be helpful to know about the process that is followed when an individual case is investigated. If someone is caring for an abused child they will have been involved throughout and if they refer an incident of abuse then they need to know what will happen, why and within what time frame.

All referrals of child abuse are taken very seriously; as has been said earlier there is a statutory duty on certain agencies to investigate and the pace of this is dictated to some degree by the urgency that the risk poses. Whichever agency receives the referral, contacts social services. If the child is in acute danger then the police can be called and they will respond immediately in order to protect the child. They have the power to implement police protection and to stand over a child to prevent a child from suffering further harm or to prevent them being removed from where they are, such as a hospital bed, or they can remove them from danger to a safe place such as a hospital, police station or children's home. They must leave a note explaining where they have taken the child. This action is time limited and if the child remains at risk then an Emergency Protection Order (EPO) can be applied for via a magistrate. Anyone can apply for this order but in practice it is usually a social worker, the NSPCC or occasionally a police officer. The applicant explains to the magistrate why they believe the child is in danger and the magistrate can then make an order for up to eight days which determines where the child shall live for that period and may include other directions such as requiring that the child undergoes a medical examination. If the parent or person with parental responsibility does not accompany the applicant when they lay the evidence before a magistrate, then they can apply for the EPO to be revoked after 72 hours; the magistrate will review the original evidence, consider what the parent or person with parental responsibility has to say and decide whether the order should be rescinded or not. At the end of the eight day period the order can be extended for a further seven days or another order can be applied for. The EPO is permissible, it does not have to be actioned. If, for example, the alleged abuser moves out of the household and the alleged risk is removed, then it may be that the child can remain at or return home and the order may not require implementation.

When it is learned that a child has been abused, a checking procedure is instigated which includes a check against the child protection register and against the social services department client index to see if the child or family are known. The health authority is contacted; as families are registered with GPs, they may have valuable information about the family or can advise on the approach to the family. If the child or a related child is of school age then the school will be contacted. The police will check their records; they may have been called to incidents of domestic violence occurring within the family or know of criminal convictions. The probation department may also hold valuable information on adult members of the household. The housing department may know who lives on the premises and whether they have rent arrears indicating possible financial stress. Mental health and substance abuse teams may be aware of issues relating to the adults.

All of these checks involve two-way consultation so that relevant agencies are alerted to concerns about the family and even if the investigation does not proceed further there is a heightened awareness and vigilance.

A meeting may be convened between social services and the police to plan the joint investigation including approaching the family, interviewing the child or children and any suspects and planning any medical or legal action that may be necessary. The first the carer may hear of all this, is if the allegations are serious and the foster carer is contacted at this point, to prepare them to receive the child should it prove necessary to remove them from home and impossible or unwise to place them with their extended family which is usually the placement of choice.

The timing of the approach to the family is particularly crucial as it is important not to pose any further risk to the child or other children in the household but also to maximise any opportunity to collect uncontaminated evidence.

Interviews of children may begin at this point but may continue once the child is in foster care. The subject child is interviewed, if old enough, as will other children in the household who may be victims or witnesses. The interviewing team collect as much information about the child as possible prior to the interview including details of their family, their routine, behaviour, friendships, and developmental age vis-a-vis their chronological age. This will ensure that the language, style and approach to the interview is age appropriate.

The timing of the interview is important to ensure the child is fresh, not in need of a meal and at their best possible state of mind. Very young children have short attention spans, teenagers are easily embarrassed so it is important to pace the interview and use language on a scale appropriate to the child. The interviewing team will include a police officer and social worker who are specially trained at putting children at ease and they will try to ensure that the experience is as cathartic as possible.

The interview may be investigative focusing on a particular incident or be a broad based assessment; it may be recorded on video for future care proceedings, criminal proceedings or as a baseline from which a treatment plan can be composed.

The interviewers will note very carefully what the child actually says and what effect the disclosure has on them. If a child being fostered is interviewed, the interviewing team may ask the carer to accompany the child and they may be asked to watch the interview through a one-way screen. The interviewing team should reassure them that they have not done anything wrong, are not in trouble and that they (i.e. the interviewing team) will try to stop it happening again.

If the child has been sexually abused they may talk about things about which one would normally be reticent and this can bring out feelings of the carer's own sexuality, sexual behaviour and experience. With physical abuse or neglect one can sometimes identify to some extent with the abuser; this is much more difficult with sexual abuse. Carers may feel embarrassed or angry, and it may bring back memories of difficult experiences. The child has had to face and endure these things, it is not their fault and they will need all of the carers compassion and reassurance to deal with this. When they return the carer should stay calm and respond in whatever way seems right, go at their pace. They should be told everyone is glad that they were able to tell what happened and now people will try to stop it happening again. Carers may be asked to record anything further the child says in relation to the alleged abuse and the interview.

When the child does begin to talk again, as is likely, carers should not prompt or stop them, they should listen but not question them.

Carers should write down everything remembered as soon as is appropriately possible. They should not raise the subject if the child does not bring it up.

The child may need a medical examination either for evidence or to make sure they have no infection or injury that needs treatment. Specialist medical examiners who are practised in examining children in such situations are used, and may be able, to reassure the child that they are whole, not injured or infected.

If it appears that the child is still at risk of significant harm a case conference will be called. This is a discussion with everyone involved to identify clearly what the risk is and what action is needed to reduce it. Everyone present will be asked to say what they know about the child; the parents may be present and the child too if they are old enough to understand what is going on. Carers may be asked what the child has said, done or drawn and how they are after contact for example. It may be helpful for carers to go through what they wish to say with their keyworker beforehand. When all the information has been collected then it will be evaluated and a decision made about whether the child is at risk of significant harm and if so, whether they should be included on the Child Protection Register (CPR).

This is an 'alert' list of children living in the area for whom there are unresolved child protection issues and for whom a child protection plan is necessary to keep them safe. The child's name will be registered under one or more of the categories, physical, emotional, neglect or sexual abuse. A social worker, will be appointed to co-ordinate the plan and members of agencies who can contribute to the plan will be delegated specific tasks. A contract will be agreed with the parents with specific objectives and tasks in order to reduce the risk within a specific timescale. Children cannot wait long for parents to effect change; their future stability and security needs to be assured. If parents do have the will and ability to alter their life style or child care practice they will do so very quickly and it will then become clear whether they can sustain the change. It may be that they undertake to undergo anger management training, or to reduce their alcohol intake and to be tested by urine samples. The health visitor may agree to weigh a young child regularly and to report any drop in weight to the keyworker; school may monitor a child's attendance and punctuality. The social worker, assisted by other professionals, may be tasked to conduct a comprehensive assessment of the family in order to take a more in depth look at their strengths and weaknesses; to identify what change needs to, and can, occur.

The plan needs to be clear, objective, achievable and conducted within a set timescale, perhaps with a caveat for non completion or a contingency plan. The plan will be reviewed at a review conference, three to six months after the initial conference although it could be convened earlier if necessary. At the review conference reports will be tabled to indicate what change has occurred and the plan may need adjustment. If the situation has greatly improved the child's name could be removed from the CPR. In extreme cases, if change is not achievable, then the child may not be able to remain at home and they may move to an alternative family within the extended family, to a foster home or children's home. Details of all children on the CPR are shared between statutory child protection agencies in order to heighten awareness and vigilance. The GP will be aware so that if the child presents at surgery, they can pay special attention to the reason for the visit; similarly hospitals will be alert and details will be fed back to the keyworker, who will maintain a composite picture of what is happening to the child, from core agencies as well as from the child and family. Children remain on the register for an average of a year and rarely beyond three years.

If a child's address changes the keyworker notifies all attendees of the conference so that the child's whereabouts are always known. If they move out of the area then a transfer conference is held to move the responsibility for the child and alert agencies in the receiving area.

Sometimes when there is concern about a baby that is to be born, a pre-birth conference is held to evaluate the risk and they may decide to put the child's name on the CPR at birth.

Conclusion

Risks to children are many, and in recent years we have become more aware of the impact on children of domestic abuse. They may be at physical risk if they intercede or are present when it occurs; they may be neglected or at emotional risk if they hear it going on and see the effect on their parents. Substance misuse and alcohol misuse are factors which can impair parenting. Parents with mental health problems or a learning disability may unwittingly put their child at risk.

The aim of statutory agencies is always to try to support the child within their family; in most cases this can be done by the provision of support and services. The child protection route is one way of providing the support if the parenting has fallen to an unacceptable level below that which can be tolerated. Agencies work with many more families and provide help without the risk to the child ever reaching a dangerous level.

In theory it could be assumed that most children look towards the foster family as providing a stable background for the first time in what may be a very long time. This is more heightened in children who have been systematically abused be it physical, sexual or emotional over a long period of time. However, it should be noted that children who have been abused and have suffered horrors that can only be imagined, may still feel that their own family is the most appropriate place for them rather than the foster family. They may view the foster home as a potentially hostile environment as opposed to a friendly one, whereas other children will seek the relief that a foster family can offer.

There is no normalisation about what will happen and foster carers should be aware that both of these behavioural traits can occur. It has been already mooted that foster carers may have to accompany the child through harrowing recollections of past abuse which can equally traumatise the child again, and for that matter the foster carers too who may well be listening to the disclosure.

The role of the foster carers is never easy; accepting children into their home who have had traumatic, abusive experiences is a challenge. The problems are not to be underestimated, but abused children can be healed if carers can live through the healing with them. In doing this they are not alone. They should have the right training, preparation and support and be prepared to seek professional advice and guidance to a greater level and extent than perhaps previously. Their contribution to helping an abused child can be immeasurable.

References

Falkov, Dr. A. (1996) *Study of Working Together 'Part 8' Reports*

Health, Dept. of *Children and Young People on Child Protection Registers Year Ending 31 March 1998 England*

HMSO *Children Act 1989*

HMSO (1992) *Memorandum of Good Practice* London

HMSO (1991) *Working Together Under The Children Act 1989*

Tardieu, A. (1868) *Etude Medico-Legale sur L'infanticide* Paris

2.13 Preparation for Adoption - Promoting a Child's Identity

Marion Burch

Setting the Scene

When we properly prepare children for adoptive placement, we hope that we are giving them and the new family the optimum chance for a successful outcome. It seems reasonable to suppose that the child who is given the opportunity to reflect on their previous experiences and feelings and anticipate their recurrence will, with support, manage them more easily and form attachments more readily. As workers and carers perhaps we need to ask ourselves this question: 'Is it right to expect a child to make a commitment to a new relationship without knowledge of their past and with unresolved issues remaining?'

We know that children within the care system quickly develop a multiplicity of negative feelings which can cause emotional damage in the long term. As caring adults, it is our responsibility to confront these and provide the information that will answer the often unasked questions: Who am I? Where did I come from? Why am I in care? What will happen to me?

A child has the right to know about their origins and the reasons for their separation from their birth family. We cannot absolve ourselves from this responsibility by rationalising that the child is not asking questions and is therefore not concerned. Neither can we use the excuse that we do not wish to burden the child with knowledge of events from the past or cause more pain. We are in fact failing in our duty to take **total** care of the child by denying them this information. Children are often unsure whom to question and what to ask. They are also frequently anxious about the answers.

It is hard for a child to hear painful facts about their birth family's inability to care for them but the truth, however painful, dispels fantasies and myths. It relieves a child from feelings of guilt and responsibility which they may carry as a result of adult behaviours. When we are honest with children we make it easier for them to accept their family as they are with their strengths and frailties.

Children feel deeply but we often minimise these feelings. We rarely consult or even debate issues with children even when they directly affect them; we only inform. Generally as adults, we are very poor at listening to their views or taking them into account.

As a result of this, children can become adept at concealing their feelings and accumulating 'emotional baggage' which moves with them but remains unresolved. We need to give children 'permission' to express their feelings. They need to hear us say that it is all right to cry and to be reassured that we will be nearby to offer comfort; they do not have to shed their tears in secret and alone.

We need to tell children that it is acceptable to feel angry and that we will be there to help them manage these frightening feelings in a safe way. We must let them know that we recognise and acknowledge their deep feelings of sadness and pain. It is such a relief to a child to know that their grief is accepted and understood. When their behaviour is less than it might be or babyish, they will not be ridiculed or cajoled into 'acting their age'.

We need to let children know that it is normal and natural to want to talk about their birth family and previous carers and that they can do so without any fear of critical or judgmental remarks. Self knowledge increases self worth and two positive ways in which we can promote this and prepare the child for an adoptive placement is through Life Story Work and by the use of Non-directive Play. These methods can give a child the opportunity to reflect, consider and express their feelings in a safe way and in a safe setting with the worker's support. Then we can help them to develop strategies to manage difficult feelings in anticipation of the next and hopefully final move.

Promoting a Child's Identity

Unless we help children in care to retain their identity it is very quickly lost. We all have a need to belong and feel accepted and children can become adept at finding ways to achieve this. One way might be to call the current carers 'mom' and 'dad' and look upon the other children in the family as brothers and sisters. This can cause confusion and the words 'mom' and 'dad' can lose their significance, particularly if the child has had a number of moves. It is important to re-establish a child's identity before asking them to accept another. For some children a change of name is exciting but for others less so. A new name can make a child feel that they are losing their last links with the birth family. One child described this feeling as "like being swallowed up". He was relieved to hear that he could, if he wished, retain his own surname and incorporate it with his new one.

We tell children that they are going to be 'adopted' but we need to explain what this really means. They need to hear that it is only their name which will change; they will still be the same. When children don't understand, they become anxious, frightened and resistant to change.

One way in which we can help children to grasp the meaning of this new word 'adoption' is to compare it to a marriage. People who love and care for each other can get married. They go to a special place such as a church, temple/mosque or a registry office. People who love and care for a child want to be a family. They go to a special place to adopt their child. A special person marries people. A special person makes the adoption - a judge. Married people have a special piece of paper with their names on which says they are married and that the wife may change her name to that of her husband - a marriage certificate. Adopted children have a special piece of paper with their name on it which says they are adopted and that they have changed their name to that of their new family - an adoption certificate. This information can be illustrated with pictures and drawings for the child.

Another way of promoting children's identity is to take them to visit the ward of the hospital in which they were born and by taking photographs and notes from the obstetric records to put in their life story book.

We can share and explain information from the child's birth certificate and those of any brothers and sisters and help the child to understand any omissions or differences. Children can be shocked or surprised to learn that parents were unmarried and that their mother is a common-law wife. This is the time to help a child to understand the meaning of words such as half brother/sister, step brother/sister, parent, separation and divorce.

We can demonstrate some of this information by drawing a family tree. The conventional way is often too complicated for a child to understand. A more simplistic but meaningful way is to draw trees with apples on, choose a colour each for the birth family, foster and adoptive family and writing the names and relationships on each apple. Then add the child's apple in their own colour. This visual aid will help the child to understand their 'beginning' and where they 'belong' and to see that they are only a temporary member of the foster family.

On the adopters' tree, the child's apple can be half coloured with the colour from the birth family and half with the adopter's colour. In this way we can reinforce the message that 'the children are who they are'; they have joined another family but their birth family will always remain a part of them.

The following case study involves loss following death. While this is not typical of children and young people in foster care, the range of emotions that can be experienced following separation are similar for all children and young people.

Michael

Michael was six years old. His parents divorced when he was two and contact with father ceased at that time. His mother, Jean, had one sister named Kay who had two children, a girl aged seven and a boy aged eight. There were no grandparents. Michael and his mother had a close, loving relationship.

Jean befriended Harry, her next door neighbour who lived alone and had retired from work early due to ill health. Jean shopped for Harry, checked that he had his medication and invited him to her home for meals occasionally.

Michael was very fond of Harry and called him 'grandpa'. In return for Jean's kindness,

Harry looked after Michael when Jean was at work.

One Friday evening Jean was admitted to hospital. She was seriously ill and one week later she died. On Sunday Auntie Kay went to Harry's house and said that she would take Michael home to live with her. Michael did not attend his mother's funeral as his aunt did not think this was a place for children. He was not involved in the family grieving. His aunt felt that he needed protecting from this pain and distress - these were private adult feelings.

Michael was well behaved for the first six weeks then his behaviour began to change. He refused food. He broke his cousin's toys. He refused to go to bed and started having nightmares. He wandered around the house during the night and got up very early. He became aggressive, shouting at his aunt and fighting with his cousins. When he finally hit his aunt, it all became too much for her. She contacted social services asking for help with Michael and he was placed with a foster family.

We need to consider how Michael's feelings relate to his behaviour and what practical help we can give him and children who, like him, are suffering separation and loss. Ideally preparation for a move begins from the first day of placement in foster care. Most children move in a state of anxiety, shock and disbelief without preparation or introduction to the new carers as Michael did. We must not repeat this mistake by expecting children to be ready to move three weeks before they meet their new family.

Children need time. Time to consider, absorb and reflect upon painful and complicated information which will have to be repeated and expanded on over a period of time. The facts must be recorded by the worker so that they are available as the child's life experience broadens and they are able to consider the information in greater depth.

We all know how difficult it is to manage silence when we are left waiting. Yet we do this to children. We avoid sharing issues with them and remain silent. Then we expect children to manage the angry and frustrated feelings that build up until they explode into difficult behaviour as Michael's did. Michael's aunt believed that she was acting in his best interests when she excluded him from his mother's funeral and the family grieving. She

was unable to make the connection between this lack of recognition of his intense feelings and his behaviour. Michael needed to be involved; he had the right to be involved in this major loss in his life.

We need to involve children in the plans for their future. We need to tell them how decisions are made, by whom, where and when and record this information for their life story book. It is not difficult to explain the composition of a case conference or an adoption panel and it's purpose. We can talk about the work of the court and how the 'wise person', the judge will make the choice about where we live, with whom and why. We need to say when we begin the search for a new family or meet one. Even if the result is disappointing, it is better for a child to know than to feel excluded. Children deserve our respect. We must learn to trust them and not underestimate their ability to survive.

Often children in care have few personal belongings and what they may have can be judged as valueless or outgrown and thus disposed of without their permission. Sometimes we put pressure on a child to relinquish a possession. This is unfair, whatever the possession, an old toy, or a shrunken jumper, it is a part of that child's past. It may be the last item bought for them by an important family member.

Even if the child voluntarily says "I don't want this any more", it may be kinder to pack it away safely with a note giving relevant personal information rather than lose a precious memory. When we thoughtlessly throw things away, we deliberately lose part of the child's identity forever. By doing this we can make that child feel that their past is irrelevant and unimportant.

Michael moved with few personal possessions but he was able to return to his home to collect them and other things to remind him of his mother. He was fortunate enough to have family photographs. One of his fears was that he would forget how his mother had looked.

This is a fear echoed by many children who are only able to recall hazy memories of people and places. When the family or previous carers are unable to supply photographs, we may have to resort to cutting out images from magazines for life story books in order to give children an idea of how they might have looked; what toys they might have had and what sort of cot and buggy they might have used.

Michael was abruptly moved from all that was familiar to him. He needed to visit his old school, meet his friends and most important of all, see Harry again.

We must give all children the opportunity to re-visit people and places of their choice to gather information, to take photographs and say proper goodbyes. Michael was taken to say 'goodbye' to his mother, place flowers on her grave and have photographs taken.

He went to the hospital to meet the nurses who had cared for his mother and this was written down for him. Harry held vital information about Michael's mother during her lifetime and in the week leading up to her death. These together with Michael's own memories were all written down as were Auntie Kay's memories of Michael's mother as a child and teenager. His aunt also had vital information about Michael's birth and his parent's divorce which were recorded for him.

It was important for Michael to know why his aunt was not able to care for him and to be reassured that it was not his fault he had to move. It is equally important for all children to know why they have been separated from their birth family and the reasons for moves within the care system. (Readers will be pleased to know that our latest news of Michael, is that he is doing well both academically and on the sports field.)

The best people to help with personal family history are parents and family members; they know what the children will need to know as they grow up. When we interview families, patterns of parenting are often revealed giving us clues as to why the parents were unable to meet their children's needs. We can diplomatically share this with the child.

Sometimes we can only obtain information from the case files. This is helpful but often limited. However it is better to have a limited edition of a life story book than no book at all. Writing a life story book (sometimes known as a 'Life Book') is much too big a task for any child or young person but they need to be encouraged to contribute. It is after all their book, not ours.

When we write sensitive information, we have to write with compassion and be aware that a life story book may be shared with parents or family members in later years. Information must be handled with understanding, not anger and condemnation.

Making a Life Story Book

Feelings

The idea of making a life story book can frighten some children. They fear that confidences shared with the worker may be repeated to parents or carers. They fear that they may be rebuked for ongoing feelings of loyalty and love for their birth family and that their sense of loss will be misunderstood. They also fear that the book will be no more than a list of their family's shortcomings.

We can reassure children about the contents by showing them a sample life story book belonging to another child (with that child's permission). We can offer them the opportunity to talk to another child and hear how understanding the past can bring a sense of relief and well being.

As adults, we may have reservations and feel anxious about delving into a child's past. We feel concerned that this will cause difficult behaviour and increase problems for the carers. Sometimes children do regress but this is part of the healing process and, at this time, they need compassionate understanding and acceptance from their carers in order that they can move on emotionally.

We may find that some teenagers can be very resistant to reflecting on their past and making a life story book. In spite of this attitude, it is very well worth while collating the information and preparing the book without their co-operation; few of them are able to resist learning more about their circumstances and the book can be left for private perusal in their own time.

We may feel concerned that children may be damaged if we burden them with knowledge of their past. This is not true: children who do not understand their life story suffer the most. Their 'acting out' behaviour, indifferent attitude to carers, family, school and life in general can be difficult to tolerate for those involved with them and can cause disruption of their placement and repeated moves.

Often it is the first opportunity a child has been given to voice their feelings and to be heard. We can begin to repair the damage that separation and loss has caused and help them along the path of healing.

The making of a life story book is not to be undertaken lightly. Never underestimate the amount of time involved; it is helpful to plan to use time effectively and delegate responsibilities. When we search for information we can find that we have opened up new areas of work. We may discover that the process of bereavement and the feelings of guilt and anger felt by parents and relatives have not previously been addressed. We may even find that a new plan evolves, restitution not separation.

When we are making a book on behalf of a very young child, we must make every effort to seek out important firsts; first smile, tooth, words, steps, etc.. Otherwise this information can be lost forever which is sad for the child and also the new family.

While we are gathering the information, we can arrange to have 'non-directive' play sessions with the child and begin to establish some rapport. The child may begin to share aspects of their life with us. It may not be in chronological order but at this stage, this is not important. What they tell us can be written down and put in the right order later when the child's life is less chaotic.

The worker must feel confident about working directly with the child and convinced that making the book is a worthwhile venture. We must also be committed to completing the task. We must not begin a book and then abandon the work as this is disappointing and damaging to the child.

We must remember that the book belongs to the child and therefore it is private and not to be shared with anyone without the child's permission. It may be wise to help the child to agree that an adult will keep the book safe for them. Though the child has right of access, they really need support when they look at the book as an outburst of emotion may result in its destruction. It is better to err on the side of caution and photocopy information and photographs in case.

We need to protect the birth family's privacy too and it is wiser to place personal information in one ring binder and photographs in an album which can be safely shared.

When we are making a life story book with a child from another culture, it is our responsibility to include information about the family's country of origin. It is also important that we are aware of different religious celebrations and rituals connected with birth, death and marriage. In this way we can show respect and not inadvertently cause offence through ignorance or arrogance.

Planning

The first point we need to consider is who will work with the child and who has the time to make this commitment, the social worker, foster carer or an independent person? It may be preferable to have two people; one to write the story and one to offer non-directive play sessions. Whatever is decided must be acceptable to the child.

The workers will need support as this kind of work can invoke painful memories long since buried. Who will give this support?

The next major decision is to choose a venue where the work can take place. Privacy is important and sessions need to be conducted without interruption. The right place might be a room in a nursery or family centre. They may be able to offer the use of suitable equipment, e.g. sand and water play and a 'home corner' which might not be available in an office setting. The child's bedroom is not the right place to use and the child may feel restricted in the foster home.

Usually sessions take place for one hour each week on the same time and same day. This consistency is important. Children usually like to know how many sessions are being offered. It is reasonable to suggest ten sessions with more if the child needs them. The majority do and they can continue for some considerable time.

We next need to consider the best time of day for the sessions. The child should be taken out of school as little as possible but experience has shown that morning or early afternoon is best as most children are too tired after school to deal with difficult and painful issues. Children may be less forthcoming and may resent being restricted to one room for an hour. Also it will be only a few hours until bedtime and it is not helpful to send a child to bed with worrying thoughts on their minds. We need to negotiate with the school, nursery or playgroup and explain that the child might be less emotionally stable at times and will need an understanding approach if they become distressed.

We need to decide who will be responsible for obtaining relevant certificates and other information, copies of reviews, court orders, case conference recommendations and anything else which will contribute to the child's understanding now and in the future.

We must decide who will contact birth parents to explain the making of the book and request their help. In this situation a personal letter is often more effective than one type written on official headed paper. If the worker is not the social worker, all correspondence must be vetted and copies kept. It is a sad fact that birth parents will often respond more favourably to someone they deem 'neutral' than to a social worker. This also applies to interviews to gather information. We then need to decide who will do these visits and who will take the child to visit people and places of their choice and other visits not chosen by the child but which hold important memories.

We need to be aware that making a life story book can be an expensive venture with a number of costs. These include the purchase of the album and binder, the cost of certificates, films and their development, play and other equipment and travel costs. Suitable funding must be made available to complete the work.

Guidelines for the worker

We all devise our own way of making a life story book. This will vary according to the age and needs of the child. It is important to be familiar with the story as soon as possible. If we stumble and change the information, it can lose its impact and importance.

We need to feel comfortable and confident when we work directly with children. We can help ourselves with this if we plan and practise how we will impart painful and sad information. While some typewritten information, reports, court orders, etc., must be included, the book itself is best hand-written. This gives a personal caring touch. The story itself must be written at the age and stage that the child is at now. We can explain this at the beginning of the book, saying who we are and how we came to be involved with the work.

It is not helpful to write 'jargon' and we may need to write three little words instead of one

long one. We can use exploratory language, e.g. the judge being the 'wise person' and we can explain the responsibilities of a social worker, Guardian ad Litem. If we need to make a sensitive reference e.g. to sexual abuse, there is no need to be explicit but it is important to open the door to communication between the child and the new family.

We can give the book a very personal feel if we incorporate the child's own expressions wherever possible and write about amusing things they have said or done. Funny little habits, bedtime routines, celebrations, holidays, first days at school, playgroup - all these will help the child to 'own' the book.

It is useful to include dates of illnesses, admissions to hospital, immunisations and the doctor's name. Also pen pictures of friends, family pets, favourite teachers and foster family members who have become special. We can include local maps to identify homes where the child has lived, schools, park and other important places which will remind the child of their time in that area.

All children benefit from a variety of approaches and this is of particular value when working with children with some forms of disability and or communication difficulty. We can consider using pictures, videos and audio tapes and computers and also use foods, perfume, objects, toys, etc., to promote the senses of taste, touch and smell and hopefully memories.

Siblings need their own life story book and photograph album. The books must hold personal information. Some of their life events may have been shared but it is not good enough to present children with identical copies. Children of different ages have their own perception of events and their own memories.

It can be useful to bring siblings together for some sessions but essentially they need to receive individual attention. Also it is very difficult to concentrate and respond meaningfully to more than one child at a time.

What can go into the book

Apart from information in the book and pictures in the album, we need to keep as much personal memorabilia as possible on behalf of the child. When they are fortunate enough to have a considerable amount, it may be more suitable to put it into a 'treasure box' rather than pockets in the book.

The following are examples of what could be kept: Christmas or other religious festival cards, birthday cards, letters, party invitations and examples of school work. Hand and foot prints, a snippet of hair, clinic information, height and weight charts, school reports as well as other official documents, medical and legal information.

We may need to put some documents in a sealed envelope to be given and shared in the future when it feels right to the adoptive family.

We must remember that the book is a cornerstone on which to build and we may only be writing the first few chapters. What is certain is that the content grows in importance as the owner grows in years. The aim of all this work is not to 'fix' the child or magic the past away but rather to offer help that heals. A life story book encapsulates the child's past, gives back a sense of identity, builds confidence and self-esteem and encourages attachment.

Communicating Through Non-directive Play

The aim of non-directive play is to give the child the opportunity to explore and express their feelings through the safe medium of play. We need to establish a warm, friendly rapport with the child so that they feel comfortable and at ease, uninhibited and free to really play out how they feel.

It is a very special time and the worker is there to give undivided attention to the child, not to ask questions or have conversations but to observe and participate if requested. We are there to help the child to recognise their feelings and to reflect them back in such a way that the child gains insight into their own behaviours, thoughts and feelings. We have to trust the child and believe in their ability to solve their own problems if given the opportunity.

Many children have difficulty in using language to say how they feel but can, by using toys, painting pictures, shaping dough and using puppets, express themselves in a safe way in a safe environment with a trusted adult. The child will go at their own pace in their own way. We must follow but not lead or direct. Play sessions belong to the child.

The toys are placed around the room ready for use. There are few limitations in this kind of play situation but we need to tell the child that they must not destroy the toys, deface the walls, break windows or deliberately hurt themselves or us. The child is free to use any of the equipment for as long or short a time as they choose. A child will sometimes check out if it is permissible to swear or use rude words.

We need to remind them that this is a 'special play time' which lasts for one hour and the child will be told five minutes before the session ends. We must not expect the child to tidy up but to leave the room exactly as it is at the end of the session. The room may be in chaos, toys having been thrown, paper ripped, paints mixed up and pictures thick with dark coloured paint. All this is indicative of how the child is feeling.

Children may use a cardboard box to represent a prison, painting stripes on the outside to represent bars and then putting the worker who represents the unprotecting parent or perpetrator who needs punishing inside. This kind of play can give messages and clues about the past which the child may never have dared to reveal before. If available, a soft play area is an invaluable place for a child to act out feelings, particularly anger.

It is useful to make notes of all the sessions as this can help us to monitor the child's progress and, with the child's agreement, it can be helpful to the new family to share some of this information. It helps to give the family a deeper understanding of the child who is about to join them. The worker should have strategies in place to help the child cope with their feelings.

When we are making a life story book with a child from another culture, it is our responsibility to select carefully play materials which do not inadvertently re-inforce stereotypes. Dolls are not always white; not only men drive cars. Children need images and information that challenge racism and gender assumptions to help them develop an accurate understanding of the world in which we live.

Saying Goodbye

The introductory period may be our last opportunity to exchange and receive personal information about the child and the new family. It is often small issues which worry children the most. They need answers to these questions before they move.

The child will be struggling with a turmoil of feelings during these last few days; excitement, sadness, fear and anxiety. We must continue to offer strong support as the child anticipates the inevitable feelings of separation and loss. We must endeavour to make the transition from one family to another as smooth as possible.

It is important to ensure that children say proper goodbyes to all the people who have played an important role in their life. This can be difficult for some children. They may feel embarrassed or worried that they may cry and look foolish. They will need our help and encouragement to organise this. Families will have their own ideas on how to manage this and make it meaningful.

One way which appeals to many children is to share a cake - a 'loving and caring cake'. These words, candles and the child's name are put onto the cake. Each candle represents a person who has loved and cared for the child. The ceremony of lighting the candles may take place at the foster home or the cake can go with the child for their first tea as a permanent member of the new family. It seems significant to celebrate and welcome the child into the new family in this way. It is in some respects a 'birth' into the new family.

A list of names can be given to the family to suggest the order in which the candles might be lighted, naming each person. The first will be the birth parents, then siblings and so on until the last of these will be the new family. The birth family's candle flames will be lower than those of the new family; their candles will be tall and bright but none of the flames will have been extinguished showing that 'loving and caring' goes on no matter where we are. This is a symbolic way of linking the past with the present and the future.

So our child is ready to move with the life story book which may already have been shared with the new family at an earlier meeting, perhaps a gift from the foster family, maybe a video recording some of their life to date, all their possessions and our good wishes.

Preparing a child for adoption is perhaps the most rewarding and satisfying piece of work which one human being can do for another. It is to be commended to all those who have the time, patience, understanding and determination to undertake and complete this worthwhile task.

References

Axline, V. *Play Therapy*

Fahlberg, V. *Attachment and Separation* BAAF

Fahlberg, V. *Child Development* BAAF

Fahlberg, V. *Helping Children When They Must Move* BAAF

Fahlberg, V. *The Child in Placement Common Behavioural Problems* BAAF

Jewett, C. *Helping Children Cope with Separation and Loss* BAAF

Macaskill, C. *Adopting or Fostering a Sexually Abused Child*

Oaklander, V. *Windows to our Children*

Working with Children Practice Series 13 BAAF

2.14 Men who Foster

Simon Newstone

Looking after children is not seen as gainful employment, and society has a view that men don't nurture, that it is not 'macho' enough'

(words of a foster father)

When I've asked foster fathers directly - either one to one, or at workshops and training events - what it is that they enjoy about fostering, their responses are often ones that most parents, and many non-parents, will recognise:

seeing the progression of a child towards adulthood

seeing children asleep and safe, feeling protective

when something works out right for the child, such as a move to an adoptive family

caring for children and feeling emotional

Many of these men, however, acknowledge that it was at their wife or partner's initiative that they first considered fostering. Many add that they view their wife or partner as 'the main foster carer'. In any case, I am told, social workers and fostering officers nearly always assume that the man's role is primarily as a support to his partner in the tasks of foster care.

In this chapter the term foster father is used to differentiate between the male and female care.

There are between 17,500 and 23,500 men currently fostering in the UK - that is, men who have been formally assessed and approved as foster carers (on the basis that estimates of the number of foster families vary from 20 - 27,000, and that there are proportionately more two parent families fostering than there are two parent families in the general population - 87.5 per cent compared to 79 per cent). What we know about these men who foster is recorded in few places, and often they seem to be overlooked in research. Bebbington and Miles' detailed study of 2694 foster homes in 1990 tells us that the median age of foster mothers is 47 (compared to 37 in female carers across the general population), and provides a range of other demographic information - such as number of bedrooms, and ages of own children - but omits the ages of foster fathers.

The expectations upon men who foster can appear ambiguous, reflecting wider social tensions between the providing and caring roles of fathers. When a social worker complains that they never get to see the foster father, the message is that they expect the foster father to make himself more available. When a foster father complains that social workers' visits are at inconvenient times, or that correspondence is only addressed to his wife or partner, he may be saying that he expects more effort to be made to include him.

The guidance on assessment of foster carers identifies that both male and female prospective carers are subject to assessment, and does not specify gender roles - it refers to 'the principal care giver', who could therefore be a man, a woman, or a role shared by both. Training and support is to be delivered to 'the foster parent', and again gender is not distinguished. Yet despite a drift towards more sharing of roles, it is indisputably still the case that more women than men in the UK are full-time primary carers, and that more men than women are full-time employed outside the family home. Given this context, it is still apparent to many involved in foster care that men have acquired an increasing role and profile, and should not be presumed to be the passive supporters of female partners (and in a minority of cases are the sole carer, or the one who is based at home).

Men are under the spotlight more, and their participation as foster carers is coming under scrutiny. Whilst many assumptions are still made about the role of women - as primary carers, as organisers of the household, and as the person with whom social workers will liaise - and whilst many of these assumptions reflect reality in some households, the roles men are taking on as foster carers seem to me to vary greatly. Some men who foster describe themselves as having a primary caring role, whilst others speak of themselves as supports to their wives or partners. There are single men approved as foster carers. In my discussions with foster fathers it has been helpful to acknowledge some aspects of the wider social context for childcare, and to acknowledge that this inevitably affects attitudes towards men as carers, including foster fathers' own attitudes towards their fostering role.

How Involved are Fathers in Childcare?

American-based research into two parent families in the wider society indicates that the extent of fathers involvement in their children's care, relative to mothers, varies according to the mother's employment status and the type of involvement. Where the mother is unemployed, a father's engagement (i.e. direct one to one interaction with children) averages 20-25 per cent of the mother's; where the mother is employed outside the home, the father's engagement rises to 33 per cent. Where the mother is unemployed, a father's accessibility (i.e. being physically available to children) averages 33 per cent of the mother's, rising to 65 per cent when the mother is employed. Maternal employment, however, seems to have no impact on responsibility - even when both mothers and fathers are employed for more than 30 hours/week, the amount of responsibility assumed by fathers tends to remain negligible. Responsibility is defined as 'a perception of responsibility for ensuring that the child is appropriately cared for at all times rather than simply being available to 'help out' when it is convenient. Responsibility includes:

- participation in key decisions
- availability at short notice
- involvement in the care of sick children
- management and selection of alternative childcare.

UK research echoes these findings. A study of 6000 parents funded by the Joseph Rowntree Foundation in 1996 suggests that two out of three fathers regularly worked unsocial hours in the evening or at weekends and that mothers, even if they also worked outside the home, still carried most responsibility for childcare, as well as cooking, cleaning and other household chores.

If we accept these findings as broadly true (i.e. not telling us anything about individual men in specific families, but giving a general picture of society), then it is worth asking what factors might encourage or deter men from taking more responsibility in childcare, as well as going on to ask a more fundamental question - what, in any case, are the advantages to children, especially fostered children, of more involved fathers?

Influences on Fathers' Involvement

Research suggests four main influences on a father's involvement in childcare:

Motivation - The individual desires and goals of fathers regarding time spent with children are affected by personal experiences of childhood as well as cultural pressures and expectations (these dynamics are clearly recognised in the current standard assessment tool for applicants to foster - the BAAF Form F).

Skills and Self-Confidence - Men sometimes express regret that a lack of childcare skills hampers their involvement and closeness with children, and point to the greater ease and competence of women in this area. The degree to which sensitivity and self-confidence are in fact innate rather than acquired is debatable. Certainly, fathers who have been primary carers since their children were born rarely suffer from these inhibitions.

Support - Strong feelings and opinions about appropriate roles for men and women also influence the amount of support men receive and feel that they receive as carers of children. This extends to both within the family home, and whether men are encouraged by partners and extended family members to be involved with children, as well as to the type of support commonly available to women outside the home. For example, women are the majority attendees at postnatal classes, coffee mornings, mother and baby groups, playgroups - it is not consistently the case that men are welcomed at, and encouraged to see themselves as potential members of, these groups.

Institutional Practices - Fathers often cite the unhelpful attitudes of employers, and rigid workplace arrangements as major obstacles to involvement in childcare and other related activities such as attending school open evenings or child health checks, and being at home for a significant period after a child is born.

None of these factors are uncomplicated and they are subject to different interpretations - for example, while long working hours and lack of flexibility around leave affect most full-time employed men (82 per cent of UK fathers in two parent families work for an average 47 hours/week), men still tend to put only half as much non-work time into 'family work' as do women (20 minutes/hour compared to 40-45 minutes/hour). If we want foster fathers to be involved carers, then all these factors affecting fathers' involvement are relevant, and need to be taken into consideration by those who assess and support foster families, as well as by foster carers themselves.

There is, however, an additional pressure on foster fathers, and it is one that is undeniably a greater burden than that on fathers generally - concerns about 'safe caring'.

Safe Caring - between a rock and a hard place?

People look at you as a man as if you're mad to foster

There is suspicion about why men foster

(words of foster fathers)

There has been a great deal of media coverage in the past few years of fathers and fatherhood, ranging from consideration of the 'new' actively involved father, to concerns about erosion of traditional roles for both men and women. It seems that coverage of men who foster, however, remains restricted to the tiny minority who abuse children - such as extensive reporting of the cases of Roger Saint, a foster carer in North Wales who sexually abused boys in his care for several years, and Sion Jenkins, convicted in 1998 for the murder of his foster daughter. The implication in media coverage is often that abusers - who are usually reported as men - have easily and extensively infiltrated their way into caring positions, and that foster fathers are to be viewed with suspicion. The Utting Report, *People Like Us*, which followed evidence of widespread abuse in children's homes, makes special mention of foster care as a place where abuse occurs.

The National Foster Care Association published its guidelines on *Safe Caring* in 1994, pointing out that its aims include both protecting the fostered child from abuse, as well as keeping members of the foster family safe from false allegations of abuse. Amongst very detailed, practical guidance to all foster carers on thinking about risky behaviour, and how to protect your own and other people's children, men are advised that: they 'should not be left alone to bath and dress children'; and that they should not oversee bedtimes alone, but 'might be able to put a child to bed by keeping at a safe distance and explaining what the child should do'. Regarding transport of children, a safe rule is 'for foster carers, especially men, to avoid travelling alone with a foster child'.

In my experience, the range of reactions from foster fathers - both new and experienced - to this guidance can be extreme. I have heard men argue passionately that they dare not place themselves or their families at risk, by ever being alone with a foster child - and that they i.e. the social services department, would always support the child, and that would be the end of fostering for them as a family. I have heard other fathers vehemently refute this approach and advocate that it should be our objective to offer an 'ordinary' family experience to a fostered child - and how can we do this if we offer children little or no relaxed, individual time, including special moments of a child's day such as bathtime and bedtime, and if we always have to be accompanied or at a distance?

The contradictory pressures on men who foster are never greater than in this area of safe caring - they are caught on the horns of a distressing dilemma. On the one hand they present a possible risk to previously abused foster children through having their behaviour misinterpreted, as well as themselves facing the risk of false allegations and their aftermath; on the other hand they are expected to be involved in the life of a fostered child, and to have something to offer as positive role models to children, many of whom will have had poor experiences of men up until then. They feel constrained through the advice given by social workers not to become too engaged with fostered children, but can then feel that they are liable to be criticised if they take on a more distant role.

Positive Effects of Fathers' Involvement

Why should it even matter whether a foster father is engaged or distant in his relationships with fostered children? What, if any, are the positive effects of a father's involvement with his children, and in particular a foster father's involvement? There has been widespread research into how highly engaged and accessible fathers influence their children's development. There are also various studies of foster carers from which can be drawn some limited evidence of the effects of foster fathers' involvement in childcare on the children they foster.

Studies in the eighties and nineties have extended the concept of paternal involvement to highlight positive paternal involvement. Briefly, these studies identify qualitative measures of involvement that can then be related to effects on children. Positive forms of involvement include: care giving, expressing affection, responding, stimulating a child appropriate to their development, helping with reading and homework, playing at home, having private talks, doing leisure activities and outings. Studies of pre-school children in two parent families with 'substantially engaged and accessible fathers' (performing 40 per cent or more of the child care) reveal:

- more cognitive competence
- more empathy
- more internal locus of control
- less gender-role stereotyping

Other outcomes for primary and secondary school age children are: increased self-control, self-esteem, life skills, sociability and social competence; as well as fewer school behaviour problems in boys, and more self-direction in girls.

A few UK and American studies of foster carers have considered the relation between 'placement stability' and foster fathers' involvement. Little research appears to have systematically dissected and examined fathers' input in the foster home and outcomes for foster children in the same way as more general population studies, but some associations have been made. Many different facets of a foster father's involvement have been linked to greater placement stability (which is usually defined in terms of duration, and consistency with placement plans):

- joint decision making with his partner in all areas
- inclusion in pre-placement planning
- a favourable attitude towards having a

social worker visit and make suggestions regarding care of the child

- equal commitment and involvement of both partners to care and management of the child
- attending training - especially about abuse - and giving thought to the role that the male carer is to play with the child

Emotional Involvement with the Child

Aldridge and Cautley's research into new foster carers in the USA in the 1970s - one study that does attach equal importance to men and women carers in its analysis - suggests that if they are seen throughout by social workers, foster fathers are likely to report difficulties in a placement earlier than foster mothers, allowing for more effective intervention. Why this should be the case is debatable. Factors that make a child's placement less stable include:

- unmotivated or loosely involved foster father
- foster father rarely or never seen by social workers
- little or no individual time spent by foster father with foster child

Yet a small scale study by Jeary of male foster carers within Shropshire Social Services found that six out of fourteen had not spent any time, or been anywhere, on their own with a current foster child in the past week. This seems sadly consistent with an NOP poll of 2000 parents in the UK in 1995 which claimed that more than half of the fathers surveyed spent less than five minutes a day one-to-one with their child. This contrasts with the wishes of children, who say what they most want to do with their fathers is go out and do things together. Coming back to the notion of 'emotional involvement', Triseliotis and his colleagues give as examples,

> taking (foster) children fishing, to football matches and attending school events.

There are clearly powerful arguments in terms of childcare outcomes for reasoning that in the recruitment of foster carers agencies should be seeking involved and active men; and that fostering services should be developing sensitive, creative and flexible approaches to maintaining and enhancing the involvement of existing male foster carers. These approaches will need to overcome the kinds of obstacles foster fathers identify in 'the system', as well as those that they create for themselves:

> *It is difficult for me to get time off work to attend meetings or training during the daytime*

> *I don't attend training as I babysit the children so my wife can attend*

> *Social workers assume I know nothing and ask to speak to my partner*

> *The social worker addresses my wife - all her eye contact is with my wife*

> *I don't like being the only man in a professionals meeting, and I'm not acknowledged*

> *I would never be alone in the house with a foster child - it's not worth the risk*

In the rest of this chapter I will outline some approaches to overcoming obstacles - real or perceived - to greater involvement and recognition on the part of men who foster.

Recruiting Men to Foster Care

We've noted that in one respect foster families appear to fit a social stereotype - there are proportionately more fathers in foster families than in families in the wider population. It would be interesting to evaluate whether this reflects the balance of enquiries to foster, or whether there is disproportionate selecting out of single carers (male or female). Either way, it is important for agencies recruiting families to see the male applicants as soon as possible: both for purposes of assessment, as well as to ensure adequate preparation, and a sense of involvement.

For those men who are clearly making a joint application with a partner, I hope that the initial agency response is always to both. However, in many cases the initial enquiry comes from a woman, and the man is borne along on the tide of his partner's enthusiasm. Details taken over the phone may not specify who else is in the home. Workers making initial visits should ensure that they know who is in the household, and home visits should be arranged at times that accommodate to a family's work and domestic arrangements. Don't assume that the man can't

take time off work - especially if he is given the clear message that his participation is essential to the process - but if he says that he can't be available during a weekday, then workers need to make evening, or even weekend visits. If an initial visit takes place on this flexible basis, then the subtext is clearly we value you, and the man's voice is likely to be heard from the outset. The quality of assessment is enhanced, because unenthusiastic or distant men are likely to be found out at an earlier stage if they are not given the option of absenting themselves from meetings because the agency itself is inflexible about visiting times. As a consequence men may have to take more responsibility at an earlier stage in the process for determining their commitment to the idea of fostering.

Most agencies now encourage men to attend preparation groups for applicants to foster. Policies vary on whether attendance is mandatory prior to fostering. Again, the more inflexible the timing of courses, the more likely that applicants in paid employment, as well as the sceptical and disinterested, will fail to attend. The basic NFCA *Choosing to Foster* pack is based on six modules, each of two-and-a-half or three hours duration. The course as it is, or adapted by local agencies, lends itself to a series of evening sessions, weekends (such as three Saturdays), or a combination of both.

Part of the feedback from men about preparation groups, is that it helps to meet a man who fosters at this stage, and ask him questions. The point was made earlier about men feeling that they are sometimes viewed with suspicion as carers of other people's children, and that the media encourages this with its emphasis on men in these situations who are abusers. We can understand, then, why the presence of a male foster carer might help reassure and encourage men who are ambivalent about their role in this process. In my experience, most trainers on fostering preparation groups are women - social workers and foster carers. The majority of those attending the National Foster Care Association (NFCA) training for trainers courses are women. However, it is still possible to bring in a male foster carer for a slot in the preparation course to lead discussion, answer questions, and demystify the experience of men who foster. To involve a man who fosters on an equal footing with other trainers in the preparation of new foster carers clearly establishes that men have a valued role to play in themselves as well as being supports to their partners.

Training and Support

Men sometimes complain that they are unable to attend training courses, even those taking place during an evening or weekend, because of childcare - they need to be at home with the children for their partners to attend. It is often not realistic to expect an agency to lay on a large-scale childcare facility for a wide age range, around one training event. Nonetheless, workers can do a great deal to plan with foster carers for attendance at training courses, to make links with other families who can reciprocate childcare (especially around foster children), and to help families arrange individual provision; for example, providing up to date lists of local childminders.

A different approach is to make provision for male-only training events. Other matters being equal, this would free up men to attend without the obstacle of childcare arrangements. I have been involved in several workshops and training days for men who foster, covering a range of issues, including gender roles in fostering, and safe caring in practice. NFCA have been offering agencies a course for Men in Childcare/Foster Care for some years. The response from men who attend such events to being in a male-only setting is usually enthusiastic:

I value the chance to talk and exchange views with other male carers

I enjoyed meeting other male carers and hearing their experiences

The idea of men who foster getting together as a group - as women have done, meeting formally or informally together for support - is anathema to some men (and women), but is welcomed by others. The opportunity to meet together and discuss some difficult issues, such as dealing with sexualised behaviour and risks of allegations, feels 'safer' sometimes in a same sex group. Connections are made, and friendships develop, that can evolve into informal support networks. To make such events happen, agencies need to be able to explain to carers the reasons for a training course being for men only, and that there is no 'preferential treatment'. If we want men involved more, then we need to try out new ways of drawing them in. I have found that the response to workshops or courses varies anyway, with some men sceptical, others enthusiastic. Afterwards, some men want more events in a similar vein, and others comment that:

Although the day was enjoyable, I'm not sure that I want to attend more with just men

This simply reinforces the message that there is a wide spectrum of men who foster, and that we need to get to know their individual roles and strengths.

The best source of knowledge about a foster father could be through his relationships with his fostering officer and a child's social worker. It is through meetings with them, and discussion about fostering itself, that a father's engagement, accessibility and responsibility are likely to be gauged. Cautley and Aldridge's research, in particular, emphasises the positive outcomes for foster children if the foster father is fully involved in planning, and has a positive attitude towards the role of social workers in offering foster carers advice and ideas. Men who foster cannot have their cake here and eat it - a willingness to meet with professionals, and to respect their experience and skills, at least at the outset, gives a good indication of the amount of responsibility a foster father takes towards the task of fostering. If fostering officers are willing to be flexible about when they visit, then they are justified in challenging a foster father who is consistently unavailable, or is about the house but not engaging with the discussion.

Then again, if social workers insist on addressing all conversation, and correspondence also, to foster mothers, it is easy to understand why foster fathers may feel resentful, and eventually take a back seat. Paradoxically, given the positions of power men generally occupy in wider society, in the field of fostering men often describe themselves as not being listened to by social workers, feeling inarticulate in professionals meetings about children, and deferring to their partner's greater understanding of the childcare issues involved. Workers can generally do a great deal more to acknowledge and include men in discussions, and need to accept the research findings that seeing and engaging with foster fathers is not an optional extra, but a positive factor in enhanced placement stability.

Once foster fathers are seeing themselves as involved carers, the potential for further involvement seems limitless. Men who foster will find all sorts of ways of meeting together - with or without partners, formally or informally - to offer mutual support. Some examples that I have come across include:

- Several families taking caravan holidays together, providing opportunities for the men to get together in small groups during the days or evenings.

- Several foster fathers meeting together weekly to play badminton or golf.

- A group of fathers preparing for, and entering a sponsored bike ride together.

- Family fun days organised by the agency, or by a group of carers, with some activities that the men get together on (such as organising a football game, or barbecue).

- A regular support group for foster fathers, promoted by the agency.

- A network of trades and skills, with fathers helping one another out with building, electrical, carpentry, decorating and other jobs.

All these will help the confidence that the man is a caring and competent foster father.

Practical Approaches to Safe Caring

Men still want to be comfortable in their role around children and young people who have, or may have been abused. The guidance carers receive is that any child may have been sexually abused, whether or not this has been disclosed. Through discussions with foster fathers, including those who see themselves as primary carers, and relevant literature, a set of 'practical approaches to safe caring' has been produced. I hope that these ideas will help foster fathers minimise the risk of their behaviour being misinterpreted and of false allegations being made, yet will allow them to maintain a relatively ordinary family life, in which they have an equal, involved contact with foster children.

- Understand the pattern of abuse that a young person has previously experienced. If all foster carers make it their business to know, to ask questions and more questions of placing social workers, then they can more realistically adapt their normal family routines.

- Agree with your partner and the child's social worker an approach to daily routines such as bedtimes and bath times that is based on the individual child's needs. Agree whether it is or is not appropriate for the foster father to bath a particular child, given what is known about the child and her family. Plan with your partner and the child's social worker your role in the treatment of an abused child, and what you can offer as a positive role model.

- Don't be excluded from providing positive childcare; decide for yourself what you think is good and appropriate time spent with a child. Do the benefits of a long drive together to visit a farm, or go fishing, developing an emotional relationship and trust, outweigh the risks of an allegation when there is no previous history of allegations?

- Respond to, rather than ignore or avoid a child's inappropriate sexualised behaviour, and offer the child comfortable, safe alternatives - so that rather than avoiding all intimacy, a foster father is able to talk about and demonstrate what a good cuddle is like.

- Make conscious decisions about 'risk' and consult with your partner - the only risk free fostering involves no children!

- Keep a diary log of significant incidents and signs - discuss with your fostering officer and social worker what recording is expected. Detailed notes of distressing or confrontational situations, or concerning behaviours, can provide clarification after the event.

- Talk openly with your partner, especially about feelings and reactions. Plan, and reflect on what has happened. One teenage girl tried to imply to her foster mother that she had had a 'secret' lift home from school with her foster father. As the incident had already been discussed between the adults, and written down, the girl's bluff was easily called, and the risk of a false allegation effectively eliminated.

- Know the procedure after allegations are made against foster carers, and identify who your supports are - is it your foster care association, the NFCA, or a solicitor?

- Inform the child's social worker immediately if you are concerned about the child's behaviour, not weeks afterwards when several incidents have occurred and a situation has escalated.

● Put sexual abuse on the family agenda - contribute to an atmosphere of openness and discussion, and don't hide from difficult emotional subjects. Children learn the ability to be emotional and to communicate from the adults around them.

● Be yourself, be confident that you are a caring and competent foster father.

However much agency support is offered, at base foster fathers need to decide for themselves what kind of involvement they want in the tasks of fostering. At the very least, I would argue, they need to allocate the roles with their partner more consciously than they might with respect to their own children. The responsibility of looking after other people's children, and the attendant risks, dictate that this should be so. They need to think about their involvement with foster children, and the individual relationships they have with them. They need to reflect on the responsibility they take regarding a child's health and education, for making themselves available for visits from workers, and for attending important meetings. They need to think about the kind of role model they themselves provide for all children, and especially those in foster care. In this way, men who foster can move on from an understandable anxiety,

the difficulty of living alongside a foster child's preconceptions of men, such as alcohol equals violence
(foster father)

to a point where more men who foster can value their own role,

helping to change a child's self esteem and ideas about himself, through offering a good male role model
(foster father)

Further Reading

Inspection of Local Authority Fostering 1995–6 National Summary Report. Published by Social Services Inspectorate, Department of Health. Available from 0171 210 3000.

The Foster Carer Market. A National Perspective. Association of Social Services Children and Families Committee Report. Available from Niki Clemo, Principal Officer, Suffolk Social Services, St Paul House, County, Hall, Rope Walk, Ipswich IP4 1LH.

People Like Us. The Report of the Review of the Safeguards for Children Living Away From Home. By Sir William

Utting. Department of Health. Price £25. Available from Publications Centre, 0171 873 9090.

House of Commons Select Committee. Second Report. Children Looked After by Local Authorities. Volume One. Price £12.50. Available from the Stationery Office 0121 236 9696.

Working With Independent Fostering Agencies. Guidance for Local Authorities in England and Wales. By Jennifer Lord. Published by the British Agencies for Adoption & Fostering. Price £2.95. Available from BAAF 0171 593 2000.

References

Aldridge, M.J. and Cautley, P.W. (1975b). The Importance of Worker Availability in the Functioning of New Foster Homes, *Child Welfare Vol LIV No. 6*

Aldridge, M.J. and Cautley, P.W. (1975a). Predicting Success for New Foster Parents, *Social Work* Vol. 20, No. 1 1995

BAAF (1998) *Understanding the Assessment Process*, British Agencies for Adoption and Fostering

Bebbington, A. and Miles, J. (1990) The Supply of Foster Families for Children in Care, *British Journal of Social Work*, Vol. 20, No. 4 1990.

Berridge, D. (1997). *Foster Care - A Research Overview*

Burgess, A (1997). *Fatherhood Reclaimed*, Vermilion

Electronic Telegraph (1995) Most fathers' prefer DIY to being with their children. 13/6/95

Electronic Telegraph (1996a) Long Hours Put Strain on Family. 4/11/96

Electronic Telegraph (1996b) Fathers Struggling to Take on Caring Role

Electronic Telegraph (1997) The Roger Saint Case. Issue 729, 24/5/97

Guardian (1998) Life for Billie-Jo's foster father. 3/7/98

HMSO (1991) *Regulations and Guidance to The Children Act 1994*

Jeary, A.S. (1993) *Men Who Foster* Unpublished Dissertation

Lamb M.E. (1997) Fathers and Child Development: An Introductory Overview and Guide in *The Role of the Father in Child Development*, John Wiley & Sons Inc.

Lamb M.E., and Openheim, D. (1987) Fatherhood and Father-Child Relationships in *Fathers and Their Families*, The Analytic Press

Lewsey, P. and Lindsay, G (1991) *A Male Perspective*, Community Care

National Foster Care Association (1997) *Foster Care In Crisis*, NFCA

Pleck, J.H. (1997) Paternal Involvement: Levels, Sources and Consequences in *The Role of the Father in Child Development* (Ed. Lamb, M.E.) pp 1–18, John Wiley & Sons, Inc

Triseliotis, J., Sellick, C., and Short, R. (1995) *Foster Care - Theory and Practice*, B.T. Batsford Ltd

Utting, Sir W. (1997) *People Like Us*, Department of Health and The Welsh Office

3.1 Training for Foster Carers

Kevin Lowe

The status of training for foster carers is perhaps bound up with the ill-defined relationship between foster carers and the authorities who recruit them, place children with them and pay varying amounts of allowance and reward.

This short paragraph from the Utting report (1997) touches the heart of many of the central issues in the training of foster carers. Training provision across the UK is extremely uneven. Few agencies have a comprehensive training and development strategy for foster carers. As the end of the 1990's approaches several factors have combined to move foster care training closer to centre stage and the possibility of significant change emerges. The reason for the changes and what might be the result are the subjects of this chapter.

Why is there Interest in Training Now?

Developments in foster care training provide valuable insights into the so-called professionalisation of foster care. Serious concerns about quality of child care services and the increasing reliance on foster care for the majority of children looked after by local authorities has thrust foster care into the spotlight.

Important initiatives to help improve quality such as the Department of Health's looking after children materials (LAC) and national vocational awards ((S)NVQs) for foster carers (first accredited in 1996) have made demands on agencies' training and development function. In many agencies the implementation of LAC materials was the first time foster carers training needs were considered as part of mainstream service development.

The setting up of the UK Working Group on Standards in Foster Care and the resulting national service standards point to the need for an appropriate organisational infrastructure to support ongoing training and development for foster carers. The government's Quality Protects initiative, announced in September 1988 establishes a wider framework for the improvement of local authority services for the children and young people they look after. Difficulties in recruiting an adequate supply of foster carers and the need to retain those who are approved adds emphasis to the need for effective training and development policies.

Foster care training then may be on the brink of a new phase in its history. But although there have been major events that punctuate its historical development, these have generally been the culmination of a longer more organic process related to the professionalisation of the foster care service. This can best be understood by exploring some of the more recent history of foster care training.

History

Currently, training input is most likely to be part of the approval process, though this is not universal. This is sometimes called 'preparation'. After approval, training becomes increasingly ad hoc, both in terms of availability and take up. Where training exists, it tends to take the form of short courses. Courses are run by local 'in-house' trainers, independent freelance trainers or specialist agencies such as British Agencies for Adoption and Fostering (BAAF) and the National Foster Care Association (NFCA). A small number of agencies have arrangements with local further education (FE) colleges for the provision of training.

The variation in training provision is confirmed in research by Triseliotis et al. (1998) in Scotland. Their survey found around a quarter of carers either had no continued training opportunities or, where these were available, they did not attend. The survey of foster carers in England and Wales which informed the ADSS 1997 report, The Foster Care Market found that only 16 per cent of foster carers reported that they always attended training, although 50 per cent said they had access to training, 53 per cent thought strongly that training should be made ongoing and compulsory. Barn et al. in their study of race and ethnicity in social services provision for children and families (1997) identified training gaps for carers (and staff). Training on equal opportunities and anti-racist practice was 'very sparse and lacked any impetus'.

Training input as part of the approval process owes much to the work of the National Foster Care Association. NFCA was established in 1974 and made foster carer training a major focus from the outset. NFCA's decision to develop training material in the 1970's did not occur in a vacuum. This was part of a wider realisation in the field that foster care was an increasingly complex activity where carers needed some form of preparation in order to achieve high quality care for children and young people.

A major thrust came from the introduction into the UK of 'professional' fostering schemes; particularly those geared to fostering adolescents. Those working on such projects aimed at fostering 'hard to place young people' concluded it was not possible for carers to undertake the tasks involved without preparation, training, post-placement support and continued training. Fines describes developing a preparation and training programme as part of the then new Westminster Community Fostering Scheme for Adolescents (1979). She concluded with the hope that

> the positive advantages experienced by specialist schemes in the use of groups for preparation and training will continue to be offered to all foster parents and not just those involved in specialist schemes.

The actual number of carers who are part of these schemes has only ever been a tiny proportion of the total number of foster carers in the UK. However, in the 25 years or so since these first schemes, the innovative ideas developed as part of the schemes have formed the basis of best practice about foster care as a whole, particularly in terms of training and management of carers. However as we have already seen, practice across the UK has not universally caught up with the ideas.

NFCA's significant contribution was the publication of a commercially available training pack, *Introduction to Foster Parenting* — familiarly known as *Parenting Plus* — in April 1980. This provided good quality materials for agency staff to use and set a pattern for foster carer preparation that remains in place today. *Parenting Plus* was based on a training pack published in the USA by the Child Welfare League of America in the mid 1970's. It combined well-designed curriculum content with participative adult learning techniques. NFCA ran courses to train course leaders to use these techniques. NFCA's leaders' courses promoted a co-leadership model of a social worker and foster carer training together so that the eventual course for prospective carers could be run in a similar way.

In April 1982 NFCA published a further training pack adapted from CWLA material, *Foster Parenting an Adolescent* — known as *Added to Adolescence. Parenting Plus* and *Added to Adolescence* were subsequently replaced by *The Challenge of Foster Care* (1988) and most recently by *Choosing to Foster* — *the Challenge to Care* (1994). The subsequent packs each reflect contemporary practice concerns within the training framework initiated by *Parenting Plus*. These training materials have been used widely. Agencies adapt them, supplementing the material with additional exercises, local case studies and input from specialists.

Choosing to Foster is designed in an adaptable format that provides a minimum of six 'core' sessions for initial preparation and a further five which explore issues raised in the core sessions in more depth. The additional sessions can be used as part of the preparation and assessment phase or as the basis of further post-approval sessions. Anecdotal feedback suggests that there is a wide variation in how agencies use the material. Many agencies only use the six core sessions. Some incorporate material from the additional sessions and others use the bulk of the pack in preparation. There appears to be under use of the additional material. The reasons for this will be explored later.

The Choosing to Foster Sessions

What is fostering about?

- listening to young people

- working together
- fostering skills — managing difficult behaviour
- fostering and your family
- moving on
- valuing heritage
- sex and sexuality
- team work
- managing difficult behaviour
- HIV and AIDS

Choosing to Foster has been translated and is used in several different countries including Hungary, Poland and Malta.

In noting the link between the so-called professionalisation of foster care and the link with training, three other unrelated developments are also significant.

- The growth of new kinds of fostering agencies.
- The emergence of payments for skills schemes in local authorities
- A national qualification for foster carers

New 'independent' agencies

Towards the end of the 1980's new, 'independent' fostering agencies began to develop - initially in Kent in England. The location is significant as Kent was also where the first teenage fostering scheme was developed (see Hazel). These new agencies gradually began to spread from the South of England to other parts of the UK. The approach of the agencies is often characterised by high levels of input to the carers including training (for example, Families for Children in West Sussex, Heath Farm in Kent and the Five Rivers, Wiltshire). Concern about the implications of the development of such agencies was one of the reasons the Association of Directors of Social Services in England and Wales (ADSS) undertook their study of foster care in 1997. These high levels of training input differentiate the agencies from their counterparts in many (not all) local authorities.

Payments for Skills

Concern about payment structures within foster care and the inequities that arose within

agencies when fees were paid only to carers as part of specialist schemes led NFCA to propose a new approach based on the expectations of carers skills. The scheme proposed three skill levels. This approach was not the first time that arrangements to pay all carers a fee were put in place. Some agencies had already done this, (for example, Lothian and Bradford) but the model provided a framework for agencies to rationalise payment structures. Westminster City Council was the first local authority to implement this approach in 1992 and over 20 such schemes were in place by 1998. The payment for skills model marked a significant step in the professionalisation of foster care, making fee payments to all carers an explicit element in local authorities' contracts with carers. Equally the model raises training issues. Agencies grapple with deciding how to assess carers in order to place them on the appropriate level of the three tiers. Also, in assessing competence levels, training issues emerge. The contracts with carers also typically make an expectation to attend training explicit.

National Vocational Qualifications

The development of the current national vocational qualification structure ((S)NVQs) began in 1986 as part of a government led drive to improve qualification levels in the workforce. The new qualification structure sought to rationalise qualifications in areas of work where an existing qualification framework was confusing and also to develop relevant qualifications for 'occupations' where qualifications had not previously existed. These vocational qualifications are not training courses. Individual practice and knowledge is assessed against a set of national occupational standards.

In developing qualifications in social care, foster carers were identified by the Local Government Management Board in 1989 as a group of workers for whom qualifications needed to be considered. This led to a feasibility study as to the appropriateness of such qualifications, which was published in 1992. The report concluded that vocational qualifications for foster carers were viable. The report also included a survey of training provision available at the time for carers and identified that training was less available once carers were approved (compared to the preparation stage) and that

> *the content of the training was determined locally and is variable in quality and quantity.*

The first national foster care qualification was accredited in 1996 with the Group and Foster care (S)NVQ Level 3 award. The standards on which the award was based were designed for residential child care workers as well as for foster carers and were developed out of a consultation that aimed to identify the functions of residential child care workers and foster carers — functional analysis. The content of the standards and the implications for training will be explored more fully below. However for some, whilst the award was welcome, shortcomings in the development process resulted in gaps in the content of the award. Fortunately this new award quickly became part of a revision of all care (S)NVQs in 1997 and the award was replaced by Caring for children and young people (Level 3) in 1998. The new award included an improved structure plus standards more suited to residential carers and foster carers. Further improvements in the content at the end of 1998 make the award dovetail more effectively with the functions required in using the, Assessment and Action records.

Take up of (S)NVQs in general within local authorities has been poor. A 1998 report from the Local Government Management Board (LGMB) and the Joint Initiative for Community Care criticised a management culture that has led to a 3 per cent completion rate across most social services departments. The implementation of awards for foster carers has taken place against this backdrop. Nevertheless, by mid 1998 over 30 assessment centres across the UK were offering the award. Agencies implementing the award such as Devon, Liverpool, Newcastle and Tameside. Care 2000 undertook pilot projects with small numbers of carers in order to decide whether the approach should be extended.

Although the numbers of foster carers achieving (S)NVQs in foster care is currently very small, there is evidence that the emergence of such a qualification has had a significant impact on the debate about the professionalisation of foster care and on thinking about training.

NFCA ran a series of eleven conferences about (S)NVQs in foster care in England, Scotland, Wales and Northern Ireland in 1996-97. These were attended by close to a thousand foster carers and fostering social workers including representatives from most authorities in the UK. Delegates were generally extremely positive about the new awards. They were seen as a way of raising standards of care for children and young people and of valuing the achievement of foster carers. Some were anxious about the implications for carers who may not wish to pursue this route. There was scepticism as to whether individual local authorities would promote them. The existence of national occupational standards was also recognised as providing the basis of a training curriculum for foster care.

The Content of Foster Care Training - Curriculum Issues

The idea of a curriculum as the basis of the content of training materials was referred to explicitly by NFCA in its 1982 review of the development of *Parenting Plus*. However, approaches to training were as much part of the philosophy as were content. Shaw and Hipgrave's comment from their then forthcoming study of specialist fostering schemes that the key issue in foster parent (sic) training was not so much what is included in a course (content), but rather how it is presented (adult learning philosophy and method).

Robin Short, writing in Triseliotis et al. (1995) summarises the value of training of foster carers in relation to helping achieve more positive outcomes for children and young people. He also notes the need for training to help carers understand why certain practices are pursued, such as the link between consistent parental contact and more settled and stable placements. Short outlines the likely content of basic training programmes (pages 46-52), drawing on NFCA's *The Challenge of Foster Care*, the Open University Course *Caring for Children and Young People* and Gray's *Study of Foster Care Training* based in part on work in Derbyshire. He also makes the point:

> *We need to look beyond a simple list of topics to make clear to ourselves what our basic concerns about fostering are and therefore what our training objectives should be.*

He notes that both the sets of material 'lack input in early child development theory such as attachment, separation and loss, socialisation, identity formation and generally early stages of personality development'.

The Child Welfare League of America's pack *The Ultimate Challenge, Foster Parenting in the 1990's* (1992) makes clear the concerns about fostering upon which it is based. These are described as the essential tasks of fostering. The five tasks were identified by the National Commission on Family Foster Care, which was convened in January 1990 by the Child Welfare League of America in collaboration with the National Foster Parent Association (USA).

The five essential tasks are:

1. Protecting and nurturing children and youths (sic).

2. Meeting developmental needs and addressing developmental delays. Advice to course leaders is that developmental needs include social, emotional, cultural, spiritual, educational and physical needs and that the trauma of abuse, neglect and maltreatment contributes to developmental delays.

3. Promoting self-esteem, family relationships, cultural identity and permanence. Course leaders are advised to explain that these are the components of healthy growth and development.

4. Preparing children and youths for positive relationships and responsibility. The Leaders' Guide notes that it is essential to teach about relationships and responsibility so children and young people can know appropriate ways to get their needs met and learn how to get along with family, friends and others.

5. Working as a member of a professional team. Teamwork is considered essential as the needs of children, young people and their families is seen as 'so complex and perplexing that no one can do all the care and casework alone'. Foster carers are regarded as an integral part of an interdisciplinary professional team.

The Child Welfare League of America's subsequent training material *The Pride Program* (1996) is a competency-based approach to promoting the five essential tasks. *The Pride Program* is made up of both a 'preservice' component for use in the recruitment, preparation and assessment stage, plus an 'inservice' programme for new and experienced foster carers. The programme materials also emphasise their value for adoptive parents.

Choosing to Foster (1994) provides material to be used flexibly, but its prime aims are linked to the preparation and assessment of carers. These are listed for course leaders as:

- To help provide general information about what fostering involves, to help prospective carers decide if fostering is right for them.

- To help prospective carers decide if they want to foster for your agency.

- To help you and the prospective carers decide whether they would be able to look after children in a way that is safe and does not discriminate against some children, young people and their families.

- To help you and prospective carers find out if they can work with you and others involved with the child or young person.

The material covers:

- Promoting the rights of children and young people, including safe care and promoting a positive sense of identity.

- Working in partnership with families and other professionals.

- Understanding child development, interrupted development, abuse and managing the behaviour that can result.

- Considering the impact of foster care on the whole foster family.

The Looking After Children (LAC) Assessment and Action records encompass the key functions required of looking after children in the public care system in the UK. The material, which in effect offers a framework for direct work, points to a core curriculum for carers which addresses the following seven dimensions:

- health
- education
- identity
- family and social relationships
- social presentation

- emotional and behavioural development

- self care skills.

The near universal adoption of the LAC system in England and Wales provides a powerful impetus to develop carers' knowledge and skills of the seven dimensions.

The (S)NVQ award Working with Children and Young People offers a more comprehensive framework of standards for use as a benchmark for practice. The standards are made up of a set of five mandatory units and a further 31 units divided into two groups. Candidates must choose a further seven appropriate to their work role (total 12). For example the following might be a fairly typical combination.

Mandatory units

- Promote equality diversity and rights.

- Contribute to the protection of children from abuse.

- Receive, transmit, store and retrieve information.

- Contribute to the development, provision and review of care programmes.

- Establish, sustain and disengage from relationships with clients.

Optional units

- Promoting health and social well-being for children and young people in partnership.

- Respond effectively to challenging behaviour in children and young people.

- Promote the educational opportunities of children and young people in partnership.

- Encourage children/young people to develop a positive sense of identity.

- Enable individuals, their family and friends to explore and manage change.

- Enable one's own family and networks to support care services.

- Develop one's own knowledge and practice.

Three key building blocks then emerge as the basis for a curriculum for foster carer training:

1. *Choosing to Foster — the Challenge to Care.*

2. The seven dimensions of the LAC materials.

3. National occupational standards — *Caring for Children and Young People*

(S)NVQ in caring for children and young people is also appropriate for carers in residential homes. The wide choice of topics enables each carer to choose areas of study specifically appropriate to them. This signals to foster carers an equality of roles which will further the debate on the issue of payment to foster carers.

The value of these materials to help establish a more coherent training programme for foster carers has been identified by some agencies. The (S)NVQ standards and the LAC dimensions to a lesser degree outline the standards required of the carer. The task of the training and development input is to help the carer achieve the standards. *Choosing to Foster* offers material to assist this process.

The value of the (S)NVQ standards are the basis of a comprehensive training programme for an individual agency have been described by Barbara Hutchinson in her work for BAAF with Wakefield Metropolitan District Council. Other agencies have also used the standards on the basis of a more comprehensive training strategy. In an article in Foster Care Magazine (1998) Noble and Davies describe the steps taken by Nottingham and the London Borough of Kingston-upon-Thames to develop a more comprehensive training strategy.

The Kingston framework established in 1997 was seen to have delivered positive results within its first year. The programme focuses primarily on time-limited foster carers, but long term carers can opt in. A preparation course based around *Choosing to Foster* is followed by two years basic training that is available both in daytime and evening sessions. After the two-year period, carers attend courses with other child care professionals within the social work department as appropriate. The training programmes are part of a wider development approach that includes the option of being assessed for (S)NVQ. The training strategy also includes a framework for existing carers who may have training gaps to fill. The agency has also identified the need to widen the strategy to provide specific training for long term carers and also for carers who are relatives or friends of the child they foster.

Nottingham County Council aimed to undertake a training needs analysis in order to establish a three-year rolling programme that is consistent across the districts in the county and compatible with national service standards and NVQ.

Newcastle (1998) also reported having devised a specific training strategy for foster carers explicitly based around an analysis of the requirements of the LAC system, departmental standards in foster care and NVQ.

Clarity for curriculum content, particularly at the preparation stage, should be further sharpened with the forthcoming publication by NFCA of competencies for foster carers as part of a new approach to the assessment of foster carers. The material highlights key requirements of carers at the assessment stage. This material will serve as a companion to the Department of Health's *Code of Practice for the Recruitment and Selection of Foster Carers*. This code, a recommendation of the Utting report, is likely to comment on issues of core curriculum for foster care training. Such welcome guidance from the Department of Health plus the new material should enable agencies to refocus initial input.

The Central Council for Education and Training in Social Work (CCETSW) has provided curriculum guidance for core material that managers may wish to commission in training for residential social workers and foster carers linked with the Caring for Children and Young People NVQ award. The guidance states that a learning package should include:

- understanding human growth and development in a multi-cultural society
- children and young people in their social context
- needs, rights, responsibilities and boundaries
- attitudes, values and beliefs
- communication
- protecting children and young people
- promoting active learning and self-reflective practice

The CCETSW guidance also draws attention to the value of managers auditing the training needs and qualifications of workers and the value in integrating the training of foster carers with other staff in the department. The Open University course material K201 *Working with Children and Young People* (1997) is recommended as useful for training programmes. It was written with foster carers in mind as potential readers.

The Delivery of Training for Foster Carers

The innovations in training in the 1970s and 1980s set significant precedents that may be seen to have both helped and hindered foster care training. The emphasis on co-leadership between fostering social workers and foster carers became the norm in theory (though often not in practice). Consequently, responsibility for foster care training has tended to be located with fostering social workers, ideally co-working with foster carers. This may have contributed to a process which, whilst providing training when it had not existed before, does not enable carers to have access to the wider training opportunities available to agency staff. It may have also reinforced the view that training department personnel do not regard training for foster carers as part of their responsibility.

There are examples of agencies where training staff feel fostering social workers resist the integration of foster carer training into central systems on the grounds that the needs are specialist, yet in doing so perpetuate the process of the marginalisation of foster care. In order for foster carer training to become part of the mainstream, those currently providing such training (fostering social workers and foster carers) need to come together with training specialists in agencies to establish new structures which build on each others expertise. These structures could also enable greater participation of young people as trainers, a successful feature of LAC training in many agencies

The tendency to locate responsibility for foster carer training primarily within fostering teams may also have contributed to the limited development of post-approval training. Training is only one of the many responsibilities of fostering social workers. The emphasis on recruitment prioritises preparation courses, but additional training may not receive similar emphasis. There is anecdotal evidence that the additional sessions in Choosing to foster are underused in many agencies because there is no system in place to run the sessions, not because the material is considered inappropriate.

The emphasis on organisational frameworks within the training service standards of the proposed Foster Care Standards is welcome. The standard relating to foster care training in the 1998 consultation document is:

> *Each foster carer is provided with the training necessary to equip them with the skills and knowledge to provide high quality care for each child or young person placed in their care.*

Two of the key components of the standard are:

> *The authority has a clear and adequately resourced management plan, derived from child care policy and practice, for the training and development of each approved foster carer*
> *Foster carer training is integrated within the relevant departmental training programme and includes opportunities for joint training with social workers.*

However, delivering foster care training in a coherent fashion requires more than a process that identifies need and devises suitable programmes. Significant practical issues can undermine the implementation of a training strategy. Certainly some agencies reported low foster care attendance to training on LAC courses. Poor attendance can be a problem, and whilst there may be many reasons for this, it seems bound up in the wider position of carers within the agency together with practical issues such as the need to provide effective child care arrangements. Discrimination may limit the training opportunities for specific groups including long term-carers, relatives and friends and short-term (shared care) carers. Black carers, lesbians and gay men may also feel training does not address some of their specific concerns. Carers working full-time (often male) may find it hard to attend training.

It is here again that the issue of training and professionalisation of foster care are linked. A frequent response from carers in the consultation meetings across the UK on the draft National Standards (Summer 1998) was

that training was necessary and wanted, but was an expectation too far, given the lack of a fee payment for most (90 per cent) foster carers.

It is significant that a fee payment was a feature of the innovative specialist schemes, which began in the 1970s. This made it easier to make attendance at training courses compulsory. Utting appears then to have got to the core of the matter in noting the link between the status of training and agencies' payment systems. The kind of contract that is in place for carers who are part of payment for skills schemes makes attending training an expectation, not an option.

At this point it seems worth broadening the discussion briefly from matters of training to consider the wider issue of development. Training should not be seen exclusively as 'courses'. Skills are developed in many ways and in practice training plays a relatively small part in this process for most adults. Developing foster carers' skills is likely to be more effective if those with the responsibility to ensure this happens (carers themselves and fostering social workers and their managers) seek to maximise learning opportunities in an imaginative way. As well as the traditional foster carer support groups, this might also include linking up with other carers with specific expertise and individual sessions with other 'experts'. The value of guided reading and the use of TV/video should not be underestimated.

Although this discussion has concentrated on the training of foster carers, it cannot be concluded without reference to the training needs of at least two other groups:

The sons and daughters of carers have specific needs that are different from their parents. They require preparation to help them anticipate the demands of being part of a fostering family. They also need ongoing support and training to help them manage these demands. In 1998 around 30 local authorities provided specific training and support for these children and young people, but in general this appears a much neglected area in need of development.

Improving foster carer training also raises major questions about the training of social workers. The developing professionalisation of the carer's role requires children's social workers to operate differently. The 1997 ADSS report *The Foster Carer Market* noted carers' criticisms about their working relationships with social workers. Carers often feel they are treated as junior partners rather than colleagues by social workers.

There are implications too for fostering social workers, the specialists who recruit and 'support' carers. Increasing professionalisation requires a more managerial relationship where notions of being the carers' advocate are replaced by a professional managerial role involving a supervisory relationship. Fostering social workers have a central role to help identify carers' training needs and also to measure how effective the training is in improving what carers do on a day-to-day basis.

The training needs of the different groups of social workers simply reinforces the point that any improvements to foster carer training would take place within a wider context related to foster carers' position in the agency.

The Future

In September 1998 two major initiatives were announced that are likely to herald a new era in foster care training. *Quality Protects* sets out the government's requirements of local authorities in order to raise the quality of care for the children and young people they look after. *Quality Protects* acknowledged the significance of the role of foster carers and to complement this, a dedicated funding programme for training foster carers was set up by the Department of Health.

Approximately £500,000 was set aside for 1998 and £2 million for 1999–2000 to be used for induction/pre-approval training; training that promotes the Looking After Children (LAC) child development approach and that which covers the knowledge requirements of the relevant NVQ units. It is hoped that similar funding will be made available for agencies in Wales, Scotland and Northern Ireland.

The Department of Health initiative may prove significant beyond the provision of the cash alone. Authorities bidding for the funds are required to provide management information about the foster carers whom they are training and to have 'a strategy which addresses the approval and induction training for carers as well as their longer term needs'. The availability of funds together with the

emphasis on strategic planning may enable foster carer training to move beyond the current ad hoc approaches and become part of more formal mainstream systems. This would mark a significant step forward in the raising of standards of care for children and young people.

Conclusion

Foster carer training appears on the cusp of a new era. Its development can be seen as both a consequence of the growing professionalisation of the fostering service as well as having a part to play in achieving it.

Changes in attitudes and new infrastructures will be needed to maximise the potential of the new funding available. It will only be then that training will be able to help achieve the high quality direct care that children and young people deserve.

References

Association of Directors of Social Services (1997) *The Foster Care Market - A National Perspective* Suffolk Social Services

Barns, R., Sinclair, R., Ferdinand, D. (1997) *Acting on Principle* BAAF

Care Sector Consortium (1992) (1995) *Care Awards Level 3 - Core Units and Care Awards Level 3: Group and Foster Care* Local Government Management Board

Child Welfare League of America (1996) *Pride*, Child Welfare League of America

Dobson, F. MP. (1998) *Quality Protects: Transforming Children's Services* Letter to Councillors

Fines, C. (1998) *The Preparation of Foster Parents Through the Use of Groups in Groupwork in Adoption and Foster Care* (Ed. Triseliotis, J.) Batsford

Gray, G. (1992) *The Training of Foster Carers* MPhil Thesis submitted to the University of Sheffield

Hazel, N. (1990) *Fostering Teenagers* National Foster Care Association, London

Health, Dept. of (forthcoming 1990) *Code of Practice on The Recruitment and Assessment of Foster Carers*, IK Joint Working Party on Foster Care London

Health, Dept. of (18 Septembr 1998) Letter to Chief Executive and Directors of Social Services, *Social Services Training Support Programme: Training for Foster Carers - 1998/99 and 1999/2000*

Hutchinson, B. (1997) Crisis or Opportunity? *Child Care Forum* p9

Jones, G., Foster, J. (1998) *NVQ Level, Caring for Children and Young People, Curriculum Guidance* CCETSW

National Foster Care Asociation (1997) *Foster Care in Crisis, A Call to Professionalise the Forgotten Service* NFCA London

National Foster Care Association (1980) *Introduction to Foster Parenting (Parenting Plus)* NFCA London

National Foster Care Association (1982) *Foster Parenting and The Adolescent (Added to Adolescence)* NFCA London

National Foster Care Association (1998) *The Challenge of Foster Care* NFCA London

National Foster Care Association (1994) *Choosing to Foster - The Challenge to Care* NFCA London

National Foster Care Asociation (1996) *Foster Carers: Payment for Skills: Making it Work* NFCA, London

National Foster Care Association (1998) Unpublished presentations to conference *NVQs and Foster Care*, 23 April 1998 London

National Foster Care Association (1982) *Foster Care Education Project - Looking Back - Looking Forward*, NFCA London

National Foster Care Association (forthcoming 1999) *A Competence-Based Approach to the Assessment of Foster Carers* (provisional title) NFCA London

National Foster Care Association (1994) *Training in Foster Care, Foster Care Service Making it Work* NFCA London

Noble, L., Davies, G. (1998) Training: No Longer An Added Extra in *Foster Care*, Issue 95, October 1998 p8-9 NFCA

Open University (1997) *K201 Working With Children and Young People* Open University

Positive Solutions: PTS Consultancy (1992) *Foster Carers: A Feasibility Study for The Care Sector Consortium* Care Sector Consortium

Pasztor, E., et al. (1992) *The Ultimate Challenge - Foster Parenting in the 1990s*, Child Welfare League of American, Washington

Shaw, M. and Hipgrave, T. (1983) *Specialist Fostering* Batsford

Triseliotis, J., Borland, M., Hill, M. *Fostering Good Relations: A Study of Foster Care and Foster Carers in Scotland* - Interim report of a survey of foster carers (1998) The Scottish Office

Triseliotis, J., Sellick, C., Short, R. (1995) *Foster Care Theory and Practice* Batsford BAAF London

UK Joint Working Party on Foster Care (1998) *Consultation Document on National Standards in Foster Care* NFCA

Utting, Sir W. (1997) *People Like Us* The Stationery Office, London

Ward, H. (Ed.) (1995) *Looking After Children: Research into Practice* HMSO

3.2 Working in Partnership - Social Workers and Carers

Sheah Johansen

Partnership - The state or condition of being a partner; participation, association; joint interest

In thinking about this chapter, I began to look for definitions of the word 'partnership' and checked in several dictionaries to establish the common threads running through the concept. Above is one of those definitions as a starting point for considering the question of partnership in substitute family placement.

In any partnership whether husband and wife, significant other interactions or in social spheres, sports, clubs, etc., we come to a sense of partnership gradually. The early meetings where we feel appreciated and wanted lead us to come back for more. We begin to have a role with the person or group of people and gain an increasing sense of worth and value. From that standpoint we are able to negotiate further involvement and develop a sense of being able to both give and receive. With time and positive experience we move to a partnership which will be mutually beneficial both to ourselves and to the person or group with whom we have become involved.

In any social work setting, we are called to work as 'partners' with many diverse and disparate groups, parents and extended families, colleagues, other professionals and agencies. The implications of working in partnership with all these and other groups could each be the subject of a chapter in its own right.

In this chapter I intend to concentrate on the issues around partnership with substitute carers and social workers, and to try to consider the difficulties which can arise in this often uneasy and unequal relationship. In doing so I feel it is important to revisit the steps in the process of firstly being approved as carers and secondly having children placed. I will then identify those points at which the relationship and thus the partnership can go wrong and look at ways to develop better practice to enable the partnership to be successful.

The chapter is a genuine attempt to put the many issues around partnership into perspective. Too often what we do is in isolation and we do not consider how our actions affect others. The aim of all working in partnership should be to improve the quality of life for all looked after children.

Note: Working in partnership with parents is not discussed here. The reader is referred to *Working with Parents - A Good Practice Guide* Wheal A, Ed., Russell House 1999 (in publication).

The Initial Enquiry

For anyone wishing to foster, the starting point and sometimes initial difficulty is finding an agency who is able or willing to meet with you, give you information and take up your application. With the need for carers, this should be a simple enough exercise but experience shows that often would be carers find it difficult to get information, often waiting several weeks for written information to arrive. It can then be even more problematic to arrange an interview.

Let us pause there for a moment and think about the initial interview. As family placement workers, we understand that for any substitute carer, there may be issues concerning weight, smoking, past criminal records and health, although some of these are now given less importance than in recent years. No worker wants to spend valuable time with an applicant who is doomed to fail at panel stage.

However most prospective carers do not have any understanding of these issues and the handling of the initial interview can either motivate and facilitate the process or end it there and then, leaving the would be carer feeling worthless and negative. It is often at this stage that some potential carers withdraw; some because there are insurmountable problems but others because they have been left to feel that what they have to offer is not required or not good enough or that the process is so lengthy and invasive that they are frightened off.

Whatever the outcome of the initial stage, the individual should be left with a sense of respect and dignity. If helped to recognise for themselves that fostering is not for them, this is a very valid outcome. If the application does proceed, the sense of being valued is the starting point for a genuine partnership between the worker, the agency and the applicant.

The Approval Stage

Let us assume that our applicant has managed not to fall at the first hurdle and has secured an application form. It is likely that they will never have been asked to divulge so many personal details or give so many consents, i.e. police and other statutory checks, medical, personal references, etc. Some applicants can manage this with no difficulty; others will struggle. If at the initial stage, the applicant did not feel encouraged or valued, it may be difficult to come back for help and advice.

Having completed and returned the form, there is often - from the applicants perspective - a lengthy period of inactivity whilst the references, checks, medicals etc., are gathered. Applicants can be left feeling that their application has already failed for unknown reasons or that they are very low priority for the agency or department concerned.

At this stage we need to consider training. Different agencies have different procedures as to the amount and content of training and when this takes place but, for many applicants, the act of attending training can be a nerve-racking experience. Some perceive that if they say the 'wrong' thing or express their views, they will be 'failed' at this point.

So far our resilient applicant has come through all the stages and shown patience and forbearance with the perceived delays. Next comes the home study where a complete or relative stranger sits in the living room and enquires into the most personal and private areas of life. This person then asks many questions which it may not be possible to answer; 'what will you do about...?'; 'how will you feel when...?'; 'can you cope with...?'

Whilst this process is essential to learn about the applicant and assess their weaknesses and strengths, it must be appreciated that home studies are by their very nature invasive and intrusive. Applicants' self belief and confidence can be easily eroded if information, views and feelings are not handled sensitively and with respect. Having survived thus far, our applicant is now faced with the approval (or otherwise) by a panel of people who will sit in judgement. Whether or not the agency invites applicants to panel, the process is a stressful one for the applicant. If invited, the applicant has to face and perhaps answer questions from a group of strangers. If not invited, the applicant has to put their trust in the worker presenting the information; not easy if the sense of partnership has not developed with that worker.

Avoiding the Difficulties

So how do we overcome the many difficulties outlined above? The simple answer is that we don't and can't. The process is invasive, it is intrusive and lengthy and should be so. If we are to trust carers with the well-being and lives of children in our care, then thorough and careful vetting and assessment is essential. There are however ways to avoid unnecessary difficulties. There is no justification for anyone having to wait weeks or even months for information. A pre-prepared information pack can easily be sent out on the day of the enquiry or at least within 24 hours. This simple but essential response says to potential applicants 'we are interested'. It can also be used to tell applicants how to proceed and to flag any possible delays they may encounter. To say to applicants 'we are at present short-staffed so there may be some delay before a visit can be arranged' ensures that applicants do not feel that delay equals disinterest in them personally.

The next point is the all-important first meeting. This may be in the office or the applicant's home. The venue may not matter too much but the right approach is essential. All too often workers can feel that they have to get not only the 'information' on the applicants at this meeting but also the applicants' feelings and views. If the applicants also have an agenda of getting further information, then the initial meeting can often be a difficult one. Why do we need so much information at this juncture? It may be that when potential applicants get all their questions answered, they may never be heard from again! The unconditional giving of information will often lead potential applicants to share personal information about themselves more willingly. The are not being asked if they have a criminal record but being told the position of the agency and the law. By the end of the first interview, having explained the agency or department's stance on various issues, those people falling outside this will often cancel themselves out.

Many people when simply seeking information do not want or expect to have to answer very personal questions. Anyone going into a building society to make a general enquiry about savings accounts does not expect to have to lay out their full financial history to get the information.

There are some areas, e.g. previous marriages, infertility/childlessness, which should be left alone on a first interview unless raised by the applicant(s). A recent example of this is a couple where the worker visited and wished to know not only the details of the husband's fertility problems but the wife's feelings about this. The couple were totally unprepared for these questions on their first visit and never went back to the agency concerned. It is important to gain information on which to base a decision to proceed but it is argued that it is also better to arrange a second meeting where needed than to leave potentially good applicants feeling 'invaded' by the worker's need to know everything.

If potential applicants feel that they have had their questions answered openly and honestly and have been respected and listened to, this positive view will form the basis of a good partnership in the future.

Looking at the balance of the process, all the checks, medicals and references are essential. However it is not an onerous task to keep applicants informed or to state at the outset that these will take a certain amount of time and contact will be made again in three months. For most applicants, it is the not knowing which creates the stress. It also sets up a pattern of non-communication which can present real problems during a child's placement. If we expect foster carers to communicate with us, we must set this example early in the process.

It is important to acknowledge with applicants that the home study can be stressful and invasive and to explain the purpose and benefits. In most instances allowing an applicant time to talk and being willing to follow the applicant down some metaphorical alleyways will produce more and honest information than bombarding the applicant with questions, many of which they cannot answer.

However the home study is approached, it should leave the applicants feeling that they have been given the chance to explore issues and think about situations. Expecting instant and concrete answers often leads to wrong answers and applicants should have the right to say 'I don't know'.

The use of self, and sharing of personal information, during the assessment period is to an extent a personal decision but there are also professional considerations on both sides. Having had a student on placement who told applicants that she smacked her children, I had to explore the professional implications of such a statement with her. I do not believe that such information is correctly shared with applicants and can lead to real problems.

However for the worker to be an information gathering robot is equally inappropriate. How can any applicant relate on the level we wish them to with someone about whom they know nothing. How old are your children?, What are your hobbies and interests?, Where are you going on holiday? All harmless questions but the answers can create a feeling of greater inequality between worker and applicant unless she reciprocates with some information. Changing the questioning technique by using open instead of closed questions may also help, for example e.g. Tell me about your holiday (if you really need to know about their holiday!).

It is essential never to belittle or negate issues of importance to an applicant. Personal views on arranged marriages, blood transfusions, monogamy and many other issues may differ from the person or people being assessed. Indeed such views may make the family unsuitable for the authority or agency's needs but the applicant has a right to have their deeply held views treated with respect.

A final point before moving on. Hospitality: If offered food/drinks, where possible take them. In the early stages it may be one of the few ways an applicant can give back for the work being done. In some cultures the offering and accepting of food serves a very important social function and continued refusal gives offence. It is important when working outside your own culture, religion or race, to make special efforts to learn about that religion, race or culture so as not to inadvertently offend.

It is argued that the manner in which an application is managed and the respect accorded to the applicant is the essential starting point in developing a partnership. If the worker has shown patience, respect and a willingness to communicate openly and honestly, the likelihood of the approved carer following the same pattern is greatly increased.

Post-Approval Working

While the pre-approval procedures are laid down in regulations and broadly follow a recognisable pattern, what happens next in terms of working together in partnership varies dramatically from agency to agency. In my own project we work at any one time with 20 plus local authorities throughout the country and I remain astonished by the differing rates of allowances, post-approval training, levels of involvement/consultation, and expectations for foster carers.

At one end of the spectrum, the expectation is 'boiled eggs and clean vests' (to quote from a long standing, highly respected foster carer) where the job of the carer is to meet the day to day needs of the child without any involvement in the wider issues and decisions.

At the other end, foster carers can become the primary decision makers and their views become paramount. An example of this took place recently where a foster carer was given complete copies of confidential reports on prospective adoptive parents with no reference to the adopters or their workers. The foster carer short listed the adoptive families and did initial visits with the worker. She ran the visits, asking very personal and inappropriate questions of the families and was more than simply instrumental in the final choice of family.

Neither of these models is appropriate but both are likely to continue to happen unless we give serious thought as to how we work in partnership with carers. This involves identifying the issues at the outset of a placement and having solutions which are

considered and balance the needs and abilities of all parties especially the child.

In any group of foster carers, there will be marked differences in attitude, ability and confidence. It is important in the first instance to recognise this and not to put carers into situations they cannot handle or at least not to leave them in the situation. We all recognise that inappropriate placements, often made as an emergency, do and will continue to happen usually late on Friday afternoons! There could be several problems, wrong age, wrong gender, wrong race, wrong number of children for that particular placement, wrong time for the carers, etc. This acknowledgement avoids carers feeling like failures as the unsuitability of the particular placement is recognised from the outset. In some authorities, such placements are acknowledged, quickly reviewed and remedied as soon as possible. Sadly in others, such inappropriate placements are allowed to drift on which results in problems for the child, birth family, carers and the agency. If because of resources, it is not possible to secure the right placement, then thought should be given to how to minimise the difficulties and support the children and carers rather than expecting carers to cope.

Even if we are lucky enough to have the right placement to meet the child's care needs, there are many other factors to consider. We need to think about and review as circumstances change the additional tasks required while the child remains in this foster home. Briefly some of the areas which could be considered include:

1. **Special needs.** How will these be met, by whom, additional equipment/financial implications, hospital and other appointments - who takes, who transports?

2. **Other children.** Does this placement preclude other foster children being placed? What are the implications for the carer's own children? What respite can be provided for the carer if needed?

3. **Managing contact.** The foster carer's role in this; whether in the foster home or neutral territory; is the foster carer in a supportive or supervisory role; management of problems?

4. **Record keeping.** Is the foster carer expected to keep general/specific records,

e.g. of behaviour, effects of contact, sibling relationships, etc?

5. **Legal implications**. Is the foster carer likely to be called to give evidence in court?

6. **Moving on**. What is the carer's role in returning a child home/moving a child on to permanency/after care work?

The above list is by no means exhaustive but gives a flavour of the issues which need to be considered and re-considered in each placement. Each area can by broken down into its constituent tasks and it may be that, for example, a carer is happy to support a child during contact but unhappy about supervising the contact.

By openly acknowledging and discussing these tasks rather than just letting things happen, possible problem areas can be identified at an early stage. Additional training and support may be needed for the foster carer. It may be that the carer needs practical help with other children if they are to keep hospital appointments or attend meetings. Help in writing records and reports is often needed in early placements.

In some instances the carer concerned does not currently have the skills or training to cope with the task. This is better known at the outset rather than letting a carer get into a situation where they are doomed to fail. By addressing the placement needs from the carer's perspective, a partnership is being forged with the carer where their views, feelings and fears are being listened to and addressed. Too often we hope that a carer will manage.

Thus far we have looked at the way in which the tasks of a placement can be identified and facilitated. There are however other issues to address if we are to achieve true partnership with carers.

As with the assessment period, it is important to respect carer's feelings. We can become so familiar with our carers that we forget that they have lives and responsibilities outside their role as foster carers. Do we always visit and launch directly into the subject of the child instead of taking time to check how the carer is and what is happening with their family? Sadly the answer sometimes is yes. We become so absorbed in the issues surrounding the child, court hearings, stressful contacts, etc., that we can fail to make time for the carer. A card or a letter of thanks are very simple ways of thanking a carer for hanging in there with a difficult situation.

An oft heard cry from foster carers is that they can never get hold of a social worker when they need one. Given the pressure of work on social workers, it is fully understandable that they cannot always be available. However setting up systems whereby a call is returned by a colleague or manager can alleviate the feelings of frustration and isolation which some carers can feel.

Another solution is an agreement at the outset of the partnership/placement that calls can be prioritised by the carer. If a call is stated to be urgent, it will be returned within a given time. If just for 'a chat', the timescale may be different. This system may take practice on both sides but can pay dividends in strengthening the partnership between worker and carer.

Sadly when a carer cannot get hold of the worker, some make decisions and handle situations in a way which may not be appropriate. The work which can accrue from having to 'put right' the decisions and actions can be greater than the time it would have taken to sort the problem out in the first instance. This also has the effect of putting the carer in the wrong for taking that action when in fact they have been left to manage without support.

The word 'dumped' is one heard all too frequently when used by many carers who feel that, having found a placement for the child, there is poor support, lack of planning and lack of communication.

Another oft mentioned problem can arise from a surfeit of workers where the carer is being given conflicting advice and information by the area and family placement workers. Add to this any advice and information coming from other professionals such as psychologists, therapists, and the result can be confusion. From a carer's view, if these people cannot work in partnership, what chance do they as carers stand?

All of these situations work against any real sense of partnership between carer and worker/agency. If repeated often enough, and sadly they sometimes are, they can lead to a complete breakdown in the relationship with serious and sometimes devastating consequences for the very children we are all trying to help. Often it can also lead to workers having no real knowledge of the child or their needs because carers do not feel able to fully share information and see honesty as a risky business. It has emerged in some adoptive placements that information about the child has been withheld by foster carers variously because they have not been asked, they did not think it was important, did not feel they should tell or felt they would be criticised in some way.

Equally as concerning, when the partnership between worker and carer breaks down or is not there to begin with, often the worker has no real understanding of the standards of care given to that child. In our work we have moved literally hundreds of children from foster carers and have all too often discovered that not only were the standards of routine care poor but too many children have received poor emotional care and a lack of stimulation in their foster placements. Such revelations often come as a shock to the worker who 'had no idea'. Often in addressing these concerns we come to realise that the child was inappropriately placed from the outset.

The concept of working in partnership should be seen not as a high flown theoretical ideal but an absolutely essential part of the service offered to children if we are to prevent further children from being damaged in this way.

Conclusion

In thinking about how to conclude this chapter, a much repeated phrase comes to mind. I have often heard workers and managers say of tasks they expect carers to carry out 'it's part of their job'. I began to wonder if the carers actually knew that or whether assumptions were being made.

When we as workers apply for a job, that job has a person specification, a job specification and a job description. We can be correctly expected to know what this job we are applying for entails and whether we have the necessary skills and ability. How many foster carers receive a similar job specification and job description at the outset of their 'employment'? The answer seems to be very few. Yet we expect carers to become involved in a wide range of tasks which fall outside the day to day caring. If we are genuinely to work in partnership with carers, should they not have the same levels of information about the tasks involved?

The process of building genuine and constructive partnerships with carers depends on the individual workers but also on the approach of the authority. Each agency or authority will have its own views on where carers sit in the hierarchy and how they should be managed. Often such views are quite covert and the mind set may have passed from worker to worker unquestioned.

Happily some authorities treat their carers as a very valuable resource, a partnership to be worked on and looked after. Carers are sensitively and appropriately assessed, trained, involved, consulted and the development of the carers seen as important. This approach motivates carers and allows them to really feel part of a team.

Not all carers can perform all tasks and every agency will have some carers who are difficult and problematic; carers who fail. By the nature of the process, we cannot always identify poor or difficult carers through a home study and we have to address such difficulties as they become apparent. This is entirely a different situation to making potentially good carers into problems. If we have our approach, both individually and at agency level right, we build a real sense of partnership, participation and joint interest from the beginning of our involvement. Such a sense of partnership can survive changes of personnel and other difficulties which arise and vastly improve the standards of care given to children.

Many workers forge excellent partnerships with carers and the results are clear to see when working with the children concerned. I believe we need to explore and re-visit good practice regularly. We should not lose sight of the skills involved and the importance of partnership with carers. If we do this the children for whom we care will have a better chance of a successful and happy placement.

References

I have drawn a blank on anything which specifically covers the approach taken to prospective carers by the worker/authority and the impact this has for future partnership. Obviously much of what I have said can be found under different guises in a good psychology text book. Similarly, social work text books which talk about empowerment, self determination etc. all inform the subject.

3.3 Managing Allegations of Abuse Against Carers

Martin C. Calder

Introduction

> *The work of a foster carer is about child protection: A foster home that is not safe is of little or no use to a child or young person'*
>
> (National Foster Care Association, 1994, p106).

Whilst foster carers are part of our child protection system, some children do get abused whilst in their care. This abuse can take many forms: physical, sexual, emotional abuse and neglect, and multiple forms of abuse is not uncommon. In this chapter, I will offer a framework for response but, given the constraints of space, this will not extend to private fostering arrangements or placements with relatives, given the additional considerations needed for these two groups.

Children removed from the care of their parents may remain vulnerable to renewed abuse. Foster carers are charged with the task of providing a safe, nurturing and stable environment for those children placed with them. In recent years, however, we have become aware that, for some children, foster care is neither safe, satisfactory or superior (Faller, 1990). There have been several child abuse inquiries into the deaths of children in foster care. For example, Christopher Pinder suffered multiple injuries and died the following day. His pre-adoptive mother pleaded guilty to manslaughter with diminished responsibility (DoH, 1991). There has also been a formal response in the central child protection guidance (DoH, 1991b).

The Scope of the Problem

The Department of Health does not currently collect figures on abuse by foster carers. Utting (1997) noted that nearly 35,000 children looked after by local authorities were in foster homes on 31 March 1996, placed with some 27,000 foster families. He noted that allegations had been made in four/five per cent of foster homes (1215 homes), of which twenty-two per cent (267) were deemed to be founded and in twenty per cent of cases (243) it was not possible to determine either way. In many cases, carers who have the allegations made against them are the most respected and tend to have been fostering for over five years.

The number of carers contacting the National Foster Care Association (NFCA) about allegations of abuse increased from 3 in the whole of 1987 to three a week in 1993 (NFCA, 1994, p. 109). One in six foster carers has a complaint or an allegation made against them at some point in their fostering career (NFCA, 1996).

Research in America has shown that foster carers are twice as likely as members of the general public to have an allegation made against them, whilst Weiner and Crosby (1988) have reported a substantiation rate of 8 per 1000 children in foster care - twice that for the population of children as a whole. Bolton, Laner and Gai (1981) found that the foster child population is at greater risk of child abuse than the non-foster child population (seven versus two per cent). This is because of the high risk nature of the children placed with them; different standards for abuse in foster families; and a greater familiarity with the need to report any concerns. Utting (1997) added to this list: 'looked after' children are considered as potentially vulnerable, particularly since a quarter of these have some form of disability; the isolated nature of foster care, particularly long-term care and private fostering situations; and the more complex needs of the children being placed. For example, in one London borough, as many as two-thirds of foster children had been sexually abused, though only one-third had known to be so at the point of placement. The NFCA have noted that unfortunately some people will be attracted to fostering because it provides the opportunity to abuse children (sexual abuse); the carers' behaviour may discriminate against the child or young person they are fostering; carers may lose their temper; are unable to cope because of problems in their own lives; members of the foster home repeating past abuse; reaction to caring for sexually abused children; and carers reacting to the impact on their own children of caring for children who have been sexually abused (NFCA, 1994, p. 109).

Benedict et al. (1994) reported on the types and frequency of child abuse in foster family care in Baltimore as compared to reports among non-foster families. They found an average of one-and a-half reports per foster home over a four-year period, representing a three-fold increased frequency as compared to non-foster families. Report frequency was highest for physical abuse (60 per cent) with a seven-fold risk of report compared to non-foster families, but the proportion of reports substantiated was significantly lower in foster care (8.9 per cent versus 36.6 per cent). Foster parents were the designated perpetrators in over eighty per cent of physical abuse and neglect allegations, compared to forty per cent of sexual abuse allegations.

Implications of fostering sexually abused and sexually abusive young people.

The reader is referred to Batty (1991), Johnson (1997) and Macaskill (1991) for a fuller discussion on managing sexually abused children in foster placements, and to Calder (1997) and Calder (forthcoming) for sexually abusive youth. These can act as supplementary tools to Rose and Savage (this volume) who have addressed the issue of safe caring.

What is clear is that the children placed with sexual abuse in their histories compounds further the foster carer task as there needs to be a neutralisation for the child's premature sexualisation (Roberts, 1986). There are a number of ways in which their previous sexual abuse can contribute to subsequent sexual activity and abuse in the foster home: children who have experienced sexual abuse may have been socialised by their offenders to behave in ways that can be interpreted as invitations to sexual activity, such as wearing tight clothing or make-up; they may have expectations that adults will be sexual with them, leading to precocious sexual awareness, such as excessive masturbation; they may

initiate sexual encounters to achieve a sense of mastery over their previous traumas; or they could go on to identify with their perpetrator and sexually abuse younger children (Faller, 1990).

The lack of supervision in foster homes, often created by the need to place larger numbers of children in fewer foster homes, and a shortfall in the child's need for nurturance, can lead to more opportunities for abuse either between children or carer-children. Stress and a lack of support can lead to role-reversal in which the foster father looks towards the foster children to get his own needs met. Indeed, Sone (1994) argued that allegations are more likely where men are isolated from the rest of the family.

False Allegations: Foster Carers as Victims

Children may make false allegations:

- as they have misinterpreted an innocent action
- as a way of drawing attention to previous abuse for the first time because the carer is trusted
- as a way for them to exercise some sort of control over their life
- to try and end a foster placement without losing face.

(NFCA, 1994, p. 110).

Whatever the outcome of the investigation, it is usually accepted that an allegation is a recognition that something is not right.

Foster carers experiences of agency responses to allegations leave them in shock, isolation, and with a sense of stigma and continuing vulnerability (Carbino, 1991, p. 239), particularly when they have a prior relationship with the agency. Many are totally unprepared for this possibility and have severe reactions to the ensuing process of investigation which can include: sudden and abrupt agency intervention; cut-off from communication with the agency; interviews from social workers or police officers they do not know; abrupt removals of one or more foster children (especially for sexual abuse); long periods of 'not knowing' what was happening; no ending to some investigations and no clarity of outcome on completion of the investigation (Carbino, 1991, p. 240).

Hicks and Nixon (1991) surveyed a group of 36 foster carers in the UK who were investigated for child abuse but where the allegations were unfounded. They uncovered some very disturbing practice.

There was no common procedural policy on how to convey the allegations of abuse to the foster carers. Thirty three per cent were told on the telephone and sixty six per cent had an unexpected visit either by a social worker (not always their own) or a police officer. If this was their family placement (link) worker, it removed an obvious avenue of support, and they felt betrayed. None of the carers were given any prior warning that there were problems in the fostering arrangement.

The interview was described as abrupt, unsympathetic and functional (police-orientated) and half were not told the details of what was being alleged. By implication, this removed any means of proving their innocence. Their feelings were disregarded by the workers, leading the carers to fear an unsubstantiated outcome was not being left as an option.

Eighty five per cent of the investigations took several months to complete, during which time they were provided with virtually no information. Their experience of being investigated aggravated their anger at the original allegation and they felt they had been subjected to unnecessary stress. The unfounded outcome did nothing to change their feelings.

Seventeen per cent gave up fostering altogether and sixty-four per cent had serious doubts about whether they would continue.

Verity and Nixon (1995) conducted a survey of foster carers who had had such allegations made against them and found that of 519 questionnaires returned, 177 carers had experienced an allegation. One-third were satisfied with their treatment, and this positive outcome is associated with:

- being notified of the outcome of the investigation
- a short period of investigation
- foster children not being removed
- the social worker being allowed to communicate with foster carers.

Six per cent of the allegations were 'founded'.

Eight per cent of cases the agency was unable to determine whether any abuse had taken place.

The false and unsubstantiated allegations originated mainly from teenagers. The majority were made by girls against a male within the household and concerned inappropriate touching, kissing, sexual innuendoes, sexual intercourse.

Verity and Nixon also found that many carers accused of abuse are abandoned by social services, who may adopt a more rigorous approach to the investigation of allegations against foster carers as against other groups.

- Twenty per cent of departments precluded contact between carers and their regular social workers during the investigation.
- Eighty three per cent offered carers support during investigations.
- Five per cent were well informed about investigation procedures, which often only started a month post-referral, thus aggravating carer uncertainty.
- Seventy two per cent used the general child protection procedures.
- Eight per cent used specifically developed procedures for the task.
- Ten per cent used a modified version of the child protection procedures.
- Forty five per cent of the investigations took eight months to complete.

At the conclusion of the process, carers did not receive anything in writing, and some never had children returned to their care-either because of continuing concerns about them as carers, because the child or carers were declining a reunification, or as the child had established a new attachment to carers.

- Ten per cent said they did not know whether the investigation had been completed nor the outcome.
- Sixty three per cent of cases were unfounded.
- Forty per cent of the foster families had children who were removed.
- Twenty five per cent of removed children were subsequently returned.

As one carer reported: 'children are vulnerable and need protecting. When you are the one who has provided the protection then suddenly you are accused of harming that child the implications are deep and the effects traumatic. They do not disappear when the investigation is dropped'.

'All Alone': The Limits of Professional Support

Allegations of child abuse are difficult and traumatic for all concerned: anger, despair, frustration, hurt, stigma, shock, surprise, and betrayal are some of the feelings most commonly reported. Nixon (1997) reported that good support systems can easily collapse under investigation. He found a shortfall in support and a lack of congruence between agency provision and carer needs. Seventy six per cent did not use any supports offered formally, and none viewed the social worker as a principal source of support. Twenty two per cent of his sample felt they had no one to turn to, and this was most acute where sexual abuse was the alleged abuse. Nineteen per cent used extended family or grown-up children, sixteen per cent used other foster carers compared to only three per cent who used the local foster care group, and eighteen per cent used their family link-worker. Seventy per cent of the workers felt unable to offer effective support during a crisis because of role conflict (investigator or supporter?), leading to fifteen per cent losing the trust of their carers.

Isolation was most acute for single carers, although couples often felt unable to discuss the issues for fear of threatening their relationship [Note. Hicks and Nixon (1991) had found that eleven per cent separated and subsequently divorced].

Towards a Framework for Managing Allegations Against Foster Carers

In 1991, the Department of Health (1991b) specifically emphasised that children who are cared for 'away from home' should have the same degree of protection as those who are in their own homes. This did not extend to prescriptive guidance, leaving a huge void for local areas. The current consultation paper (DoH, 1998) reinforces this line, intimating that revised guidance will address the procedures for dealing with such allegations against carers, which protect the child but which also support the carers and their own children (p. 40).

The local authority has a duty to respond to the lack of central guidance as, without this, managers and workers have no way of knowing what is expected of them. In order to effectively discharge its responsibilities, each local authority has to provide an integrated framework which includes clear procedural guidance, an incremental training package and outcome indicators, all influenced by good supervision (Calder and Horwath, 1998). I will now offer a conceptual framework for this purpose, summarised in figure one.

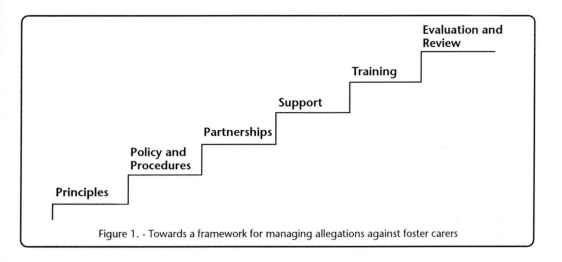

Figure 1. - Towards a framework for managing allegations against foster carers

Recruitment and Selection: Safeguarding the Image of Fostering

It is clear that particular care must be taken in the recruitment and approval of those who foster children. Whilst all carers must be regarded as having the potential to abuse, most abusive carers will not be screened as there are few predictive features of sexually abusive behaviour (Benedict et al., 1994), and many carers have raised their own children well. Police checks that reveal convictions are rare. However, care needs to be taken as abusive carers have been known to choose foster children from advertisements which include pictures and descriptions of the child (Utting, 1997, p. 36). A thorough assessment during the selection process is important as it provides a benchmark against which to judge any subsequent allegations of abuse (DoH, 1991, p. 95). There needs to be a wider range of checks: such as references from past and present employers, proof of identity, the vetting of extended family members who play an active role in the foster carers lives, and checks against the Department of Health Consultancy Index

There needs to be more wide ranging questions including: exploring any history of sexual abuse; any previous allegations against them; any sexual dysfunction; their motivation to foster; any history of mental illness or substance abuse, and whether they have a clear concept of proper behaviour, boundaries and discipline.

> *The role of men in foster care is not straightforward and they often evade regular contact with the professionals. This is worrying since we know that they are disproportionately responsible for physical and sexual abuse, and because of this are more likely to have their behaviour misinterpreted by children and young people. They must be interviewed in detail, as should significant extended family members, and any failure to do so reported*
>
> (Humberside CPC).

Simon Newstone in Chapter 2.14 discusses the issues of men who foster. Many would challenge the above statement and certainly more research needs to be carried out in this respect.

The above recommendations are clearly difficult to implement in an environment which has few placements and where there is the temptation is to expedite approvals.

Decision Time: Colleagues or Clients; Partners or Parents?

> *Arrangements between carers and authorities would be improved if foster carers are treated as full partners. The increased complexity and difficulty of the foster care task sits uneasily with the traditional voluntary service ethos*
>
> (Utting, 1997, p. 28, 32)

The status of foster carers is crucial as it will influence the way in which the investigation into any allegation is conducted. This is more important when we consider anecdotal evidence which points to a change in status from that of colleague to client when an allegation of child abuse is made (Capewell, 1997). The least that a carer can expect is equality with parents, yet the carer is often left without an opportunity to express their point of view, has fewer legal rights, has children removed without recourse to the court and often cannot attend child protection conferences.

Foster carers differ from other parents in the sense that they have a prior collaborative relationship with the authority, yet they also pose a great legal liability threat to them (Carbino, 1991, p. 234). The social worker/foster carer relationship must be based on trust. The professionalisation of foster care within local authorities should match independent fostering agencies many of whom provide a high standard of support and training to their carers. A relationship should develop in which all concerns can be discussed, as co-workers. This is important given the magnitude of the consequences for carers when an allegation is made against them, which may include:

- de-registration as a foster carer
- removal of their own children and other foster children
- loss of control over their lives
- criminal prosecution
- loss of partner (in marriage or in trust)
- loss of self-esteem and dignity
- loss of status in the local community
- possible suspension from their employment

Agency Contributions to Allegations Against Carers: Sharing the Responsibility

This can be broken down into several parts:

Overloading by the agency: in which the authority exploits the kind-heartedness of the carers by placing more children and of different types than for which they were approved for example age-range, sex, the degree of disturbance exhibited by the child, the length of placement

Lack of matching: where workers fail to carefully match the carers and the child together, particularly black and mixed race children, siblings, those with a disability and adolescents. There should always be an initial agreement giving the aims, objectives, length of placement, roles/responsibilities and projected outcomes. A failure to do so is correlated with a higher rate of breakdown and long-term damage to the child. Thoburn (1995) strongly advocates matching and suggests we ask:

- What sort of placement?

- For how long?

- What will be the appropriate legal status for the placement?

- What sort of contact will be appropriate, where and with whom?

- What services, support or therapy will be needed by those involved in the placement ~ the child, the carers and members of their own families, the original family members and relatives?

- What financial help and practical support will be needed to maintain the placement? (p. 449).

Lack of information on the children placed with them: Carers often feel that workers have been less than open with them about the background of the children they foster, leading to situations where the carers are subsequently suing the local authority for damages (see W and Others v Essex County Council and Another, Court of Appeal, 9,10 March, 2 April 1998). They need to know the child's history, what is suspected if not proven, what help has been offered to them (if any) and with what outcome, what problems are anticipated in the placement

and how these may be managed, how they can minimise the risk of allegations against them- particularly if the child is known to have made previous allegations against carers.

Failure to comply with statutory requirements: These are set out in detail in the Children Act and associated regulations and guidance, and cover statutory visits (content and frequency), medicals, care plans, recording, placement agreements and statutory reviews. Utting (1997) reported that only seventy nine per cent of authorities were complying with these requirements. This is worrying considering these are only the minimum standards to safeguard vulnerable children. Several child abuse inquiry reports also endorse this particular failing. Even where documentation is completed, it is of variable (but usually poor) standard. Where workers visit carers infrequently, this reinforces their sense of isolation and heightens anger when an allegation is made. Many carers are hesitant about contacting workers for fear of being viewed as unable to cope.

A failure to provide a clear and accessible policy, procedure or practice guidance for the management of allegations against foster carers

Lack of training, support or supervision for carers.

It is essential that agencies acknowledge these factors as they can create a climate in which placements become abusive.

Principles

- To support and protect children in their families, including their foster families.

- To produce accessible and clearly understood procedures for the investigation of allegations of child abuse against foster carers.

- All allegations of child abuse should be dealt with seriously.

- The vulnerability of carers and the unique relationship between carers and the agency must be recognised.

- The agency must explore their contribution to an abusive situation by over-stretching the abilities and the resources of carers.

- Allegations against foster carers must be prioritised and dealt with quickly.
- Investigations should be dealt with openly and honestly with all those concerned.
- Investigations should be conducted by competent and experienced people who are independent of both the child and the carer.
- Consideration of the total picture for the child and the carer and not simply the presenting incident is needed.
- There is a need for a full assessment of the child's needs, safety and total care to be considered before a decision is made to continue or terminate the placement.
- The investigation should be clearly recorded, including details of all decisions made and actions taken, and should be shared formally with the carers.
- Support should be provided to all those involved throughout and following any investigation. This support must be acceptable to the individual concerned.
- The carers should have a right of appeal.

Policy Issues: Putting the Subject on the Record

Policy needs to provide a clear framework for response that is clear, credible, resourced, monitored, and reflects local conditions and arrangements. It is recommended that this should be in the children's services plans where issues can be addressed within the wider context of the development and resourcing of fostering services. It needs to include what criteria will be used to remove carers from the register and in what circumstances the information would be referred to the Department of Health Consultancy Index; how allegations against carers will be recorded, where they will be placed on the carers and the child's files, and what accumulation of allegations would lead to a review of the carers continued use (Utting, 1997, p. 28, 39).

There should also be an agreement with Independent Fostering Agencies on how they will manage complaints and/or allegations of

child abuse (DoH, 1998, p. 40) A reciprocal arrangement with a neighbouring authority or the NSPCC may be helpful if a truly independent investigation is needed.

Procedures: Plugging the Gap

Procedures are a double-edged sword: they can help workers by providing a structure for the work, in clarifying professional roles and in resolving inter-agency difficulties; yet they can also constrain practice if they are perceived by workers as an added burden, leading to a rigid and unresponsive service. Where no procedures exist, workers may have no sense of direction and believe the work to be of low priority (Calder and Horwath, 1998). Agencies must have procedures as a guide to action, although they should never be seen as a substitute for good practice.

Input of carers who have experienced an allegation may help construct a sensitive yet thorough framework. The procedures need to address the following:

- Foster carers should be advised of the allegations made and the process of investigation that will follow, in person, and with the link-worker present as soon as is possible.
- They need to know how the investigation will be conducted and by whom.
- They need to know how their views and responses to the allegations will be elicited, and the time-scales involved.
- There needs to be clarification on the roles and responsibilities of the investigating officers and the link-worker, as this impacts on the provision of support services.
- The carers need to know how the interim and then the final outcome will be communicated to them, and in what forum (e.g. child protection conference, home visit, or both).
- Information sheets on avenues of support and a copy of the procedures should always be made available to the carers at the outset of the investigation.
- There needs to be guidance on when and how foster children are to remain, be removed or returned to the carers.

- There needs to be agreement between the agency and carers on mutual responsibilities. For example, the agency should commit itself to providing the resources to enable the carers to carry out the work and ensure there is regular social work contact, whilst carers should record carefully any incidents which might become potential material for subsequent allegations (Lowe and Verity, 1989, p. 18-9).

- There needs to be scope for the agency to identify and acknowledge any contribution they may have made to the allegations, and this may well influence who is asked to conduct the investigation.

- The procedure should integrate the complaints, child protection and criminal aspects for streamlining purposes.

- There should be a link between the child protection procedures and the report to the Adoption and Fostering Panel. Under the Children (Protection from Offenders), (Miscellaneous Amendments) Regulations 1997, a carer convicted or cautioned of a specified offence can no longer be considered as a suitable person to act in this capacity. Where these regulations do not apply, the panel should give consideration to the future wishes and needs of the foster child when considering whether the approval of the carers should continue.

- Where the allegation is unfounded, the agency should convey in writing to the carer the outcome of the investigation, in writing, and clarify what information is to be given to future social workers when placing children and what information has been recorded on the carers file and the child's file.

- There must be a clear right to, and process of appeal, and/or the resolution of any complaints under the agency's Representations and Complaints Procedure.

All these procedures should be time limited and all parties should be informed of the timings.

Hicks and Nixon (1991) found variable procedures in their survey, with the majority being destructive and insensitive (p. 254). No positive benefits were noted by the carers,

leaving doubts on how this assists workers approaching an investigation.

The Conduct of Child Protection Investigations: Neutrality is the Key

Any local authority receiving an allegation must investigate it in law and their first priority and responsibility is to the children, yet they cannot overlook the carers vulnerability, rights or integrity (Hicks and Nixon, 1991, p. 249). This is important as carers often do not understand that the Section 47 investigation applies equally to fostered children, carers and to children living in their own families. Historically an investigation does not always follow on from an allegation. Where it does, there appears to be a presumption of guilt from the outset. This is important as the way in which the investigation is conducted has a direct bearing on both the recruitment and the retention of carers.

When social workers are charged with investigating allegations against a carer, the obvious conflict of interests must be openly recognised. Indeed, particular attention must be given to the process in order that there is no collusion or 'cover-up' of unprofessional or unacceptable practices; the child is not subject to avoidable pressure through impartial investigations; and that the welfare of other children cared for within the setting is taken into account, including the carers' own children. Social workers approaching the task in a non-judgmental way is associated with better outcomes. Where the carers have concerns about the workers neutrality, an independent agency or neighbouring authority should be considered. Investigations are often painful for all concerned, yet attention to procedures and good practice can help ameliorate, but not remove, some of these negative (unintended) consequences. Foster carers remain a very valuable resource and should be treated accordingly.

Supporting Carers: a Problem Shared

Support can be in the form of information, advice and comfort. Non-judgmental advice and someone to listen can reduce their sense of isolation. The construction of procedures that frees the link-worker to act in this capacity removes any potential role confusion or divided loyalties and is also correlated with positive outcomes (Hicks and Nixon, 1991, p. 253). Workers cannot totally distance themselves from being agency employees, but their involvement in an investigation might be problematic for anyone who was involved in their approval and have personal issues to reconcile.

The provision of support should not be dependent on whether the abuse is corroborated or unfounded and should include: practical information such as addresses of national organisations (e.g. National Foster Care Association, British Association of Adoption and Fostering, Parents Against Injustice, etc.); information on counsellors and advice/mediation services; the development of local independent support groups; and the pairing of carers together.   The link-worker can be identified as the initiator and facilitator of any such support provision.

Outcomes

Allegations can either be founded (valid, substantiated), unfounded (not valid, not substantiated), or there is an inability to substantiate the validity of the report. Risks often have to be considered and managed in the majority of situations where no clear conclusion can be reached. Whatever the outcome, there should be a mechanism for debriefing the workers and the carers; the outcome should be confirmed in writing to the carers, embracing the future placement of children and the future status as foster carers. Retention of good foster carers is essential and many are being lost due to poor responses to child abuse allegations.

Safe Care

This has been addressed in detail by Rose and Savage (this volume and NFCA in their paper *Safe Caring*), but it is important to reiterate that abuse can occur in any family and that clear boundaries and limits must be established. The creation of a safe caring environment also enables the carers to be more aware of any signs of abuse that may emerge. Some writers advocate self-protection work with both fostered and birth children (Elliott, 1985).

Training

Training is pivotal in equipping workers and carers with appropriate knowledge, skills and values, and in modelling what is expected in practice (Calder and Horwath, 1998). It is an encompassing structure as it influences every part of the suggested framework, yet it is only effective if it is used as part of a wider strategy to promote and develop practice — not to compensate for gaps in policy or procedure.

The expanded role and expectations of carers should be matched by additional training, which should be provided at a number of different levels and at a number of different stages (preparation-post approval-refresher) and to a wide target audience (carers, workers, managers).

The training programme needs to include:

- Safe caring/discipline: how carers can protect themselves against the sort of misunderstandings which may lead to allegations against them.

- Child protection procedures: what they say and why. The high risk of allegations against carers needs to be explored. The reality is that the agency treats them differently if an allegation against them is made. This needs reinforcing at various stages in their career. The development of support plans in advance is needed.

- The management of difficult behaviour.

- The law and legal rights.

- The effect on the carers' own children and family life.

- Child sexual abuse: management of abused children and sexually reactive and abusive young people; management of their feelings and fears; normal versus abusive behaviour, knowledge and attitudes, profiles of male and female abusers, etc.

- Placement agreements: mutual expectations, including the need to review child protection procedures and safe caring at the point of each new placement.

Evaluation and Review: Keeping Your Eye on the Ball

This is important as abuse may emerge as a stress reaction to a particular fostering situation. Utting (1997) identified that long-term carers are a major risk for child abuse allegations because of:

- the reduced level of supervision and external involvement

- increased confidence that the situation is 'settled' and needs no intervention

- confidence in the carers themselves

- lack of training opportunities and annual review

- lack of agency support (p. 38)

There are cases where carers have won considerable confidence and respect but where this has masked abuse. Ryan, McFadden and Wiencek (1987) reported that 18 per cent of families where abuse was substantiated had received no contact from a worker in the previous six months. Utting is suggesting that a reduction in visiting frequency from 12 to 8 weeks for children in placement for over a year will help address this point. The Department of Health (1991) is also indicating the need, as a matter of high priority, to explicitly review carers whose care structure has changed (p. 96).

Conclusions: Joint Solutions to Shared Problems

Foster care is a traumatic experience for many children without the added burden of maltreatment...

(Benedict et al., 1996, p. 569)

In order to achieve some resolution to this problem, we must see foster carer well-being and foster-child well-being as complementary rather than competitive. This chapter has attempted to provide a preliminary framework for changes to the way in which we have been managing allegations against foster carers. This may ease, but will not resolve, the multiple consequences of the painful process. It is essential that we engage carers in the process with the aim of resolving shared problems with joint solutions.

References

Batty, D. (Ed.) (1991) *Sexually Abused Children-Making Their Placements Work*. London: BAAF

Benedict, M.I., Zuravin, S., Brandt, D. and Abbey, H. (1994) Types and Frequency of Child Maltreatment by Family Foster Care Providers in an Urban Population. *Child Abuse and Neglect* 18(7): 577-585

Benedict, M.I., Zuravin, S., Somerfield, S. and Brandt, D. (1996) The Reported Health and Functioning of Children Maltreated While in Foster Family Care. *Child Abuse and Neglect* 20(7): 561-571

Bolton, F.G., Laner, R.H. and Gai, D.S. (1981) For Better or Worse? Foster Parents and Foster Children in an Officially Reported Child Maltreatment Population. *Child and Youth Services Review* 3: 37-53

Calder, M.C. (1997) *Juveniles and Children Who Sexually Abuse: a Guide to Risk Assessment*. Dorset: Russell House Publishing

Calder, M.C. (Forthcoming) (Ed.) *Towards an Understanding of Juveniles Who Sexually Abuse*. Dorset: Russell House Publishing

Calder, M.C. and Horwath, J. (Eds.) (1998) *Working for Children on the Child Protection Register: an Inter-agency Practice Guide*. Aldershot: Arena

Capewell, V. (1997) Foster Carers: Clients or Colleagues in Child Protection? In Bates, J., Pugh, R. and Thompson, N. (Eds.) *Protecting Children: Challenges and Change*. Aldershot: Arena, 237-247

Carbino, R. (1991) Child Abuse and Neglect Reports in Foster Care: the Issue for Foster Families of 'False Allegations'. *Child and Youth Services Review* 15(2): 233-247

Cavanagh-Johnson, T. and associates (1997) *Sexual, Physical and Emotional Abuse in Out-of-home Care: Prevention Skills for At-risk Children*. NY: The Haworth Press

DoH (1991b) *Child Abuse: A Study of Inquiry Reports 1980-1989*. London: HMSO

DoH (1991b) *Working Together Under the Children Act 1989*. London: HMSO

DoH (1998) *Working Together to Safeguard Children: New Proposals for Inter-agency Co-operation*. Consultation paper. London: HMSO

Elliott, M. (1985) *Preventing Child Sexual Assault*. Bedford Square Press

Faller, K.C. (1990) *Understanding Child Sexual Maltreatment*. Newbury Park, Ca: Sage

Hicks, C. and Nixon, S. (1991) Unfounded Allegations of Child Abuse in the UK: A Survey of Foster Parents' Reactions to Investigative Procedures. *Child and Youth Services Review* 15(2): 249-260

Humberside Child Protection Committee. The report of a panel of enquiry instituted by the Humberside Child Protection Committee into the quality of foster care provided by Mr and Mrs 'A' for children placed in their charge-with special reference to allegations and instances of sexual abuse

Lowe, M. and Verity, P. (1989) The Right to Dignity, Fairness and Compassion. *Insight*, 17 January, p18-19

Macaskill, C. (1991) *Adopting or Fostering a Sexually Abused Child*. London: BAAF

NFCA (1994) *Choosing to Foster: The Challenge to Care*. London: NFCA

NFCA (1996) *Child Abuse: Accusations Against Foster Carers*. London: NFCA

Nixon, S. (1997) The Limits of Support in Foster Care. *British Journal of Social Work* 27: 913-930

Roberts, J. (1986) Fostering the Sexually Abused Child. *Adoption and Fostering* 10(1): 8-11

Ryan, P., McFadden, E.J. and Wiencek, P. (1987) *Analysing Abuse in Foster Family Care, Final Report to the National Center on Child Abuse and Neglect*, Ypsilanti, MI: Eastern Michigan University

Sone, K. (1994) A Safe Haven. *Community Care* 1-7 September, p7

Thoburn, J. (1995) Out-of-home Care for the Abused or Neglected Child: Research, Planning, and Practice. In Wilson K and James A (Eds.) *The Child Protection Handbook*. London: Bailliere Tindall, 447-469

Utting, Sir W. (1997) *People Like Us: The Report of the Review of Safeguards for Children Living Away from Home*. Norwich: The Stationary Office

Verity, P. and Nixon, S. (1995) Allegations Against Foster Families: Survey Results. *Foster Care*, October 1995, 13-16

Weiner, R. and Crosby, I. (1988) Fostering Sexually Abused Children- The Catch 22 Situation. *Foster Care*, September 1988

3.4 The Children of Foster Carers

Pat Doorbar

Introduction

The following chapter summarises and discusses findings obtained whilst working with children and young people in families who fostered.

Our research aimed to give these children and young people an opportunity to express their views on fostering and how it affected their lives. *We're Here Too* was carried out with the Hampshire Foster Care Federation and Hampshire Social Services Children's Department.

The bulk of the findings reported in this chapter are based on conferences held in Portsmouth, Southampton and Aldershot.

Background

A number of issues relating to children in families who fostered have been raised that were used as a basis for the research. Fostering is voluntary and does not yield the financial or social rewards of paid employment. For this reason, presently, fostering is usually carried out for altruistic reasons. Whilst this may be beneficial to the children looked after, it can have unforeseen consequences for the families concerned.

Children and young people who are looked after by the local authorities and who are candidates for foster care are likely to be troubled and to have undergone experiences outside the scope of the children and young people within the family offering foster care. They may have been victims of physical, emotional or sexual abuse, or may have experienced family misfortunes, illness or bereavement. They may also have been unwanted or at odds with their families. The results of such traumatic experiences are likely to produce a range of emotional and behavioural difficulties. These difficulties will undoubtedly have an effect on those who have close contact with them.

Traditionally, it has been believed that the principal responsibility for fostering rests with the adults who enter into contracts with the local authorities. These adults are provided with training, support and counselling before and during their time as foster carer.

At present, it is commonly assumed that the children of foster-carers do not have the same needs for training and support. Despite this, children of foster-carers face specific and real challenges. Sharing parenting and parent time, pets, possessions and personal space are likely to create potential problems for even the most phlegmatic child.

In addition, exposure to disturbed and frequently violent behaviour combined with the general disruption of the family can present additional difficulties for children living in families who offered foster care.

Whilst it is likely that all parents who offer their services as foster-carers discuss the implications with their children, it is also believed that they may not be fully aware of the effects that foster care may have on their children, as our research demonstrates.

The research methodology used was important. The research techniques used were deliberately designed to give children and young people the maximum opportunity to express their opinions in the way that they found easiest and most appropriate. The principles that underpinned the consultation process were consistent across all groups.

Historically children and young people have not been asked for their comments or opinions on issues that concern them or have an impact on their lives. The Children Act (1989), Children Act (Scotland) 1995 and the Children Order (Northern Ireland) 1995 give legal recognition to the importance of listening to their views. Giving children and young people the right to comment on issues that concern them is also enshrined in Article 12 of the United Nations Convention on the Rights of the Child. Whilst this may be seen as good or desirable practice it has often been difficult to adhere to. Only articulate and confident children and young people are able to respond directly or to fill in traditional questionnaires. Children and young people who are less articulate because of age, ability or culture have not been regarded as able to give their views. This however is a misapprehension. Results from a number of projects and ongoing work with children and young people show that this group is both able and willing to give their views of services and practice.

Children and young people have given their views in projects and ongoing work on health care, education and residential care settings. Represented in these groups are children with social and/or emotional problems, children with learning difficulties and children who have physical disabilities.

The unifying factor in all these projects has been the methodology that has a number of key features. These are as follows:

Communication

The onus is on the researcher to find a means of communication that is accessible to the child or young person. Use has been made of drama, visual art, sentence and picture completion, play scenarios and role play.

Comprehension

Again, as above, the onus is on the researcher to tailor materials to suit the needs of individual children and young people.

Attention span

Responses made by children and young people are likely to be more meaningful if their attention is focused. If children and young people are to be engaged the interaction must be fun.

Motivation

The engagement must have meaning for the child or young person. Children and young people need to feel that their trust and involvement is respected. They also need to know that something will happen as a result of their involvement in terms of change or further consultation.

The Research

In our research children and young people were involved from the beginning of the project so as to ensure that they were able to give direction and shape to the process. A wide variety of active techniques were used, such as drama, video, art etc. so as to provide a wide variety of means of expression that allowed everyone to have their say in the way most appropriate to them, and also to take into account the shorter attention spans of younger children and prevent boredom setting in. A sealed post box was provided so that the participants had an opportunity to express views anonymously and without fear of recriminations.

Participants in the research

A total of 145 young people and children completed questionnaires at three locations in Hampshire (45 per cent boys 55 per cent girls). The children's parents had been foster carers for a wide range of time periods, from a few months to over ten years. There was however a polarisation cabbage, with 62 sets of foster carers having fostered for less than three years, 48 for 10 years or more yet only 31 between four and nine years.

The number of foster children sharing each household showed a distinct result with over 50 per cent of children saying they shared their home with more than six others. The next highest figure represented two other children (c15 per cent) with all the numbers of children sharing representing seven per cent or less.

Sharing families, home and possesions

Consultation with children was felt to be important so that children could adjust to the situation and could retain a degree of control over events close to the centre of their lives. Consultation did not frequently occur, however. Although the majority (75 per cent) of children and young people reported that their parents had told them that foster children would be coming to stay with them, only 35 per cent said that they were also told that their involvement would be needed. A fifth of the children and young people who participated in the project reported that the issue of fostering had not been discussed with them.

She didn't say nothing

They just told me where they were going to stay, the bedroom and that

We are going to have children so don't drive them out like devils

Many of those who said that they were made aware that their involvement would be required said that information mainly related to their behaviour:

Don't be horrible because she can't hear

Although people outside the family were reported as discussing the arrival of foster children, the involvement of outside agencies varied. In two regions only a third of children said that they had been consulted or had discussed this with outside agencies. In most cases, social workers were the main person who had talked to the children and young people.

Information ranged from general advice and comments, ensuring that children supported their parent's decision, enquiries as to how children would cope with some of the issues that could arise, such as sharing possessions.

Sharing family and possessions with foster children also produced mixed feelings. Participants frequently showed a high level of understanding about the issues involved in sharing parents, although they also found this difficult:

Fine because I know they love me

Normal, I've grown up with it. In the beginning I didn't like it because the other kids got more attention

Was OK but then she tries to take my Mum and Dad off me and calls her 'Mum'

Horrible I hate it

Many children in the research found it difficult to share their personal space, such as bedrooms, with foster children.

Great fun, we can talk to each other at night

Horrible, especially now I'm sharing with a 15 year old

Sharing possessions revealed anxieties about losing possessions or breakages occurring. Responses included:

OK if it's my foster sister who has been here since I was a baby

Hard because they steal

I don't [share things] because things get broken

When asked which possessions they least minded sharing, toys, TVs, computers and CDs were most frequently mentioned. Pets were the most frequently reported things that participants did mind sharing, with parents and siblings and 'special' possessions also being mentioned. The majority of participants (more than 75 per cent) reported that sharing was a problem for them.

Participants enjoyed some of the positive aspects of sharing their homes with foster children but found that competing for parental time, and adjusting to children become integrated into the family and then leaving were difficult.

It's really hard when they only stay for a few days

Living with Foster Childen

Although a sizeable proportion of children and young people reported positive experiences about the first day that a new foster sister/brother came to live with them, over half said that they were anxious or had negative feelings.

Fun to have someone to play with

Going to be an unpredictable experience

Once I knew him, I wanted to get out of the house

Like I was unwanted

Feelings about having a foster brother or sister on a more long-term basis were also mixed. When asked to complete the sentence 'Having a foster brother/sister made us feel…', responses included:

… Proud that I can look after someone

… A bit uneasy

… Inadequate

… Unvalued

Participants in the research were asked what were the best and worst things about having a foster sister/brother. Responses included altruistic feelings such as:

> When we looked after two little boys (aged three and five). The five year old was deaf and couldn't talk and the little one couldn't talk, but he got to know us and started talking.

However, negative responses demonstrated distress in some instances:

> They did not like me

> When a girl wrote a letter about me and I had to go to the police station

> When mum told me off I couldn't cry I was too embarrassed

Participant's views on foster children leaving the family were evenly divided between distress and relief. Comments included:

> Glad they are going

> Depends. When the younger ones leave its difficult if they are attached. I was upset when one child left who we'd cared for five years and I wasn't told that she was going. I felt unprepared, it would have been better if I'd known.

The overwhelming majority (95 per cent) experienced problems when foster children were rude to their parents. Children and young people also found it difficult when foster children were allowed to get away with things, although some participants demonstrated an attempt to understand the reasons for the foster child's behaviour. Comments included:

> They blame things on me

> Like my parents like them more than me

> OK because I know they need attention

Many of the children and young people who participated in the research said that they found visits from the parents of foster children difficult. Problems included difficulties with the foster child getting special attention and with being excluded from the situation. Children also reported finding the parents themselves difficult.

> Sometimes people seem quite nice, but sometimes you can understand why the child is in care

> Unhappy because I have to go to my room as if I'm naughty

> Sometimes they don't like me

Children reported more positive feelings about visits from social workers. Comments included:

> Happy because I can talk to her

> Glad, because she calms him down and he's out of my way for a couple of minutes

Some children did report that they were uncomfortable about social worker's visits. Concerns centred on saying 'the right thing'.

> As though I have to be polite and say what I think they want me to say

> Scared

How to make it easier for children in families who fostered

The main issues that were raised by children during the course of the research were that they needed to be consulted about fostering, and that they needed to be given information that would help them to understand what was going on. The need for a forum where they could discuss problems and issues was also considered to be important. Many children in the project did not feel that they were listened to. There was an absence of anyone with whom to discuss issues such as bullying, sharing personal possessions, families and space.

A number of suggestions as to how it could be made easier for children in families who fostered were put forward by the steering groups (which were made up from young people and children in families who fostered). Children participating in the conferences were then asked to express their opinions on these suggestions.

Having regular meetings with other children in families who fostered was widely thought to be very helpful (supported by 80 per cent of participants). Over half (60 per cent) of participants thought it would be helpful to be able to talk to someone outside the family.

Three quarters of children who participated in the research said that it would help if someone could explain to them why some children behave in the way they do.

Sixty per cent of children felt that it was important for people to take notice of how they felt about fostering.

Other solutions were a phone help line for children in families who fostered, and the provision of books and videos explaining what it was like to have someone else living in your family.

Children who participated also had messages for parents who offered foster care, or were considering it:

I like it when we play football together

I know they need the money but they should not take the abuse they get

I need to have some quiet to get my homework done. I am worried about passing my exams

I would like to tell them that sometimes the children beat me up

We are the ones who have to put up with it but we get nothing out of it

Conclusions

Some children and young people appear to have a view of themselves as providing opportunities for others at the expense of their own personal development and welfare. There are also feelings of being overlooked and undervalued by those for whom they provide a service. Their perception of themselves is of being of less value than the children they look after, constantly playing the role of 'Cinderella' - expected to do all the work but not invited to the ball. A number of children and young people are able to both cope with and gain from the experience of fostering.

It is important to establish the key factors that enable this group to be happy in making and meeting the complex relationships and requirements demanded of them. In order to improve the current situation it is important that:

- initial discussions involve children in the family as partners in arrangements and agreements.

- children and young people are given a formal opportunity to talk about their feelings concerns and expectations; if possible in private, separately to parents and social workers.

- children and young people are given appropriate training.

References

Doorbar, P. (1993) *Listening to Children*, Hampshire Social Services

HMSO The Children Act (1989)

HMSO (1991) *Working Together Under the Children Act (1989)*

Middleton, L. (1992) *Children First*, Venture Press

Newell, P. (1991) *The UN Convention and Children's Rights in the UK*, NCB

NFCA (1994) *Safe Caring*

Utting, Sir W. (1991) *Children in the Public Care - A Review of Residential Child Care*

3.5 Independent Agencies

Felicity Collier

For many years, the provision of foster care was almost wholly the domain of local authority social services departments. The only other providers of foster care services were some of the large voluntary child care agencies (such as National Children's Homes (NCH) and Barnardos) which developed a network of foster carers around their 'village' residential homes to allow some children to live in the local community. As a result of this virtual monopoly, there was little competition between agencies and loyalty generally developed between carers and particular social workers or teams with whom they had developed a good working relationship. Foster carers, more usually described as foster parents in the seventies and eighties, tended to be two parent families where the women did not work outside the home. These foster carers looked after children in care for a few days or weeks and sometimes, of course, for many years. They gave freely of their time and expected little reward other than basic allowances. Most older children or children with challenging behaviour were considered more suitable for residential establishments and when they were placed with foster carers, extra resources were usually made available.

Over the last fifteen years, there have been major societal shifts which have caused dramatic changes. Far more women are in paid employment outside the home, more families are now dependent on two breadwinners and, most significantly, a much higher proportion of families are now headed by single parents. These changes in family structure make it harder for parents to successfully juggle extra child care responsibilities and also be available at home during the day which can be important for a number of children now being looked after by local authorities.

While these social changes were taking place in the family there were important shifts taking place in the organisation of public care. Concerns were being raised about the quality of residential care for children and large numbers of residential units were closed. As a result almost double the proportion of looked after children were placed in foster care — from 32 per cent in 1976 to 65 per cent in 1996. It is important to remember that these figures represent proportions, not actual numbers which have not changed dramatically. The Children Act of 1989, and the corresponding Acts for Scotland and Northern Ireland, emphasised the importance of keeping birth families together, wherever possible, and this led to a significant reduction in the number of children in care away from home. It was therefore the case that those children who were placed with foster carers were inevitably some of the more troubled and challenging. Many would not have been considered suitable for fostering in the past and would have been thought to warrant specialist residential care.

Unfortunately, the savings accrued by the closure of residential establishments were re-directed to other aspects of general social services provision and usually not reinvested within the 'care system'. There was little increase in resources for the foster care services even though they were clearly caring for some of the children who would previously have been in residential care.

The changing patterns of family life, referred to above, combined with the increased demands made of foster carers and insufficient additional support, has, unsurprisingly, meant that there is a growing shortage of new foster carers. This shortfall has created the opportunity for the emergence of a new entrepreneur, the independent fostering agency. The first independent fostering agency (IFA) was set up in the UK in 1987, and since then the growth has been rapid. In 1993 there were 11 IFAs and by 1995 there were 19. We now know of the existence of over 60 independent agencies.

In the beginning many IFAs were founded by disillusioned foster carers, often in collaboration with disillusioned social workers. They came together with the intention of offering a better service to foster carers and the children for whom they cared. They were originally formed as a way of providing a specialist service for fostering of teenagers. There is a school of thought who would have preferred them to stay in that area of work. Opinion is divided in local authorities as to whether the development of the new agencies is a positive step for foster care in the UK, particularly in the absence of a regulatory framework. Nonetheless, the agencies are widely used.

Although they offer greater financial rewards to foster carers, the carers who work for them generally say their primary motivation was to have access to better support. Support is of crucial importance to foster carers. The SSI report in 1995 identified the excellent support offered by many IFAs. Foster carers were very appreciative of support which was 'highly flexible and immediately responsive' to their needs. Further support, either provided in house or purchased from independent providers, is often available to meet the child's educational needs and to arrange input from the child and adolescent mental health services may also be secured. In addition, many of these independent agencies provide excellent training for foster carers which in turn benefits children. They have quicker access to special allowances and grants for equipment; access to 24 hour support appears to have developed.

IFAs have also given rise to fear by many carers of the growth of two-tier provision. Indeed, many local authority staff refer to carers in such agencies as 'professional carers'. This term inadvertently conveys messages about the perception of the carers in their own agencies that may or may not reflect actual levels of competence. The growth of the new agencies then can be seen as exerting some impetus towards the wider professionalisation of foster care with implications for training provision.

This so-called professional service provides an attractive alternative to working for a local authority which can on occasions appear bureaucratic, inflexible and have frequent changes of key social workers. As independent agencies have become an increasingly attractive proposition for existing local authority carers, social services departments have found it difficult to retain carers, particularly in areas well served by independent agencies. Some local authorities have found themselves buying back the services of foster carers they had originally recruited and trained from the new agencies at a much higher prices.

But the SSI study also found examples of very bad practice among IFAs. There were concerns that young children were placed at some distance from their home area; the mingling of social work and financial management could create commercial pressures for the retention of children in placements; it was difficult to get adequate information about quality assurance issues; and placements were costly by comparison with local authorities' own provision. Common criticisms which have been raised recently include some evidence that some IFAs have 'poached' carers from local authorities, thus disrupting current placements and effectively holding local authorities to ransom over increasing fees for children already settled with carers.

The *Foster Care Market* report, a 1996 survey conducted by an ADSS project team of which BAAF was a member, demonstrated that about 75 per cent of social services departments used independent fostering agencies, some only occasionally and in emergencies but many on a regular basis. The additional cost per child ranged from £500 to £1,000. As a result the cost of foster care has increased and two income classes of foster carers have developed with many local authority carers feeling increasingly undervalued.

Another problem has been that independent agencies have been clustered in particular areas — in 1997, 21 were based in Kent, 19 in London and the south east and the remaining 22 spread throughout England and Wales. Inevitably the risk is that some children are placed at a distance from their families and communities and this may prejudice subsequent rehabilitation or make regular contact difficult. The number of agencies that can offer an appropriate service to black children is small and too many black children and children of mixed parentage have been isolated in white rural communities, where foster carers are available but where the child's racial and cultural needs cannot be fully met in the local community. Indeed the potential for racist abuse may be more prevalent in such areas.

However, the greatest problem, as both Burgner and Utting recognised, is that there is no official national inspection and approval process for the independent agencies and no way in which standards can be properly monitored. In fact there are no agreed standards, although this is being addressed currently by the work of the UK National Working Party on Foster Care Standards. Although local authorities are expected to vet agencies with whom they place children — including assuring themselves that all the proper checks have been made — it is time consuming when they must organise this themselves. This is compounded when local authorities are placing children outside their own areas and using a range of different agencies. The Utting Report stated that 'this area cannot be left outside the inspection and regulatory framework if children are to be properly safeguarded'. The House of Commons Health Select Committee report stated, 'We support the call by many of our witnesses for stricter regulation of independent fostering agencies. We recommend that all foster agencies should be subject to a mandatory requirement that they be approved, registered and inspected. The Government should bring forward legislation as soon as possible to achieve this'.

There is also currently some confusion both among local authorities and independent agencies about the provision for delegated powers which can allow IFAs to approve their own foster carers. BAAF has provided clarity on this issue in a recent Practice Guide. Since delegation is not possible for a non-voluntary IFA, operating on a 'for profit' basis, careful examination of the financial arrangements are necessary. Again, in the absence of an agreed inspection process, each local authority has to set up its own systems for establishing and monitoring its requirements of independent agencies. Arrangements for comprehensive criminal record checks have proved difficult due to the lack of access currently for new voluntary agencies; they are therefore dependent on gaining access through local authorities, and there is evidence that some IFAs have relied on inferior checking procedures which can be unreliable. This is very worrying.

The Select Committee report also recognises that 'the best independent fostering agencies

show what can be done in support of carers, given the availability of sufficient funding'. However, they also temper this with concern that 'the proliferation of these agencies is diverting resources from local authorities which might be more effectively spent in other ways and may be leading to very distant placements for some young people'. While recognising that independent agencies will continue to have a role to play within the care system, they felt it undesirable for local authorities to become too reliant on them.

As stated earlier, not all the independent agencies are genuine 'voluntary organisations', a number are profit making partnerships. The injection of the profit motive into the fostering service can potentially introduce a distortion. Cost apart, who is to say that the implementation of a permanency plan - be it a return to birth family or adoption - may not be delayed by an agency or indeed a foster family which needed to maintain its income base to survive? Indeed, in the USA some believe that heavy state subsidies for foster care reduced the chances of adoption for a generation of children.

Some of the smaller agencies also do not have the financial security which can ensure that services will be maintained over time. This may mean children moving once again if the agency does not survive. Alternatively, local authorities may have to move children from very successful placements to reduce the cost of an independent placement. When we know that one of the most important ways we can safeguard a child's mental health is to minimise changes of carers this cannot be right.

Lack of standards regarding the structure and management of these agencies means there is not always an appreciation by them of the importance of avoiding potential conflicts of interest. Foster carers may occupy management positions or be on the board of directors. While fostering children for the agency, they are also determining policy, supervising other carers, negotiating with local authorities and sitting on the agency's foster care panel. It is much more difficult to challenge 'an expert' and, as Utting says, a small number of abusers in high places can wreak untold damage with children's lives, children who are 'a captive group'.

Voluntary adoption agencies are providing an increasing number of foster care services and find that the description of independent fostering agency sits uneasily with their SSI approval to provide adoption services and their adherence to SSI standards for adoption. Approval is confirmed every three years by the Secretary of State following inspection by the SSI. Some of these agencies have worked with foster families for many years whilst others have started foster schemes recently. Many work specifically within geographical, ethnic or faith based communities. Foster carers recruited and assessed by them can either be approved by the local authority or the local authority can delegate to the voluntary agency the power to approve the foster carer on their behalf — this is exactly the same provision as relates to voluntary independent fostering agencies.

BAAF welcomes Utting's clear statement that the work of independent agencies 'cannot be left outside the inspection and regulatory framework if children are to be properly safeguarded' and his support for the urgent implementation of the Burgner recommendations. The responsibility for the inspection must be vested in a single agency and not delegated to local authorities where inevitably there would be wasteful duplication of effort and an unfair burden on those where large numbers of new agencies are in place. A model akin to that currently used for voluntary adoption agencies has much to commend it, with SSI approval and regular inspection against national standards.

Indeed recent research findings demonstrate how effective voluntary adoption agencies have been in providing high quality services. It would seem cumbersome to set up two different regulatory frameworks when the expertise currently exists. It is hoped that the development of national standards on foster care will provide the basis for the inspection process. Independent agencies would certainly welcome this seal of acceptability and have indicated their agreement to being judged against high standards of practice. Indeed, many of them would say, and would be right in saying, that they provide a service to foster carers and children which is superior to that of some local authorities. A genuine partnership with local authorities is essential however, if they are to assist in providing a comprehensive

and safe foster care service for children, a service which does not allow financial considerations to override the best interest of children.

In conclusion, the growth of independent fostering agencies is accompanied by the growing difficulties of local authorities in recruiting, supporting and retaining high quality foster carers. This shortage of foster carers has been influenced by changes in family life and compounded by the particular challenges that children with special needs present to foster carers. The failure by local authorities to invest sufficient resources in the proper support of foster carers to these new and challenging children, and to offer the rewards in fees which would compete with the attraction of the external workplace, have led to these support services and fees being provided by the independent sector. The irony is that the local authorities, with nowhere to place the children whom they are looking after, have to purchase back foster carer services at much higher prices by buying the services through the independent agencies. It is surely time for a major re-examination of where these fees for independent agencies are coming from and consideration of a reinvestment in local authority fostering services. The lessons for local authorities are clear. The challenge also is to develop effective collaborative partnerships with the independent sector and ensure that children looked after are provided with the continuity, care and permanence which they need and which will facilitate their development through childhood and into adulthood.

References

Association of Social Services Children and Families Committee Report *The Foster Carer Market: A National Perspective (1996)*

BAAF *Working With Independent Fostering Agencies*

Health, Dept. of *Inspection of Local Authority Fostering 1995-6 National Summary Report.* Families Committee Report

House of Commons Select Committee *Report on Looked After Children*

Utting, Sir W. *People Like Us, The Report Of The Review Of The Safeguards For Children Living Away From Home.* Department of Health

3.6   Financial Matters

Pat Verity

One can only speculate why there have always been problems associated with money and foster care. Is it a hang up from the days of the Poor Law when babies were placed with wet nurses who were paid for their care, and where payment continued after the babies had died at the hands of their carers? Or is it perhaps linked to the work of those great philanthropists who built huge orphanages and large children's homes and villages to house destitute children in the 18th and 19th centuries? Whatever it is, the attitudes that extend to foster care and finance must be examined, if the needs of children requiring care away from their own home are to be met.

Traditionally, valuing a service and receiving payment did not necessarily go together. Indeed many of the UK's services are still run on a volunteer basis, for instance the life-boat service and mountain rescue. But increasingly, as individuals are being held to account for their work, and the expectations on them increase, society is questioning whether such services can still be maintained on a volunteer basis. These same questions are raised by those in the foster carer service.

Requirements of Carers

Foster carers are probably the most heavily scrutinised group of workers in any country. They go through a long assessment process that includes a number of interviews, are questioned about their background, their upbringing, their attitudes to sex and sexuality, their abilities, and have police and medical checks, before being accepted as foster carers. The majority, at the end of this process, will qualify as acceptable volunteers, receiving no payment for their work, although they will be looking after children 24 hours a day, 7 days a week, 365 days of the year. Foster carers also have their approval reviewed annually, by a salaried group of people who judge the carers abilities and quality of work over the past year

to enable the latter to continue to practice as foster carers.

The way in which the fostering service has developed means that there is a large workforce carrying out tasks set by the State for a group of children for whom the State is responsible. This workforce is outside the normal workforce because they are not employees, and are therefore seen as 'volunteers'. Unfortunately 'volunteer' often also equates with amateur but caring for other people's children is not a task for amateurs! This is particularly true for fostered children, many of whom will rank among our most vulnerable and troubled youngsters.

The task of fostering is much more than looking after children. The policies that local authorities have to tackle, problems with children's families in their own homes, mean that by the time children come into the care system they are likely to have had damaging experiences which will affect their behaviour. Foster carers are expected to work with the child and their family to try and put the two back together again. Even in long term placements, there is an expectation that work will be done to ensure that children remain in contact both with their brothers and sisters and with their parents, and sometimes with wider family and friend contacts too.

As long ago as 1977, Parker in *Decision in Child Care* was arguing that fostering breakdowns occurred because fostering agencies 'ask unskilled and untrained foster parents to do a difficult job in what for them may be an unnaturally difficult way: by eschewing the role of parents'. He further argued that 'The requirement that they act as foster parents rather than parents may mean that fostering has to be recognised as a skilled and semi-professional task', and thought that some 'professionalization' of foster care needed to take place.

The Barclay Report (1992) included foster homes within the spectrum of residential and day care services, and explained:

We have included private family homes...because it is our view that people placed (fostered) with families should be considered as recipients of day services or residential services just as much as those placed in centres or homes... To think of children (or adults) living with foster families as receiving one form of residential care, diminishes the sharp differentiation often made between fostering and residential care and puts the relationship between them in what we believe to be a more helpful perspective.

Foster care has increasingly become more specialist and task-orientated than providing a home for life for a child. Like residential care, foster carers are required to achieve work with children and young people that is recognised in a residential setting as requiring skilled and committed workers.

Financial Aspects of Fostering

There are a number of financial aspects associated with fostering. Firstly, there is the maintenance allowance for the needs of the child. Secondly, there are the costs to foster carers of providing a foster care service, and thirdly, there is the question of paying foster carers for their work.

Maintenance allowances for children vary greatly. In UK law there is an expectation that foster carers will be reimbursed for the costs of the child they foster, but there is no standard for payments which are left to the discretion of each individual fostering agency. So the maintenance allowances for the needs of the child vary greatly. For instance the maintenance allowance for a seven year old in 1998 varies between £48 a week and £180 per week depending upon which local authority is placing the child.

In 1975 NFCA set a minimum fostering maintenance allowance which it wished to see paid by any fostering agency. This minimum allowance was calculated using the Family Expenditure Survey and the Equivalence Income Scales. Average family expenditure showed how much families were spending, and the Equivalence Income Scales provided a percentage for how much of a family's income was spent on different age groups of their own children.

This formula has continued to be used. However, it can be argued that the costs of looking after a fostered child are much greater than looking after one's own child. There are the increased costs associated with parental visiting, social workers calling, keeping in touch with the agency, as well as direct costs of a child who is entering a family for the first time. Children who come into care often have high expenditure associated with them — their eating patterns can be very different to the family they are now living with, they may be destructive of equipment, toys, furniture etc. Their unhappiness at being in care may show itself by them running away, with their carers needing to search for them. Many will have missed opportunities for expanding their horizons and foster carers will be keen to help to make up these experiences. Whilst foster carers' own children may have already had some of these opportunities, it is important that the newly fostered child is included with the other children of the family, making outings and hobbies more expensive for the carers.

NFCA makes a clear statement in its book *Foster Care Finance* that the costs of fostering are higher than the minimum recommended maintenance allowance, and suggests 25-50 per cent higher should be considered normal. However, many local authorities have used the minimum fostering allowance recommended by NFCA as their maximum, and have sought to include within this any further discretionary payments which might have been payable to carers prior to moving to the NFCA recommended minimum maintenance payment.

The additional costs for the foster carers are similar to other businesses. There is the cost of supplying beds, bedding, and equipment, etc. as well as the rooms that are required for fostering. Many carers have either extended their homes, or live in houses that are larger than they need in order to foster. They may be paying increased mortgages, council tax, or higher rent to accommodate foster children. Most foster carers require a car that is larger than the average family needs in order to be able to transport children safely. This means that every journey that a foster carer undertakes, whether or not it is connected with fostering, is probably more expensive than their neighbours.

Lastly, in terms of costs there are the opportunity costs for carers. By fostering, many carers have had to actively remove themselves from the work market, and are unable to earn an income from any other employment because of the demands that fostering makes on their time. These are known as the lost opportunity costs for carers. Alternatively, if foster care was a paid occupation, it would compensate carers for these lost opportunities.

In her book *The Adequacy of Foster Care Allowances* Nina Oldfield identifies the indirect costs as the 'time spent by foster parents on foster caring tasks, tasks that would not occur in non fostering households'. These were described by carers as personal care of foster children, general household care, travel time, therapeutic time and time spent in administering the placement. The average time spent on caring for the foster child (including those who reported no extra time and those who reported on foster children with 'special needs') was between 13.2 and 14.5 hours per week. These averages did not include the time spent on the emotional care of foster children, that is counselling, talking and reassuring as these were considered secondary tasks to be done at the same time as other tasks.

Why Pay Carers for the Work of Caring?

Everyone needs money to live. Society sees nothing wrong with paying people who work closely with children in other fields, so why should there be an automatic assumption that paying foster carers will produce a group of people who will be fostering for the wrong reason?

If all carers were paid, fostering would be opened up to people who currently cannot afford to foster, or who choose to take on employment which gives them an income, rather than stay at home and look after other people's children, even though the latter would be their preference.

Foster carers effectively remove themselves from the work market place, and if they have no income they are not in a position to pay contributions towards a retirement pension. They take on an important and demanding job for which they will not be entitled to a pension when they reach retirement age.

Children's Families

In the 1970s the terms inclusive and exclusive foster parents were introduced to differentiate between those who wished to work with and include children's families in their lives, and those who wished to exclude them. The former saw fostering as a service for children and their families. The latter tended to see fostering as rescuing children from their original families, and indeed some might even have thought that the service was about providing children for foster families. Some social workers could also have been described as inclusive and exclusive.

The attitudes of exclusive carers and social workers led many parents to feel that foster care was dangerous. They feared that if their children went into the care system, they would be lost to them for ever. Yet residential workers, who can become just as emotionally involved with children as foster carers, are rarely viewed as a threat. Parents know that, for a residential worker, caring for a child is a job, and one for which they get paid. The payment of a salary confirmed that the residential worker was doing a job, and was clearly seen as a worker by the parents and therefore not someone in direct competition with their parental role.

Fee Paid Schemes

In the UK, specialist schemes started in the early 70s when model schemes for the placement of teenagers were developed. Their remit was to prove that it was possible to recruit more foster carers for teenagers by remunerating them for their work on top of the maintenance allowance for the young person; by providing good support; and having a contract that everyone was working to, including the young person. This model is still in use today.

The problem with this model was that it was limited to a certain number of places and particular age groups of young people, mainly teenagers. If a scheme was set up with 20 carers offering 30 placements between them, then when all these were full, the next young person needing a family placement, and fitting all the criteria, would have to go to a traditional carer not entitled to a fee, or the additional support. This caused enormous tensions. Carers questioned why they should not get the same level of payment as someone else, especially when they had the skills to hold a young person in their home who previously had absconded from a number of different 'specialist foster carers'. Some local authorities then tried to distance their specialist carers from the rest by not allowing them opportunities to meet together. This only made the problem worse.

Many of the placements were time limited, and at the end of the allotted period of time, the young people were transferred into 'ordinary' foster homes. Again these carers questioned why they were being asked to do similar jobs to the specialist carers but without payment. The rift grew larger.

The majority of these schemes had been developed to place teenagers in foster care. They were seen as the hardest group to place. Yet what became clear to many workers early on was that if it was possible to pay people, then in fact there were people who would take on the challenge. In some local authorities, incentives caused so great a shift that whilst the majority of teenagers needing a foster care placement were found one, under fives were being denied placements. Alternatives were also developing which allowed people to take on a caring role and be paid for it. Women became child minders and received realistic remuneration, rather than subject the whole family to the rigours and time commitment of fostering

Allowances and Fees

Concern both about the low level of maintenance allowances, and the type of work that social workers were asking carers to do, led some social workers to try and ensure that carers received higher payments. They disguised these by using enhanced payments, and arguing with managers that children's needs were greater. Such systems are open to abuse, and some carers benefited to the detriment of the majority.

NFCA sought to address this problem. Recognising that the basic fostering maintenance allowance did not cover the costs of fostering, NFCA developed a scheme based on a Canadian model. It considered the child's problems, identified these and the additional costs associated with them, and then paid the carers for the costs and the work that they would need to do.

The Canadian model had not taken into account the extra costs involved, nor were there any recommendations about the length of time the work would continue at the agreed payment. These were important considerations in NFCA's view and needed to be addressed. The scheme that it developed had two parts. The first looked at the time, energy and skill that carers needed to have in order to care properly for the child. The second part looked at the extra costs involved. The association made a clear recommendation that the time, energy and skill payment should be constant throughout the placement on the basis that, even if a child's behaviour improved, it was because the carers were continuing to use their skills. The maintenance costs, however might reduce as behaviour improved. For instance if a carer had been skilful enough to get a child to stop smearing, then the costs of laundry and cleaning would reduce. Equally, if a young person's eating habits were under control, the food bill might decrease.

Unfortunately most local authorities reduced the skill payments when a child's behaviour improved — not a good incentive for carers to do a good job!

Kind notes in *Caring for Children — Counting the Costs* (1992)

> The use of enhanced allowances as a means of rewarding foster carers is questionable, not least because it stigmatises the child, and portrays him as part of a problem for which special payments have to be made. Such payments may also act as a perverse incentive, since they may be renegotiated once the problem that led to the enhancement has abated. When the problem disappears so too does the payment.

Sellick in *Supporting Short Term Foster Carers* (1992) makes a similar point that this is a system that is analogous 'to one which would reduce a teacher's salary once her pupils had learnt to read!'

A number of good things did come out of these schemes. It provided social workers and carers with an opportunity to consider together the work that needed to be done. It was an opportunity to build up a picture of the child, and at the end of the assessment social workers had an understanding of the work of the carers.

It acknowledged that young children could have more complex needs than teenagers, and that the work that carers did with parents was time consuming and very involved. The scheme showed that those caring for young children were often involved with a variety of professionals, and that the work that they did tied them to their homes, ruling out the possibility of part-time employment.

The downside of the scheme was that in order to pay carers, there was a need to label children as problems, and in order to continue to pay carers, the children had to have continuing problems.

The development of this system had a knock-on effect in some low paying local authorities who realised that their basic fostering payments were not meeting the costs of children. Basic fostering maintenance allowances began to increase to nearer to the recommended minimum.

For NFCA the challenge was to find a system that was fairer to carers, and paid them appropriately for their work, whilst not disadvantaging children further. Knowing that you have to be seen as a continuing problem in order that your carers continue to get paid was not a message that the association wanted children to have, nor a burden that they should carry.

Payment for Skills

Could agencies be encouraged to show carers that they valued their work? Could the work that carers do be valued? What could be done to stop carers with valuable experience leaving the foster care service? How could the wastage be reduced? If there was a career structure on offer to carers, would they continue fostering, possibly taking on different tasks? Was there a way of identifying the skills and knowledge that people bring to fostering, and identify those skills that are learnt through undertaking the work, or taking advantage of training opportunities?

In consultation with carers and social workers from across the country, NFCA set about developing a model 'payments for skill' scheme which could be adapted by fostering agencies.

The scheme is based on three levels of skills that are tied into a residential child care grade;

as salaries rise in the employed sector, so too would the reward to carers. The three skill levels recognise that all carers, following assessment and training, will come into the service with some skills. Whilst undertaking the work, they will develop and some will want to increase their skills more than others. Many carers do develop specialisms, working intensely with parents, developing their direct work with children, or perhaps developing training courses.

The scheme enables carers to know exactly how much money is for a child's maintenance and how much is theirs as a reward for their skills, and to know that their money is to be paid to them every week of the year. An important principle is that there is a 52-week of the year payment that is not reliant on a child being in placement.

The model scheme suggests only one payment per household, no matter how many children are placed. Moving from the previous specialist schemes means that this can be a contentious area. Many of the specialist schemes gave carers additional reward payments if they took more children. This approach is not consistent with the idea that the fostering agency is agreeing a package of care with the carers when they are recruited, and does not equate with other areas of social work where larger case loads do not increase salaries.

The model scheme would ensure, however, that a fostering agency knew its financial commitment to the rewards of carers, no matter how many placements were made with them. It is acknowledged that there may need to be some incentive to make an increased payment for additional children, but not at the same level as the original fee. Some agencies have written into their schemes that there is an expectation that carers will take two children in order to qualify for the scheme. This seems to be in keeping with the Department of Health's view that smaller numbers of children in a foster home are compatible with ensuring that children get sufficient attention.

However, it is essential that the payment to meet the maintenance needs of the young person and the costs of the carer in providing the service are fully met, so that the reward to the carer is clear.

A clear contract should spell out the conditions of the service that the carers are providing, and what the authority is providing in order that the carers can do their job. The contract would set out the carer's status, and identify responsibility for national insurance, pension and income tax payments.

A period of notice on either side should be required to end a foster carer's involvement with an agency, with the carers having the right to appeal against dismissal.

This model scheme highlights the need for carers to have respite, and suggests that paid holidays, as well as regular breaks to prevent stress can be instrumental in preventing fostering breakdowns.

The expectation that carers should take part in training is a requirement of the scheme, and this is mirrored by the agencies ensuring that training and specialist support is available. Those with responsibility for supervising foster carers can use their regular meetings to assist with training, and through support develop the carers' abilities.

The payment for skills model is now being used widely across Britain but is still in its early days. Most agencies who have introduced it have not used the payment levels suggested in the scheme, nor have the majority extended it across all their carers.

The independent fostering sector, that has grown significantly over the past 10 years has taken a different approach. Agencies pay carers a total sum per placement, which includes the young person's maintenance costs.

Other agencies are developing loyalty bonuses which guarantee a one-off payment per year as long as the carers have provided a certain number of placement days during the year.

Friends and Family Carers

Friends and family carers who have children placed with them by a local authority are not treated, financially, in the same way as other foster carers by many authorities. Yet the children's needs are the same as other children who are looked after by local authorities. A survey of calls from family and friend carers to NFCA's Helpline found they were almost exclusively related to finance, or lack of it. Carers had been encouraged by local authorities to take care of a child known to them, only then to be told there was little

financial support. The variation and considerable discretion in practice for payment to these carers was also apparent in other studies. This causes carers a great deal of stress. In particular, it is clear that grandparents, who with aunts and uncles were the majority of this group of carers, struggled financially at a time when many had planned a comfortable retirement. The National Standards in Foster Care final document will include a standard on reward/payment for foster carers' skills.

Employment Status of Carers

The employment status of carers has been agreed in the past as self-employed by inland revenue. However, the move by some agencies to have explicit contracts with carers can move them into an employer/employee relationship. Fostering agencies are urged to seek advice from their local inland revenue nominated status inspector on draft contracts, for their view, before finalising arrangements. It is impossible to give general advice on such contracts as it is the actual contract between agency and carers that count.

Insurance

Insurance cover for carers continues to cause problems, and is a major financial problem for many carers, particularly those who foster children or young people who cause damage. When the 1988 Boarding Out Regulations were introduced the then Minister stated that 'it was unacceptable for any local authority to state that it had no insurance cover for foster carers'. Foster carers themselves cannot readily get insurance cover for their foster children's actions. Even where fostering agencies have policies to provide such cover they demand that carers seek redress through their own insurance company knowing that they will be refused. Carers then build up a history of claims, and some have been refused insurance for their own family needs, even though they have not received any reimbursement from their insurers. Fostering agencies need to develop their insurance arrangements so as to remove carers' fears that they will find themselves uninsured because of their fostering activities. Some foster carers can find their mortgage at risk where this is tied in with an insurance policy.

Conclusion

When asked, many foster carers would wish to be altruistic in offering their services to fostering. Indeed many came into the service with this in mind. However, the reality of the cost to themselves and their families has led them to re-think their attitude to money and foster care, whilst acknowledging that no agency could compensate them for what they give of themselves over and above what could be expected in any other form of employment. Of the foster carers who responded to the Association of Director's questionnaire for their report *Foster Carer Market Place* 69 per cent thought that fostering should be a paid job.

All carers need to have maintenance allowances that fully cover the costs of the young person and providing the placement. Whilst it is recognised that some placements will be more costly than others, foster carers would prefer to receive a regular level of allowance that, in the majority of cases, would cover the costs. Foster carers do not wish to have to argue the case for additional payments, but would prefer a fair system which ensured that everyone had a reasonable level of allowance. The Health Committee in its second report states:

> The question of payment to foster carers needs to be tackled at two levels. Firstly we believe it right that all foster carers should be adequately reimbursed for actual expenses incurred. The current situation, in which local authorities pay less than the NFCA recommended rates for reimbursement of expenses, is not only unfair to carers, it acts as a strong incentive to the recruitment of carers on low incomes... Secondly, ...there should be a stepped scale of payments to carers, with the level of payment being linked to the level of their skills and experience in dealing with difficult or demanding children.

Being paid for the work of fostering is not a reality for most carers. Between 10 and 20 per cent of carers receive a reward payment which is not eaten up by the maintenance costs of the placement, and which carers can depend on for their own needs. Whilst advertising that agencies can pay carers a reward for fostering may open the market up to more people, it is not necessarily the only aspect that attracts potential carers. They have to know that they will also receive good support and training — in fact a package of care that shows that the agency also cares about them. Paying carers will help to stem the loss of experienced foster carers who have learnt to adapt, change, and take up the challenges presented to them in the interests of doing the best for children.

But perhaps the biggest challenge still lies with local authorities. They must decide what sort of foster care service they want in order to enable their carers to provide quality care. If they do not provide carers with good training, high levels of support and a clear structure within which to work, and which recognises the expertise of carers, then they will not only fail carers, but also fail the children and young people for whom they have responsibility.

References

ADSS (1997) *Foster Carer Market Place*

Barclay Report (1982) *Social Workers and Their Role and Tasks.* Bedford Square Press for N.I.S.W.

Foster Care Finance. NFCA annually

Health Committee (1998) *Second Report Children Looked After By Local Authorities*

Kind, P. (1992) *Counting the Costs of Caring for Children.* York University Centre for Health Economics

NFCA (1997) *Payment for Skills (Making it Work Paper).* NFCA

Oldfield, N (1997) *The Adequacy of Foster Care Allowances.* Ashgate

Parker, R. *Decisions in Child Care*

Sellick, C. (1992) *Supporting Short Term Foster Carers.* Avebury

Summary

John Hudson

Foster care has a long history during which it has had to reinvent itself many times over; this volume highlights many of the current dilemmas for which resolutions will be needed in the 21st century. But, however hard the dilemmas may appear, we can take some comfort from the fact that previous generations have had to face similar dilemmas and come through.

We have seen considerable change in the children thought suitable for fostering - from under sevens only up to the early 19th century through able-bodied children and young people for the next hundred years to children with quite severe disabilities, emotional disturbance or challenging behaviour and, most recently, offenders.

We can be reasonably sure that the children and young people themselves are no better or worse than children and young people in previous generations. Adults have always had problems with the younger generation, two and a half thousand years ago a Babylonian scribe wrote:

> *This youth is rotten from the very bottom of their hearts. The young people are malicious and lazy. They will never be as youth happened to be before; our today's youth will not be able to maintain our culture.'*

We also know that the range of children thought suitable for fostering has expanded greatly, not only in the UK but also abroad and some countries have gone even further than the UK in using foster care for children with very considerable care needs.

In the UK foster care has been caught up in a huge shift of emphasis in child care. A hundred years ago most people believed that children in need were best taken away from their 'bad' home environment and placed in a 'good' home environment, whether that 'good' home environment was a foster home many miles from where they lived or a family in the colonies.

Though child care workers began to question this in the 1920s (Heywood 1978) and

Winnicott (1954) argued strongly from her experience of working with evacuees that it was essential to maintain family links. Even when researchers like Trasler (1960) began to produce the evidence that children did better where links were maintained between the foster family and the child's family, it was to take another forty years before this idea became official policy in England. Even as late as the 1980 Child Care Act, social workers were being given even more powers to separate children from their families.

In this respect those working with children with disabilities have often been ahead of other child care workers. Because it is no longer assumed that a family with a disabled child is automatically a 'bad' family (an idea which was very widespread 100 years ago at the height of the Eugenics movement), those working with families with disabled children have usually stressed the importance of shared care and of continuity of experience for the child. There is no reason why family link schemes of the sorts pioneered for children with disabilities should not be more widely used to support families with children with challenging behaviour, for example, but such flexible arrangements have been slow to come into mainstream foster care.

The past fifty years has seen a gradual increase in our awareness of rights, first through the Universal Declaration of Human Rights signed fifty years ago and more recently through the UN Convention on the Rights of the Child. Many people have found this last difficult to come to terms with. One reason has been that we have found it difficult to come to terms with the idea of children as 'meaning makers' (Verhellen 1998).

Even today, the CCETSW (Central Council for Education and Training in Social Work) recommended curriculum for DipSW students (CCETSW 1991) is based on very traditional child development theories taught to me as a student 25 years ago. Within these theories, adults are responsible for shaping the world of children; the idea that children shape their own world, even though it is a key theme running through, for example, Lucy Maud Montgomery's *Anne of Green Gables* written seventy years ago, is rarely taught in the UK. A generation of social workers brought up on this traditional diet has found it very difficult to come to terms with the idea that children have the capacity, let alone the right, to contribute to shaping their own world.

Of course, there have always been foster carers and child care workers who have known that this was important but they have usually picked this up from their experience, not from any formal teaching they have received.

We also know (George 1970; Berridge and Cleaver 1987) how important placing children with their siblings is for the success of a placement whilst there is growing evidence that we may have underestimated the potential contribution grandparents can make to a child. This last may become even more important in the light of earlier divorce. Twenty five years ago, relatively few divorces involved younger children, now, half of all marriages involving children are of marriages which have lasted less than ten years, so grandparents are increasingly the main link with the 'missing' parent.

Pulling all this evidence together, we can be reasonably sure that good child care practice in the 21st century will increasingly involve much greater contact with all members of a child's family.

We have known that children in care were losing out educationally since the early 1970s when the *National Child Development Study* highlighted this but it has taken fully twenty five years for any real attempts to counteract that trend to be announced.

Over those years, the importance of school as the place where children make and sustain peer group relationships has increased. Increases in road traffic, which have made streets increasingly dangerous as play areas, and the decline in youth and community services have meant that, for many children, a major source of peer group experience is the school playground or, if they are lucky, after-school activities. But even these are often limited by the need to catch the school bus home.

Children in care who, with the fashion for short term placements, have to change schools frequently find they have to make new peer group relationships every time they move and, if they cannot find a pro-social peer group to join, will either 'drop out' or join an anti-social one.

So education does not simply give access to higher education or employment; it gives access to one of the major sources for the development of our identity and the quality of our life - the friendships we make amongst our peers.

For all carers, both foster carers and residential staff, the biggest obstacle to continuity of schooling has been the short termism that has informed so much child care planning. The government's Quality Protects programme will go some way towards addressing this. Weiner and Weiner (1990) found that foster children who had had more than five changes of placement in fourteen years did less well than those who had not. Sadly, the present government's target, whilst applauded, is well short of that standard!

The past fifteen years has also seen increasing awareness of the needs of children from cultural backgrounds different from those of their carers. Though we have moved from assimilation through race-awareness and anti-racist practice to greater understanding of the need for children to have access to the culture of their parents in order to develop a true sense of their identity, we have generally been less willing to explore the patterns of family and community relationships in other cultures which might provide us with new forms of alternative care for children.

The UN Convention explicitly recognises kafalah but there are other patterns of alternative care among families and groups which might usefully become part of the range of alternative care provision, not just for members of those groups where it is part of their culture but also for white, European or other children where such patterns of relationships, while unknown in their own culture, might better meet their needs as children than traditional British approaches to foster care.

If our attitudes are changing towards the children we care for and their families, so our attitudes also need to change towards the foster carers and the children of foster carers. If we want foster carers to take children with difficulties, we must not end up turning carer's children into children in need for the sake of someone else's child.

In the last fifty years the majority of foster carers have come from the over-35 age group but this group has changed considerably over that time. Within the earlier generation most people got married, many women did not expect to have a career of their own and most had completed their families by thirty. Now 20 per cent of adults choose to remain single, many more women expect to have a career and many women do not begin child rearing themselves until their thirties, or even forties. Many more foster carers will come to foster care now with the experience of having held a responsible position and the respect that goes with that and will expect a similar level of respect from professionals to that to which they have become accustomed in employment.

The fact that many people have not yet come to terms with these changes is amply illustrated in the growth of independent fostering agencies many of which have been set up explicitly to provide, in the best sense of the words, a more professional service.

However, foster care also suffers, like all alternative care in the UK, from an assumption that it is largely an unskilled job capable of being undertaken by unskilled but 'motherly' types who may have to do a short course if they are to deal with more difficult children.

We have not gone the direction, for example, of the VHG (1991) in Switzerland who recruited qualified and experienced residential workers, who had high professional expectations and the experience of working together as a team, to provide foster care for very severely disabled young people who hitherto had lived in a specialist hospital. The organisation provided weekly support groups in which foster carers from a particular locality met for support. Within five years, nearly all the young people were able to move on to more independent, community based care.

Even though we have not gone that far, there is still very little recognition in the UK of the wide range of relationships which foster carers do or might offer to children and their families from respite care through short and long term non-specialist alternative care to short and long term therapy or intensive care of the type developed by VHG. Some of the existing diversity is well represented in this book but barely acknowledged outside it.

One suspects that, apart from ignorance of the diversity of foster care, the main impediment is that acknowledging the range of possibilities within foster care will open the floodgates of training demands and increased pay and allowances.

As long ago as 1982 the *Barclay Report* (NISW 1982) acknowledged that foster carers were just as important a part of alternative care as residential staff; but, from reading Utting (1997) 15 years later, you would hardly believe it. Foster carers reported insufficient training, inadequate advice and assistance and lack of involvement in planning.

Part of the lack of recognition of the changing situation of foster carers is expressed in the lack of training. Just as the education of children in care has been a low priority for most of the past twenty five years, so has the education and training of alternative carers, whether foster carers or residential staff.

I would argue that every foster carer should automatically be entitled to professional training in child care if they choose to go down that line. We can only do this if we have a comprehensive child care training strategy which begins with the preparation for becoming a foster carer and enables each foster carer to build on that training at their own pace and in their own way to suit the needs of the children and young people for whom they care. It should be part of lifelong learning and it should enable a foster carer, who chooses, to become professionally qualified.

Many people are afraid of professionalism because it has become associated with training courses for young high flyers without life experience. Perhaps we need to change the word 'professional'; but, whatever we call it, we do need a way of recognising the knowledge and skills that people have acquired through study and experience as signifying a special level of expertise in the care of children.

Alongside this, we need to grasp the nettle of pay and allowances. The long shadow of Lord Shaftesbury who 150 years ago declared that only voluntary carers were trustworthy and railed against those who cared for profit still hangs over carers in England. We are also partly at the mercy of the UK tax system which, unlike those of several other European countries, does not recognise 'not for profit' organisations other than charities whose legal obligations do not always make them the best vehicles for flexible child care practice.

We would do much better to listen in the late twentieth century to Charles Handy who points out that all of us can do three types of work - voluntary work for which we may get expenses but no pay, work for which we get paid at a rate below the economic cost to us of doing the work and work for which we are paid at an economic rate.

There is no reason why, within the range of placements which foster carers provide, there should not be those who care for expenses only, those who care in return for pay below the economic rate and those who care for pay at the same rate as anyone else caring for a child with a similar level of difficulty, whether that person is a teacher, a nurse or a social worker.

To do this, we need a radical shift in the way we cost alternative care. Because local authority finance has for many years been linked to central government finance, local authorities have traditionally been concerned with current cost and, if you can get someone to do something free now rather than paying them or someone else to do the job, so much the better.

The costs of doing something badly can wipe out all those savings over time. Thirty years ago Howard Skeels (1966) found that the average additional cost to the state of putting a child in a poor home compared with a good children's home for just under three years was around £50,000 a year every remaining year of that child's life. It certainly would not have taken £50,000 a child to improve the quality of care in the poor home so that the children received a good experience as a child and the state would have saved all those £50,000 a year they were paying out for the rest of those children's lives. As far as I know, this is the only study ever to attempt to cost the difference between doing something well and doing something badly in a child's life partly, one suspects, because politicians are less bothered about whether their decisions will have an impact ten, twenty or thirty years after they are out of office than whether they will affect taxes next year.

Such shortsightedness in politicians should not blind us to the fact that 25 years after they had been in care, the children who had been in the good home had a vastly improved quality of life compared with those who had been in the poor home. None were a burden on the state and many were in productive employment and contributing taxes to the state; those who were married but unemployed were married to spouses who were contributing taxes to the state.

We know that many foster placements break down because of poor preparation and lack of support from local authorities (Berridge and Cleaver 1987; Jones 1975); but complaining about the charges levied by independent fostering agencies to ensure good practice is hypocritical and dangerous. Of course, we need to ensure that the quality of care is satisfactory but, as the government's Quality Protects programme has so dramatically demonstrated, quality is precisely what has been lacking in the arrangements for the alternative care of many children and young people. And, if quality costs money now, we should be prepared to pay for it now.

If, as a society, we have any commitment to our children and to the quality of ther lives, then the 21st century will see an expansion in the range of placements offered by foster carers, greater recognition of the value of diversity and of arrangements for alternative care from different cultures, the availability of training for foster carers working in every type of placement and a proper recognition that 'the labourer is worthy of their hire' whether that hire is support for and recognition of a voluntary contribution, remuneration for using specialist skills and expertise or a full salary for full-time work by a professional child care worker.

References

Berridge, D. and Cleaver, H. (1987) *Foster Home Breakdown*, Oxford, Blackwell

Department of Health (1998)

CCETSW (1991) *The Teaching of Child Care on the Diploma in Social Work*, London, CCETSW

George, V. (1970) *Foster Care: Theory and Practice*, London, Routledge & Kegan Paul

Heywood, J. (1978) *Children in Care, 3rd Ed.*, London, Routledge & Kegan Paul

Jones, E.O. (1975) A Study of Those who Cease to Foster, *BJSW*, 5, 1, pp. 31-41

NISW (1982) *Social Workers: Their Role and Task* (The Barclay Report), London, Bedford Square Press

Skeels, H.M. (1996) Adult Status of Children with Contrasting Early Life Experience: a Follow up Study, *Monographs of the Society for Research in Child Development*, 31, Series 105, pp. 3-57, partly reprinted in Wolins M (Ed.) (1974) *Successful Group Care*, Chicago, Aldine

Trasler, G. (1960) *In Place of Parents*, London, Routledge & Kegan Paul

Utting, Sir W. (1997) *People Like Us*, London, HMSO

Verein Heilp, Dagogischer Grossfamilien (1991) Konzept (5th edition), Wengi, Switzerland, VHG

Verhellen, E. (1998) *From protection to partnership*, Paper presented at the 50th Anniversary Congress of FICE, Paris, 27 May

Weiner, A. and Weiner. E. (1990) *Expanding the Options in Child Placement*, London, University Press of America

Winnicott, C. (1954) *Casework techniques in the child care services* Paper presented at the UN European Seminar for the Advanced Study of Social Casework, Leicester, August 1954 reprinted in Winnicott, C. (1964) *Child Care and Social Work*, Hitchin, Codicote

The Way Forward

Ena Fry

On 16 December 1998, John Hutton MP, Parliamentary Under Secretary of State for Health stated that:

> nothing will improve for children in care unless we acknowledge that these children and young people have been let down by the system.

He also noted that:

> ...we have had reviews, scandals and failures, now we must have action. Together we need to strengthen the reality of corporate parenting. One lesson we can learn from the scandal is the need to listen to children and young people.

(from notes of the meeting of the Associate Parliamentary Group for Children and Young People In and Leaving Care, 16.10.98)

There are three government initiatives:

- **National Standards in Foster Care** — ch. 2.1

- **Quality Protects** which includes local authorities providing plans showing how they will reduce the number of placements and moves of looked after children; expanding the range of foster carers and developing new voices for children 'in care'.

- **The Social Services White Paper** — proposals include:
  - a new regulations and inspection service with independent inspections applying to foster carers as well as residential units
  - removing quality controls from local authorities so there is no confusion of their role
  - reducing bodies with responsibility for children's services from 250 to 8
  - children rights officers in each social services commission area
  - a new duty on local authorities to support care leavers up to the age of 18

In addition to the above, what is needed is a concerted effort to work together by all those involved in foster care — voluntary agencies; foster carer organisations both local and national; local authorities; professional associations; interagency workers and academics.

As we approach the end of the century, foster care is in crisis (Jan. 1999) — but this is a time of change. We have the opportunity to build on the many good things referred to in this book and we have the chance to respond to the views and experiences of:

- fostered children and young people
- care leavers
- carers and their families
- the children of foster carers

We also have the chance to put in suitable evaluating and auditing systems to ensure appropriate standards are maintained and any necessary changes are made.

Resources are being put into service but, alongside this, there needs to be changes in attitude and approach. We must all think and act together so the opportunity is not lost and the next decade really does see us improving the foster care service.

What a great start that would be to the 21st century.

Useful Addresses

British Agencies for Adoption and Fostering (BAAF)
200 Union Street
London
SE1 0LX

National Foster Care Association
87 Blackfriars Road
London
SE1 8HA

Who Cares? Trust
Kemp House
152–160 City Road
London
EC1V 2NP

Index

Author Index